Leeds Trinity
University College

Florida A&M Un
Florida Atlantic U
Florida Gulf Coa
Florida Internatio
Florida State Uni
New College of F
University of Cen
University of Flor
University of Nor
University of Sou
University of Wes

Nonviolence and Peace Building in Islam

Theory and Practice

Mohammed Abu-Nimer

University Press of Florida

Gainesville · Tallahassee · Tampa · Boca Raton · Pensacola
Orlando · Miami · Jacksonville · Ft. Myers · Sarasota

Copyright 2003 by Mohammed Abu-Nimer
Printed in the United States of America on acid-free paper

First edition 2003. First paperback edition 2008
13 12 11 10 09 08   6 5 4 3 2 1

Library of Congress Cataloging-in-Publication Data
Abu-Nimer, Mohammed, 1962–
Nonviolence and peace building in Islam : theory and practice / Mohammed Abu-Nimer.
p. cm.
Includes bibliographical references and index.
ISBN 978-0-8130-2595-7 (cloth : alk. paper). ISBN 978-0-8130-2741-8 (ppk)
1. Nonviolence—Religious aspects—Islam. 2. Peace—Religious aspects—Islam.
3. Conflict management—Religious aspects—Islam. 4. Religious tolerance—Islam.
5. Religious pluralism—Islamic countries. I. Title.
BP190.5 V56A28 2003
297.2'7—dc21   2002043033

The University Press of Florida is the scholarly publishing agency for the State University
System of Florida, comprising Florida A&M University, Florida Atlantic University,
Florida Gulf Coast University, Florida International University, Florida State University,
New College of Florida, University of Central Florida, University of Florida, University of
North Florida, University of South Florida, and University of West Florida.

University Press of Florida
15 Northwest 15th Street
Gainesville, FL 32611-2079
http://www.upf.com

Contents

Acknowledgments

There are many people to thank for the completion of this project. I am first of all grateful to the many individuals and groups who granted me the opportunity to converse with them on the subject of peace, nonviolence, and Islam. Since I began working on this project in 1997, I have had the privilege of interacting with many Muslim and non-Muslim peace builders and gaining from their experience. In almost every workshop I have led since 1997, I have asked for input directly from the participants on the notion of peace building and nonviolence in Islam. Thus, I am especially grateful to those participants who took part in peace-building workshops from Mindanao, Cairo, Amman, Gaza, Sarajevo, and Washington, D.C., to Harrisonburg, Virginia. Thank you for sharing your life experiences with me and for awakening my interest in religion and peace.

Many thanks are due to my research assistants, Amal Khoury, Lynn Kunkle, and Patrick Ncgoya, and others who reviewed this manuscript again and again and who helped me in collecting updated data for each of the sections. Thanks to Amr Abdullah, who was among the first readers of this manuscript; his constructive feedback and encouragement validated the need for this type of research among Muslim scholars. Thanks also to Lou Kriesberg, Michael Nagler, Asma'el Muhaiyaddeen, Mubarak Awad, Abdul Aziz Said, and David Smock (director of religion and interfaith initiative at the United States Institute of Peace) for their extensive suggestions.

Without the help and contribution of Joe Groves of Guilford College this manuscript would not have been completed. His field research on the Palestinian Intifada was crucial to the analysis and writing of the chapter on nonviolence and Islam in the Palestinian Intifada.

I gratefully acknowledge the institutional and moral support I have received from Guilford College Dean's fellowship, the School of International Service and International Peace and Conflict Resolution at American University, the United States Institute of Peace, and the Joan B. Kroc

Institute (Rockefeller Fellowship for Religion and Peace) at the University of Notre Dame, all of which made the completion of this project possible.

Finally, without the unwavering support of my wife, Ilham Nasser, and my beautiful children, Ayman and Luma, this project would not have been achieved. Ilham has truly been the source of my inspiration as well as my lifelong companion. This book is dedicated to her, and to my parents, who have consistently striven to practice Islamic peace-building values within the continuing context of a minority.

Note on Translation and Transliteration

In translating and transliterating people's names, places, and books' titles, I have followed the Library of Congress system of transliteration, without the diacritical marks. Exceptions include names and titles quoted directly from other sources, as well as terms familiar to many Western readers.

Introduction

Throughout the world's most volatile regions, a novel approach to peace building is taking hold. In Eastern Europe, Latin America, Africa, South and East Asia, and the Middle East the quest for peace is increasingly taking the form of conflict resolution training workshops, projects for building civil societies, nonviolent resistance and mobilization of resources, and civic education programs. The United Nations, along with regional organizations in Africa and Latin America, has been leading the way in fostering these methods of nonviolent conflict resolution (Rubenstein 1992; Laue 1991; Scimecca 1991; Ronald Fisher 1997).

This approach is also surfacing in academic studies and institutions. Hundreds of new conflict resolution and peace-building projects and programs have emerged in university and college course catalogues and are offered by a wide range of departments: international relations and development, economics, religion, education, psychology, social work, sociology, anthropology, and political science. New multidisciplinary academic programs are now granting formal degrees in peace building and conflict resolution. While originally dominated by Western models developed by scholars in the United States and Europe, the field of peace studies is increasingly incorporating indigenous and local cultural methods of intervention and analysis (Avruch 1998; Lederach 1995; Abu-Nimer 1996a).[1]

Efforts to apply peace-building approaches to the Middle East and other Muslim communities (such as the Philippines and Indonesia),[2] have been hampered by the widespread assumption that Islamic religion and culture are inimical to the principles of peace building and conflict resolution. Such presuppositions are evident not only in studies that examine the compatibility of Islam with democracy, human rights, and conflict resolution, but also in group discussions at peace-building training workshops.[3] The stereotype of a bellicose and intolerant Islamic worldview, so widely purveyed in the Western media, has wide currency among Western policymakers as well.[4]

Since 1990, images of violence have emanated from politically troubled Islamic countries such as Algeria, Lebanon, Egypt, and Sudan, where harsh government crackdowns against popular resistance have helped to reinforce prevailing Western images of Islamic culture and religion as inherently violent (Shaheen 1985). This Western preconception has been an impediment to discussing and promoting nonviolence and peace building in Islamic nations.[5]

The academic literature on the subject is no less tendentious. A search of the Library of Congress subject catalogue for resources on "Islam and nonviolence" produces fewer than five items. "Islam and Violence," by contrast, floods the screen with thousands of entries. This orientation is evident in the research of Western scholars and orientalists alike, both Muslim and non-Muslim.

There are many reasons for the pejorative cast of Islam in Western eyes: selective reporting (print and electronic), lack of academic research on positive and nonviolent activities and traditions in Islamic society, the legacy of colonial subordination of Islamic countries to the West, ignorance of cultural differences, failure of Muslims to convey their message, and the Arab-Israeli conflict. The result has been a persistently negative view among policymakers and many scholars (Norman 1993; Esposito 1992; Said 1981; Hippler 1995). Edward Said's description of such a notion in 1981 is still valid: "Yet there is a consensus on 'Islam' as a kind of scapegoat for everything we do not happen to like about the world's new political, social, and economic patterns. For the right, Islam represents barbarism; for the left, medieval theocracy; for the center, a kind of distasteful exoticism. In all camps, however, there is agreement that even though little enough is known about the Islamic world, there is not much to be approved of there" (1981, 15).

Joe Montville, in his foreword to Abdul Aziz Sachedina's pioneering study on pluralism, accurately captures the perception of Islam in the West and the motivation for the new study of pluralism and Islam: "In this environment, the image of Islam in the West, where knowledge of the faith and values of the more than one billion Muslim souls was almost nonexistent, became simplified and often ominous" (Sachedina 2000, viii).

The discussion of nonviolence and peace building in Islam threatens to derail those scholars and policymakers accustomed to traditional frameworks—apologetic, defensive, or orientalist—in the study of Islam. Now, at the beginning of the twenty-first century, with unprecedented opportunities for communication, the human density and passion of Arab-Muslim life have impinged with unprecedented sharpness on the awareness of even professional analysts of the Islamic world. Yet instead of fresh insights we continually reproduce crude, essentialized caricatures of contemporary Islam, freighted with geopolitical imperatives: the West, then, purveys the image of a belligerent, confrontational Islamic culture at odds with Western notions of the *normal* (Said 1981, 26).

This book is an attempt to address the potential and practices of nonviolence and peace building in an Arab-Muslim context. It aims to examine some of the basic misconceptions and misinformation abroad in Islamic studies about Muslims' views of nonviolence and peacemaking, not only by providing Qur'anic quotes and examples from the Prophet's life and sayings (Hadith), but also by offering examples of current peace-building practices and values among contemporary Muslims. The use of the sacred scriptures in this study is mainly intended to support the assumption that Islam is a lived religion and tradition that promotes peace building and the nonviolent settlement of conflicts. I will endeavor to show how such practices can be extended further in modern Islamic culture. Neither defensive, apologist, nor proselytizing Islamic faith, this study seeks to actively promote peace-building and nonviolence strategies and values rooted in the indigenous Islamic cultural and religious contexts, focusing on the identification of Islamic values, rituals, stories, and worldviews.

The present volume has two parts. Part 1 provides a theoretical framework and identifies the various Islamic values and principles supporting peace building and nonviolence. Chapter 1 sets the parameters and basic definitions for research on this subject. Chapter 2 highlights the basic assumptions, principles, and values of nonviolent methods and their place in Islamic religion. Part 2 presents three case studies derived from a Muslim-Arab context. Chapter 3 reviews traditional dispute resolution methods in Muslim-Arab communities, illustrating the daily application of nonviolence and peace building in Islamic social and interpersonal contexts. Chapter 4 examines the obstacles to applying nonviolent methods in Muslim-Arab frameworks and presents some options and strategies for overcoming them. Chapter 5 focuses on the Palestinian Intifada (1987–92) as an illustration of the possible political use of nonviolence in a Muslim community context. These include the function and role of cultural and religious values, norms, and the general sociocultural context for the massive application of nonviolent strategies and actions in the Intifada. The book concludes with a discussion of key issues in future theoretical research and applied projects in peace building based on indigenous methods and worldviews, focusing especially on the challenges facing both Muslim and non-Muslim scholars. Identifying and discussing nonviolence and peace building in Islamic religion, tradition, and culture contribute to a positive and much needed dialogue between West and East.

1

Peace Building and Nonviolence in Islamic Religion and Culture

A Theoretical Framework

Research that seeks to combine cultural analysis with conflict resolution requires an interdisciplinary approach. This book draws on anthropological methods and emerging conflict resolution theories in researching the application of peace-building principles and values in Islamic religion and culture, relying on a combination of emic and etic approaches to the study of culture. A major feature of the emic approach is the identification and use of native terms or institutions as key organizing concepts for description or analysis. It is a "thick description" of cultural institutions that uncovers the details and roots of the relevant cultural context of practice (Avruch 1998, 57). In conflict resolution, an emic approach would "emphasize the elucidation of the native's own understanding and theories of conflict, and their own techniques or processes for resolving it" (63).

An etic approach is characterized by the "identification of underlying, structurally deep, and transcultural forms, expressed in terms of certain descriptors that are putatively capable of characterizing domains across all cultures" (63). The structural and generic generalizations made by the etic approach can be based either on a large set of data gathered from many respondents or deduced from a particular theoretical orientation. Studies on high- and low-context cultures[1] are classic examples of an etic analysis, where diverse cross-cultural categories and tendencies are reduced into a "few manageable dimensions" (68). The etic scheme allows comparison across cultural contexts and allows the processing of a tremendous amount of data and variation in one or more cultures. In the study of conflict resolution, an etic approach allows us to group and conceptualize different cultural patterns of responses to conflict and violence.

An emic approach to Islamic culture and conflict resolution is centered on the actor and his or her context. The present work examines the various subcultures and the subjective factors that influence various conflict resolution practices in Muslim communities. An in-depth analysis of the Palestinian Intifada seeks to capture the role of religious values in the practice of nonviolent resistance and reflects an emic approach. This approach also applies to the analysis of Islamic peace building as put forward in the Qur'an and Hadith and in the discussion and "thick description" of the process of dispute resolution in Muslim communities.

When concepts and practices of peace building are introduced at a macro level, an etic analysis of the challenges to the study of peace building in Islamic culture and conflict resolution draws on the generic patterns of Islamic cultural behavior. In such an approach, the researcher focuses on the "objective" conditions of the conflict—political, socioeconomic, and geopolitical factors (Avruch 1998, 57)—to understand and classify the cultural patterns.

The purpose of examining those macro and generic obstacles to conflict resolution in a Muslim context is not to construct a list of cultural and social attributions that are valid in all Muslim societies but to identify those factors that might assist in the analysis and design of conflict resolution approaches in a given Muslim community. Integrating both emic and etic approaches to the study of Islam and peace building is the best way to understand the diversity and complexity of violent and nonviolent micro and macro responses to conflicts in a Muslim community and thus to forge specific and effective conflict resolution methods for these contexts.

These theoretical principles are reflected in each case-study discussion, which is guided by Avruch and Black's (Avruch, Black, and Scimecca 1991) anthropological framework of ethnoconflict theory and praxis and their transformative approach to conflict resolution. The assumption underlying these approaches is rooted in a relativist approach that does not view indigenous culture as inferior or in need of adaptation to outside, foreign, or imported models.

The present study also focuses on Muslim perceptions, metaphors, rituals, and other considerations that are rooted in Islamic belief. The study not only utilizes cognitive approaches to conflict resolution and culture (Avruch 1998, 59) but also focuses on rituals and metaphors adopted by Muslims as central to their own understanding of approaches to conflict resolution. These rituals are often deployed in all phases of the conflict resolution process, providing social and cultural meaning while connecting the form of resolution to the context of the conflict process. For example, when an old Arab-Muslim man walks bareheaded (without a *kufiya,* a square kerchief diagonally folded and worn as a traditional head cover for Arab men) in a Middle Eastern village, he is agreeing to pay one of the highest forms of compensation in exchange for settlement with his enemy. In addition, the analysis of the symbolic and immediate function of a public handshake, when hundreds of people are observing a traditional dispute resolution, is another illustration of the type of approach that is employed in this study, which allows the understanding of the subjective and objective factors that shape conflict resolution in indigenous communities.

This perceptual (cognitive and affective) approach to the study of Islam, culture, and conflict resolution is conducted through the eyes of Islamic actors, and the various case studies aim to illustrate metaphors and schemes in their communities. Tracing static patterns (attitudinal or behavioral patterns) is not an effective approach to the study of Islam and peace building because Islam is not a monolithic culture (or community), nor is it independent of specific geographical and historical contexts. On the contrary, there is a dynamic relationship between Islamic culture and ways of dealing with conflict, a relationship marked by changing patterns found within multiple cultures and subcultures (national, confessional, organizational, occupational, and so on) (Avruch 1998, 59). For example, an Indonesian Muslim community's ways of handling conflict might differ markedly from those of a Lebanese Sunni community in key respects. Thus, focusing on a general mode of conflict resolution is not sufficient; what is needed is a cultural analysis based on the ethnoconflict theory and praxis proposed by Avruch and Black. Such an approach of examining the dynamism of sociocultural institutions can assist in understanding how a specific Muslim group reacts to conflicts (Avruch 1998, 11).

This study makes no assumption of systematic "cultural coherence," or of an overarching "cross-domain" way of life or value, for all Muslim communities. Even if such a coherence exists, contradictions always emerge from the social practice in the "interdomain" (Avruch 1998,12). For instance, the analysis of hierarchy as an Islamic cultural value does not preclude the possibility of countervailing subcultural and social practices in Muslim communities. The use of generic concepts such as collectivism or hierarchy in studying Muslim society and culture is aimed at helping conflict resolution researchers and practitioners make initial observations, which are to be followed by more complex and contextual analyses that incorporate emic approaches.

This study also makes the assumption that Islamic culture resides in the individual as well as in institutions. Thus, both the individual cognitive and affective components of Islamic society, as well as its institutional components, are incorporated in conflict resolution. As Avruch argues (1998, 19), culture is not merely psychological or social; rather, Islam as a culture and religion is socially and psychologically distributed throughout a Muslim community.

Avruch (1998, 154) warns of six typical, inadequate ideas often adopted by researchers and practitioners when studying culture and conflict resolution. The present study avoids those ideas by assuming no homogeneity even within a single Islamic culture. To begin with, there are many internal paradoxes and subcultures within every Muslim community. Therefore, traditional dispute-resolution practices in Egypt, Palestine, or other Islamic societies do not constitute a single culture. Second, Islamic culture is not a "thing" that can be reified into a single object or dimension. Such a view overlooks the dynamism, diversity, and complexity of a Muslim cultural context. Third, Islamic culture is not uniformly distributed among all Muslims or members of a Muslim community. Even in a Palestinian Muslim village, members of the community will react to conflict and interact differently, and therefore the impact of such gauging of the influence of culture will be different for each individual. Fourth, a Muslim possesses many subcultural identities at the same time. The religious aspect of his or her identity is only one dimension, one that is not generic among all Muslims. Thus, there is no single religious Muslim method of dealing with conflicts. Fifth, Islamic ways of dealing with conflicts are not reducible to traditional dispute resolution, but tradition is one of the factors, along with social and political institutions. Sixth, Islamic culture is not timeless; it has changed throughout history. Thus, the values, norms, and practices of Muslims may keep their form but change dramatically in significance over time. (For example, Meccan-period norms and rituals are perceived differently in the twentieth century.)

To avoid these pitfalls, this study assumes that Islamic culture and its relationship to peace building is best examined from a "local-actor" perspective of a "local Muslim actor," an approach that is sensitive to sociocultural changes, processes, and the dynamics of subcultures. Understanding the practice of peace building from such a perspective is useful for countering the prevailing tendency to generically regard Islamic religion and culture as potential ideological foes.

Culture in this study is used as an analytical tool to understand conflict resolution. In Avruch's words, "Culture consists of derivatives of experience, more or less organized, learned or created by the individuals of population including those images or encodement and their interpretations (meanings) transmitted from past generation, from contemporaries, or formed by individuals themselves" (1998, 17).

Culture here is a discourse or a way for researchers to talk about the world, including social, political, religious, economic, and psychological contexts. Islamic culture can provide us with ways to address the relationship of individuals to social groups and institutions. Thus, Islamic religion is one system or way to organize individual meaning in Muslim societies. There are other elements (e.g., ethnicity, race, gender, region, tribal affiliation) that can influence responses to conflicts and methods of their resolution in a Muslim community.

Theories of conflict resolution and peace also constitute an integral part of the theoretical analysis in this research. Human-needs theory as developed by John Burton (1990) identifies the causes of conflicts as unfulfilled basic human needs that are generic and universal. The satisfaction of those needs, however, is culturally bound. Humans are deeply motivated to satisfy their basic needs of recognition, security, and identity. If any of those needs remain unfulfilled, individual or group conflict will result. A genuine resolution of conflict occurs only when those basic human needs are fully satisfied. Values and perceptions play a major role in defining the satisfaction of those needs. For example, self-esteem, identity, and security can be satisfied in different ways by different cultures, depending on the sets of values that govern the perceptions of individuals and groups. Identifying Islamic values and notions of quality of life for an individual and a community are keys to understanding how basic human needs are satisfied in Muslim communities.

From this perceptual framework, conflicts arise from both systemic and individual perceptions. Therefore, a lasting resolution for any conflict requires both systemic and individual analysis and intervention. Conflict resolution and peace building thus call for a collaborative approach that addresses both of these levels. The parties to the conflict are the experts in defining their needs and how to satisfy them. The role of a third party is to assist parties in identifying and understanding those needs and values when negotiations have deadlocked. Imposing outside resolution may provide temporary relief, but a lasting arrangement can only be designed and implemented by the parties themselves.

The approach in this study combines instrumental and cognitive or perceptional approaches to conflict resolution (Pruitt and Rubin 1986; Fisher and Ury 1981; Kriesberg 1991; Kelman 1990). It assumes that resolution of a conflict requires changes in the perceptions and attitudes of the parties and in the distribution of resources. The main assumption in this research is that mediation, arbitration, or other processes of conflict resolution and peace building are more effective if they are carried out by the parties themselves and if they are comprehensively and inclusively designed and implemented.

|

The Study of Islam, Nonviolence, and Peace

Conflict Resolution and Peace Studies

Before identifying the principles that underlie methods of conflict resolution and nonviolence and their applicability in Islamic religion and tradition, we must establish a specific set of distinctions and definitions to guide the discussion of pacifism, nonviolence, and peace building in Islam.

Peace researchers have long recognized the differences among various types of pacifism (Johnson 1987; Yoder 1992). "Prudential pacifism" calls for the use of nonviolent methods in the pursuit of pacifist goals, while conceding that such methods may entail coercion, or compelling people through reason or forcing them against their will to perform or refrain from acts by threats. "Absolute pacifism of witness," however, insists on noncoercive means and ends, using pacifism as a starting point and deploying strategies solely from within a pacifist framework. From the absolute pacifist perspective, the use of nonviolent tactics for resisting evil can be challenged or condemned as not being true pacifism on the grounds that the use of coercion, for any aim, is in principle unacceptable. Reinhold Niebuhr criticizes this absolutist distinction and argues that it is wrong to say that violence, as a policy, is intrinsically evil, since only motives can be interpreted as intrinsically evil. Violence and nonviolence are both forms of coercion and the differences between them are relative and not intrinsic. These differences exist in degree, not in the use of coercion to achieve certain goals. However, those who argue for absolute nonviolence reject these distinctions and insist that violence and nonviolence are different in their nature, kind, and motive. "They appeal to fundamentally different forms of morality. All problems of social morality must be regarded in pragmatic rather than absolute terms" (Childress 1982, 31–32).

James Childress (61) asserts that there are significant differences between violence and nonviolent acts; using examples from Tolstoy, Gandhi, and Arendt, he concludes that nonviolence has moral priority. Absolute and pragmatic pacifists take different stands in their attitudes to war. The pragmatist might see some justification for violence under certain circumstances, while the absolutist consistently rejects all forms of violence.

Absolute religious pacifism is a perfectionist approach ruled by a norm that requires nonresistance instead of nonviolent resistance. From this perspective, the ideal to strive for in this world is the achievement of perfect love in individual life. Absolute religious pacifism was not put forward as a rationale for strategic political activism but emerged instead as a rejection of mundane or political reality. Nevertheless, this argument provided a powerful platform from which to make political choices, such as refusing to participate in wars.

Nevertheless, refusing to engage in the world and fighting injustice are also criticized as politically irresponsible, particularly in regard to neglecting social responsibility toward other people living under injustice. It is this type of nonresistance that is feared or opposed by many Muslims and other oppressed groups when nonviolent and peace-building strategies are preached by peace workers.

Thus, one difficulty in studying pacifism lies in its diversity as a multifaceted phenomenon. As a working definition, pacifism refers to a set of overall principles that guides the application of nonviolent strategies. Pacifism can be grounded spiritually or instrumentally (Nojeim 1993), "absolutely" or "strictly" (Sisk 1992), or as creed or policy (R. Crow, Grant, and Ibrahim 1990), depending on whether the opposition to violence is a matter of principle (often based on spiritual beliefs) or of strategic, rational cost-benefit calculations. Regardless of the different types of pacifism identified by researchers (see Yoder 1992, which identifies twenty-nine types of pacifism; Johnson 1987), and regardless of whether the motivation is moral or pragmatic, there is a common opposition to the use of violence. The opposing parties may also differ in the degree and level of commitment to such principles.

However, James Johnson (1987) traces the development of the concept and practice of absolute pacifism and limited war in Western culture and devotes a significant portion of his study to the various reactions of religious and humanist pacifists to the political reality of war and violence. J. Howard Yoder (1992) also identifies many arguments made by pacifists to explain their absolute pacifism and antiwar positions, ranging from patriotic stands to a means of self-defense.

Johnson details three distinctive traditions in Western culture on approaches to peace, providing useful links to modern social, political, and religious movements. First, in the "just-war tradition, . . . violence is permitted in the service of good (including order, justice, and peace), but it is also restrained lest it adds to the burden of evil" (1987, 280). Peace then is the result of a balanced action between doing good and fighting evil. It is not a state of being but is rather an active process of maintaining balance through perpetual adjustment. Violence can be used for good or evil. The role of politics is to make sure that violence is used for good.

The second tradition identified by Johnson is the "utopian tradition," which promotes an amoral vision of the ideal human community in which all live at peace. The use of violence is rejected as evil itself and not permitted as a means to settle conflicts. However, nonviolence as a defensive or resistance tool has emerged. Followers of this approach do not necessarily remove themselves from the reality of the world. They seek active, pragmatic methods of nonviolence to resist evil.

The final approach is known as sectarianism, which combines elements of the two previous traditions; it is more pessimistic than the just-war tradition and more idealistic than the utopian. Adherents of sectarianism perceive earthly realities as polluted with evil. Peace will not take place on this earth but beyond it. The most that can be done is to create communities of peace that are "living the life of the new age already," and strive to keep the secular world outside their communities for fear of dragging them into worldly concerns and necessities (Johnson 1987, 281–82). Sectarianists express their quest for peace through an absolutist, pacifist rejection of violence and war. However, for them, either war or no war are the only options available in a "sick world."

Of the three traditions, the just-war doctrine has been developed most among theologians, historians, and scholars. The just-war doctrine has many criteria to justify the use of violence, which include legitimate or competent authority, just cause, right intention, announcement of intention, last resort, reasonable hope of success, proportionality, and just conduct (Childress 1982, 64). Johnson traces the roots of "just war" in the West and explains how these arguments historically developed and were later used to justify the colonization of the New World (Johnson 1991).

Childress (1982, 94) summarizes the relationship between just-war theories and nonviolence when stating that the just-war criteria do not answer the question of the justification of war in general but, more narrowly, the justification of particular wars. Thus they do not determine whether the existence of war institutions are legitimate or justified. Just-war and pacifist doctrines need each other. The pacifists rely on the just war arguments as permanent institutions to regulate fighting, and to maintain degrees of justice, order, and humanity within violent warfare.

For the purpose of comparative theological studies and for practical applications of pacifism, it is important not only to identify the above various distinctions between nonviolent methods and pacifism in Western culture but to expand and illustrate their links to Islamic civilization. However, for the purpose of examining nonviolent practices and change in Muslim communities, all forms of nonviolence utilized by Muslims will be explored and discussed, regardless of whether they were carried out as a result of deeply rooted spiritual beliefs or more pragmatic considerations of resisting evil. This study is mainly concerned with approaches that reject violence and actively oppose its consequences rather than advocating passive withdrawal from world reality (such means are used by Christian groups such as the Amish or the Church of the Brethren).

Nonviolence is a set of attitudes, perceptions, and actions intended to persuade people on the other side to change their opinions, perceptions, and actions. Nonviolence uses peaceful means to achieve peaceful outcomes. Nonviolence means that actors do not violently retaliate against the actions of their opponents. Instead, they absorb anger and damage while sending a steadfast message of patience and an insistence on overcoming injustice. The major features of nonviolent action are: (1) "It is non-aggressive physical, but dynamically aggressive spirituality." (2) "It does not seek to humiliate the opponent" but to persuade the opponent to change through new understanding and awareness of moral shame so as to reconstruct the other's "beloved communities." (3) "It is directed against forces of evil rather than against persons who are caught in these forces." (4) Nonviolence seeks to avoid not only "external physical violence but also internal violence of spirit." (5) Nonviolence is "based on the conviction that the universe is on the side of justice."[1]

Nonviolent resistance becomes successful only where there is sufficient preparation for it. The group has to be ready to engage in such resistance, particularly in actively establishing the conditions necessary for effective mass nonviolent resistance. At the end of the Second World War there was an increase in the interest in nonviolent methods of resistance, which allowed scholars to begin systematically exploring conditions for effective resistance. For example, Sibley (1944) identified four major conditions for successful strategic nonviolence: (1) no service or supplies to be furnished to invaders; (2) no orders to be obeyed except those of the constitutional civil authorities; (3) no insult or injury to be offered the invader; and (4) all public officials pledge to die rather than surrender.

Childress (1982) distinguishes between just-war and nonviolent approaches as being based on different ethics of responsibility. By analyzing the notion of trust and responsibility, he arrives at nonviolent resistance as morally right and effective.

This conclusion is premised on the sanctity of human life: the nonviolent resister puts his life in the hands of his opponent. Childress highlights three features of effective nonviolent resistance: (1) a recognition of sacred boundaries of action, (2) a voluntary assumption of risk, and (3) a sense of equality (1982, 98). The nonviolent resister makes him- or herself vulnerable to physical assault, injury, and death, not to mention imprisonment. The resister takes a greater risk through a reliance on (but not full confidence in) the opponent's sense of moral responsibility, making the assumption that the opponent can control his or her actions and refrain from killing or injuring the resister.

Such an approach is in alignment with Gandhi's differentiation of passive nonviolence into "nonviolence of the weak" and "nonviolence of the strong" as an effective force for transformation. This is similar to the distinction between the notion of unviolence, where violence is not possible, and nonviolence, which involves a voluntary decision or commitment. These distinctions affect the opponent in different ways. Childress (1982, 20) argues that it is more powerful and ultimately more effective to allow opponents to feel secure because their resister will not harm them physically, instead of deriving a sense of security from defending themselves with weapons.

Suffering is generally accepted as an inescapable component of successful resistance. "Not to be confused with passive suffering or nonresistance, nonviolent action involves suffering in resistance, in noncooperation, or disobedience" (21). It is the suffering generated by nonviolent campaigns that often stimulates a sense of injustice in third parties, and not suffering from the opponent, as would be expected.

Separating the person from the problem, or separating the evildoer from the evil deeds, is a third important feature of effective nonviolent campaigns. If the nonviolent resister targets the deeds and not the people who perform them, the conflict becomes depersonalized, allowing a sense of trust to emerge in the opponent, while keeping attention relentlessly focused on the sources of injustice.

The discussion of nonviolence is important to the study of Islam and peace building because nonviolence is at the core of all peace-building programs and approaches. Any application of peace-building methods must, therefore, presuppose an understanding of how the culture and religion of a given society relate to nonviolence. In this study the emphasis is on the nonviolent methods and values within Islam, and not on the debate of whether Islam is an "absolute" pacifist religion or not. Thus when discussing nonviolent applications and values in Islam, the study does not necessarily seek to imply that the religion or its adherents should subscribe to theologically absolute pacifism. The purpose instead is to identify the religious sources that promote and support the use of nonviolent methods in resolving disputes. Although pacifism and nonviolence are not identical, the use of these terms in this study will refer to the common principles and practices of rejecting war and violence (nonviolence), regardless of whether it is motivated by spiritual, moral, cultural, or political considerations.

Peace Building: A Bridge between Peace and Conflict Resolution

The field of peace studies is made up of scholars and peace activists who have a long history of struggle for social and political change. Peace studies researchers and activists have traditionally promoted values of cooperation instead of competition; dialogue, protest, and peaceful resistance instead of violence; and persuasion instead of coercion. During the Cold War, peace research and activism focused on nuclear disarmament and promoted mutual security arrangements. Beginning in the 1950s, when pioneers of peace research began challenging the dominant realist and power paradigms of political science and international relations, they were known as idealists.

Peace activists have also historically been involved in struggles against racial and ethnic discrimination. An important contribution of peace studies is the emphasis on structural analysis of a conflict (Galtung 1969) as a means of identifying underlying causes of social inequity and discrimination in society. Justice and peace are viewed as correlative concepts, so that the advocacy of one naturally entails the advocacy of the other.

In contrast, the professional field of conflict resolution has a short history. It emerged in the 1960s out of various social and political movements in the United States. The industrial arena was the first to develop the concepts of cooperation and collaboration among employees within companies and to utilize collective bargaining strategies in settling labor disputes. Burton (1969) was among the first scholars to bring conflict resolution concepts into international relations. Community dispute resolution and Alternative Dispute Resolution (ADR) practices emerged in response to the Civil Rights movement in the United States and the crushing caseload in the U.S. court system. As a result of these developments, there are two distinct domains in the field of conflict today: (1) ADR, in which mediators or arbitrators settle disputes informally or via court orders. This widespread practice constitutes a major segment of the field (for dealing with conflicts relating to divorce, the environment, labor, and public policy). (2) Conflict resolution as applied to international and community (training and other intervention), education (school peer mediation programs), community problem-solving centers, and academic programs in conflict resolution.

There are several key distinctions between ADR and other conflict resolution models and approaches. The main distinction pertains to conflict resolution as a vehicle for long-term change as opposed to the short-term approaches advocated by the ADR models. Some scholars of conflict resolution (e.g., Scimecca 1991) have argued that ADR can be used as a means of social control, while conflict resolution can promote social change.

Among the assumptions that guide the various conflict resolution processes (mediation, facilitation, conciliation, and negotiation) are the following:[2]

Conflict is not necessarily evil or a failure of an existing system. On the contrary, conflict often is a creative force that generates new alternatives and solutions.

Conflict is a natural process that can have either constructive or destructive outcomes or both.

Conflict is an intrinsic part of all relationships.

Conflict is caused by many different kinds of events.

People are not problems.

Having clear and explicit expectations is a crucial and essential part of any resolution process and of reaching an agreement or understanding the issues involved.

Conflict can be positive when it increases communication and trust; the problem is solvable; it results in development and growth; it releases pent-up feelings; it improves work and performance.

Conflict can be negative when it develops into war or violence; prevents and blocks personal and group development; prevents people from addressing the real issues; motivates people to become uncooperative.

Conflict can be managed or settled constructively through communication. However, not all conflict can be resolved by improving communication.

Not all conflicts lend themselves to joint or negotiated endings. But when mutually satisfactory outcomes can be found, they tend to be more self-enforcing, efficient, and durable.

Conflict resolution process can be creative. It can lead to new or improved relationships and can help identify new criteria, resources, and outcomes.

These points reveal a great deal of overlap between the fields of peace studies and conflict resolution as defined in this section. Thus, in spite of the continuing debate between conflict resolution and peace studies on the boundaries and distinctions of each field, both are still searching for and defining their parameters and unique characteristics. Nevertheless, in this study no distinction is made between conflict resolution, peace building, and other nonviolent approaches. They all share the assumption that to resolve a conflict, parties must be committed to nonviolent approaches and methods. Such a common assumption does not exclude diplomacy or similar activities carried out during a war, but the term *peace building* excludes any strategies that encourage or actually use force and violence to resolve differences among conflicting parties (For further literature on such conflict resolution approach see Burton 1990; Diamond and McDonald 1991; Ronald Fisher 1997; Lederach 1997).

Islam and Nonviolence: Basic Research Assumptions

When addressing social and political phenomena, scholars and practitioners operate within a framework governed by certain assumptions. Uncovering these assumptions when examining Islam and nonviolence will contribute to a deeper understanding of the discussion and the objectives of the research. As in other social science studies, all knowledge is interpretation, so that interpretation must be self-conscious in its methods and aims if it is to be vigilant, humane, and useful. A choice faces every intellectual and scholar: whether to put intellect in the service of power or of criticism, community, and moral sensibility (Said 1981, 164).

When applying this postmodern approach to research into Islam and nonviolence, scholars must be prepared to acknowledge and uncover their own cultural and religious interpretations and assumptions that govern their worldview. They should ask themselves, when addressing the relationship between Islam and nonviolence, whether they are serving the power of the status quo or promoting constructive criticism, community, and moral sensibility.

The possibilities for addressing social and political problems through Islam have yet to be fully realized. Islam as a religion and as a tradition is replete with teachings and applications about peaceful resolutions of conflicts and thus provides rich resources for nonviolent values, beliefs, and strategies. For Muslims, inquiry within the Islamic scripture is highly valued and encouraged, particularly in developing an awareness of the Qur'an, the Prophet's tradition (Hadith), and the early Islamic period. These sources have remained a source of inspiration for Muslims and Islamic movements in every age (Esposito 1992, 25), a legacy that is especially evident in Islamic developments in philosophy, ideology, law, and science. Moreover, the influence of early Islamic thought and scripture are clearly discernible even in Gandhi's philosophy and methods of nonviolence, as suggested by Sheila McDonough (1994)[3] and Chaiwat Satha-Anand (1993).

A second assumption is that when dealing with Islam and nonviolence, there is a need to constantly reconsider and reevaluate our understanding and application of Islam in various historical periods, especially as a way of understanding the collective and individual survival of Muslim communities.[4] In the words of Edward Said, "For Muslim as for non-Muslim, Islam is an objective and also a subjective fact, because people create that fact in their faith, in their societies, histories, and traditions, or, in the case of non-Muslim outsiders, because they must in a sense, fix, personify, stamp, the identity of that which they feel confronts them collectively or individually. This is to say that the media's Islam, the Western scholar's Islam, the Western reporter's Islam, and the Muslim's Islam are all acts of will and interpretation that take place in history" (1981, 40).

Because Islam is subject to diverse interpretations, knowledge of it should not be treated as the property of small, privileged elites. Said's concept of "communities of interpretations" is an important addition to the effort to grasp Islam as both subject and object while viewing its religious and cultural traditions through the lenses of nonviolence and peace building (1982, 26).

Third, there is still a severe lack of comprehensive knowledge and hermeneutics in the area of nonviolent conflict resolution among Muslims themselves. Most of the academic research and writings that have been carried out (not only by orientalist but also by Muslim scholars) is aimed at the study and interpretation of war, violence, power, political systems, or legal arrangements. This limited perspective underutilizes the vast resources available to the Muslim community for dealing with contemporary challenges. Abdul Aziz Sachedina states that "if Muslims were made aware of the centrality of Koranic teachings about religious and cultural pluralism as a divinely ordained principle of peaceful coexistence among human societies, then they would spurn violence in challenging their repressive and grossly inefficient governments" (2000, 13). Approaching Islamic tradition and religion from narrow perspectives and neglecting research into peaceful Islamic methods of conflict resolution can inadvertently perpetuate negative images and perceptions among policymakers, nonobservant Muslims, and non-Muslims while narrowing the possibilities and dynamics for change.

Fourth, it is the Muslims' duty to project an image of Islam that is closer to how they perceive it, rather than leaving it to popular writers whose knowledge of Islam may be simplified or leaves out important aspects of its complex nature (Satha-Anand 1993). In addition, it is the peacemakers' duty, regardless of their faith, to identify both the religion's violent and *religio-centric* values, beliefs, and practices as well as its constructive and *religio-relative* side. Emphasizing the latter set of values, beliefs, and rituals is in itself an act of peace building that promotes conflict resolution between religions.

Fifth, the discussion of nonviolence and conflict resolution in Islam can not be limited only to the holy book (the Qur'an) or the Prophet's tradition. Muslim cultures and traditions are rich in values, belief systems, and strategies that facilitate the application of nonviolence and conflict resolution. Such a comprehensive approach to the study of conflict resolution and nonviolent peace building in Islam can be effective in promoting values and strategies of peace building in day-to-day economic, social, educational, and political interactions. Including culture and tradition in the study of conflict resolution and nonviolence in Islam is an important step of inclusion for non-Muslims living in a society in which Muslims constitute the majority. In such societies, the sociocultural context has been deeply shaped by Islam. Both Muslims and non-Muslims adhere to these traditional and cultural values and beliefs regardless whether their motivations are grounded in religion or not.

It is crucial, then, not to limit the meaning and definition of the religious context to the scripture and the Prophet's tradition and to include cultural and social norms and values derived from Islamic history and tradition. Depending on the region, religious norms and values have often been culturally and socially adopted and modified by both Muslims and non-Muslims in Middle Eastern societies (Tibi 1988; Zubaida 1992b).[5] Typical examples of those values include the emphasis on honor, shame, faithfulness, brotherhood, and wisdom (*hikmah*). These are often emphasized by indigenous peacemakers (mediators and arbitrators) through the use of certain stories derived from the scripture or the Prophet's tradition (Abu-Nimer 1996a,b; Barakat 1993).

Sixth, Islamic religion and tradition offer various teachings and practices that can be applied to building peace and resolving conflicts. The nature and validity of these teachings depend on the various levels and types of interaction—family, community, interpersonal, Muslim, or non-Muslim. However, there is a set of peace-building values that, if consistently and systematically applied, addresses all varieties of conflict. Some of those values—justice (*'adl*), beneficence (*ihsan*), and wisdom (*hikmah*)—have already been identified by scholars. They are core principles for peacemaking (see the discussion of these values later in this section).

Seventh, it is important to differentiate between the terms *Arab* and *Muslim*. Although most Arabs are Muslims, many are not; non-Muslim Arabs are mostly Christians who are nevertheless Arab in their cultural and national identity despite living in predominantly Islamic cultures. Hence, Arab culture (including language and shared common experiences) functions as a common denominator for Muslims and non-Muslims in the Middle East. Using the terms *Arab* and *Muslim* interchangeably, so common in Western media, is inaccurate and misleading, even though 90 percent of the Arabs in the Middle East are Muslims by faith (Barakat 1993, 41).

Likewise, the term *Muslim* does not refer only to Arab Muslims; in fact, the majority of Muslims are not Arabs. Most Muslims live outside Arab countries. While there are many common religious and cultural traditions shared by Arab and non-Arab Muslims, there are differences that preclude any facile generalizations about "all Muslims." For instance, an Indonesian Muslim, due to different sociohistorical and cultural factors, is likely to take a different view of nonviolent peace building than an Egyptian or Palestinian Muslim.[6]

This study is chiefly concerned with the Arab-Muslim culture of the Middle East, whose Islamic roots extend back to the fifth century C.E. The empirical data that relate to cultural aspects of nonviolence and peace building are all derived from Arab-Muslim cultural contexts such as Egypt, Palestine, and Jordan.

Awareness and adoption of the foregoing assumptions in research on Islam and peace building can (1) assist both Muslim and non-Muslim researchers in expanding their perceptions and understanding of the relationship between the concepts and practices of nonviolent peace building on the one hand, and Islamic culture, religion and tradition on the other; (2) reduce the possibility of pejorative, stereotypical preconceptions about Islamic society and religion, which may inhibit resolution processes; and (3) provide researchers with a way to avoid being caught in a rigidly literal interpretation of Qur'anic verses and the Prophet's sayings, without consideration of historical context or social, political, and cultural forces that have influenced the lives of Muslims and non-Muslims alike.

Studies of Modernity, Democracy, and Nonviolence in Islam: A Compatibility Approach

Studying the compatibility between Islam and peace building involves the analysis of a large body of scholarship that has focused on the study of democracy and Islam (Abed 1995; Anderson 1994; Clawson 1994; Dunn 1992; Esposito 1988, 1992; Esposito and Piscatori 1991; Garnham and Tessler 1995; G. Jansen 1992; Kramer 1993; Lewis 1993; Mernissi 1992; Miller 1993; Norton 1993; Sivan 1990; al-Suwaidi 1995; Voll and Esposito 1994; Wright 1992; Zartman 1992; Zubaida 1992a,b).

Our search for conflict resolution and nonviolent peace-building principles and values in Islamic religion and tradition is inherently different from the traditionalist and conservative trends in Islam that spread in the nineteenth century in response to the challenge of modernization.[7] Moreover, in most instances, modernization has fostered a rise in the degree and scope of violence in society.[8] Thus, nonviolence and peace-building strategies are not the exclusive domain or concern of modern, urbanized Western societies. Nonviolence and peace-building strategies are authentic components of the traditional, pre–nineteenth-century Islamic sociocultural context as well, with solid roots in Muslim culture and history. Uncovering and reconstructing nonviolent peace-building values and strategies can help indigenous Muslim communities to develop economically, socially, and politically.

Nevertheless, the comparative study of Islamic and non-Islamic cultures dates at least to the eighteenth-century emergence of Muslim and Arab reformers, who debated the applicability of modernism to Muslim societies. The collapse of the Ottoman Empire further fueled the development of such studies. In the mid-1950s and 1960s another debate over the compatibility of socioeconomic development with Islam began, followed in the 1970s by a classic postcolonial debate regarding democracy and Islam. From these debates, two viewpoints have emerged: the liberal and the Islamist (Sisk 1992). Each has attempted to provide proofs of the validity of its argument through the Qur'an and Hadith. The liberal view allows for broad interpretation of the holy scriptures, whereas the Islamist approach adopts a literal, restrictive interpretation. At the heart of the debate is the degree of infallibility of the Hadith—the authenticity of the Qur'an is not debated—and their applicability to modern life.[9] There is a wide range of middle-ground views between these divergent interpretations in which compatibility with democratic values emerges for some points but not others (Sisk 1992, 17).

The study of Islam and nonviolent peace building can thus be viewed historically as an extension and continuation of the study of the debates over Islam and democracy of the 1970s. Scholars in the peace and nonviolence field can examine these issues in Islam using the same methodology. Underlying both arguments are the assumptions that the hallmark of the perfect Muslim community is law and reason and that Islam as a world religion is capable of reforming itself and adapting to an ever-changing world (Sachedina 2000, 2).

The debates over nonviolence and pacifism and their compatibility with Islam are also similar to those in the field of human rights and Islam. "Muslims have espoused a wide range of opinions on rights—from the assertion that international human rights are fully compatible with Islam to the claim that international human rights are products of alien and Western culture and represent values that are repugnant to Islam" (Mayer 1991, 3). Between those two extremes, there are moderates who accept many but not all aspects of international human rights, or who endorse human rights with certain reservations and qualifications. There is no definitive guidance in the interpretation of the modern Shari'ah in regard to nonviolence, and with similar human rights issues there have been no settled doctrines in contemporary Islamic thought.

Some of the arguments in the debate between democracy and Islam provide greater insight into the role of interpretation in Islam. William Zartman stresses the elasticity of the scripture as an interpretive source for democratic values: "There is no inherent incompatibility between democracy and Islam. Like all scripture, the Qur'an can be interpreted to support many different types of political behavior and systems of government. It contains no direct support for democracy, the closest statement being an indication that 'what is with God is better and most lasting for those . . . who [have conducted] their affairs by mutual consultation [*shurah*].' As would be expected, its emphasis is much more on the pious qualities of a ruler than on the way in which rulers should be chosen" (1992, 32). The ruler in Islam does not derive his authority directly from God but from God's law as expressed in the Shari'ah, in what Majid Khadduri (1984, 4) calls a "nomocracy." Nevertheless, "no human institutions can claim representation of God's interest on earth" (Sachedina 2000, 5–6). Such principles allow Muslims the flexibility to evaluate their rulers.

However, if Zartman did not exactly capture the duality of Islamic religion and democracy, George Weigel, in the context of Islam and nonviolence, points out the multiple possibilities that exist in many religions, including Islam: "It would be foolish for people of faith to deny that religion can be a source of violent conflicts. . . . But it would be imprudent, unwise, and just plain wrongheaded for both religious skeptics and statesmen to ignore the fact that religious convictions have also functioned as a powerful warrant for social tolerance, for democratic pluralism, and for nonviolent conflict resolution" (1992, 173). After reviewing in detail the impact of Christianity and Judaism on Western democratic and pluralist societies, Weigel briefly mentions three examples of researchers who are exploring the relationship in Islam between human rights, democracy, peace, and just war. However, in his response to those who do not see the links between Islamic values and human rights and democracy, he warns, "on the bases of these realities, one should not prematurely dismiss Islam as a potential religious ally in the pursuit of peace and development of nonviolent means of conflict resolution within and among the nations" (185).

Similar to the argument against the inherent compatibility of Islam and democracy, the Islamic scriptures can be interpreted to support many different types of peace-building activities, both among Muslims and between Muslims and other peoples. The above argument on democracy and Islam illustrates the need for an interpretative approach to Islam with regard to nonviolence, similar to Said's communities of interpretations, which reflect both the objective and the subjective sides of Islam. The assumptions discussed in this chapter can be guiding principles for such communities in the study of Islam and nonviolent peace building.

Current Studies of Peace and Nonviolence in Islam

There is a large and growing academic literature that addresses the question of whether and how Islam as a religion supports principles and values of nonviolence, peace, and war. These studies can be divided into three main categories, each with its own research issues, perspectives, and interpretations of Islamic religion and tradition: studies of war and jihad, studies of just war and peace, and studies of nonviolence and peace building.

Studies of War and Jihad

Scholars in this group attempt to support the hypothesis that Islamic religion and tradition lend themselves easily and uniquely to both war and violence as means of settling conflicts and differences. This group argues that Islam is a religion of war and that violence is an integral part of the Islamic religion and tradition. Therefore, nonviolent methods are not even broached by such writers, who consider such notions inimical to the Islamic tradition. Their analyses typically exclude Qur'anic verses or Hadiths that counsel the pursuit of peace by Muslims (see Pipes 1992; Lewis 1993; Sivan 1990).

Instead, members of this group have overemphasized (and, to some extent, have been "obsessed" with) the principle of violent jihad (holy war) in Islam. They point to jihad in both Islamic history and religion. Violent jihad has been described as an ultimate method that Muslims employ to settle their internal and external differences. These scholars and policymakers tend to view the behavior and writings of Muslims mainly through the lenses of violent jihad. Interpretations of contemporary Islamic groups or organizations (for instance, the statements and actions of Algerian, Egyptian, or Iranian Islamic movements) are viewed as byproducts of a violent Islamic penchant for jihad.[10] Ignoring the nonviolent aspects of Islamic religion and cultural tradition, such studies usually focus on fundamentalism and the recent emergence of radical Islamic movements.[11] (See, for example, Dunn 1992; Emerson 1993a,b; J. Jansen 1986; Kepel 1994; Kramer 1993; Lawrence 1986; Pryce-Jones 1992; Wright 1985.)[12] In addition to the typical studies mentioned above, a new type of study, neo-orientalism, has been identified by researchers like Joel Beinin and Joe Stork (1997) and Sachedina (2000). These studies refuse to see the potential of Islamic society to produce or develop civil society or democratic entities, due to the historical development of the culture and religion.

Studies of Just War and Peace

Studies in this category hypothesize that Islamic religion and tradition justify the use of violence under certain limited and well-defined conditions. When compared with the first group studying war and jihad, these scholars and writers differ markedly in their approach. First, these scholars view Islam as a religion upholding peace and justice, and they consider the use of limited force in jihad as one of many ways to pursue peace and justice, but not the central or only way to resolve differences. This group has focused on the conditions and circumstances under which Islam as a religion and tradition has allowed the use of force to settle internal or external conflicts. (See, for example, Ahmad 1993; Ayoub 1997; Carmody and Carmody 1988; Hashmi 1996; Kelsay 1993; Khadduri 1984; Rahman 1996; Sachedina 1996; Saiyidain 1994.) Many of the studies in this category aim at objectively presenting the Islamic interpretations of just war and peace, but they tend to approach this topic from a framework of security and power politics, strategic studies, or classic Islamic studies and not peace and conflict resolution. They therefore tend to focus on the specific conditions that allow the use of force in Islam, while nevertheless assuming that it is a religion of peace and justice.

Al-Farabi was the first Muslim scholar to characterize wars as just or unjust on the basis of whether they served the individual interest of the ruler or promoted the general good of the people (Khadduri 1984, 172). Peace and war are fundamental to the Islamic worldview, although war and violence have tended to receive more attention in popular media representation of Islam (Martin 1991, 93). In fact, Khadduri stated as early as 1966 (Shaybani and Khadduri, 17) that Islam makes a strong claim that both peace and war are ultimately rooted in the divine purpose of human history. From this view, the ultimate objective of the Islamic worldview is peace, not war. No purpose for war exists, except one that aims to defend the interests of the Ummah (worldwide community of Muslims).

The works of Sohail Hashmi (1996) and Abdul Aziz Sachedina (1996) are representative of this group. Hashmi (1996) identifies several essential assumptions based on the Qur'an: (1) Man's fundamental nature is one of moral innocence—that is, freedom from sin. (2) Man's nature is to live on earth in a state of harmony and peace with other living beings—hence the responsibility assigned by God to man, his khalifah (caliph, vicegerent) on this planet (Qur'an 2:30).[13] Peace (*salam*) means therefore not merely an absence of war, but also the elimination of the grounds for conflict and the waste and corruption (*fasad*) it creates. Peace, not war or violence, is God's true purpose for humanity. (3) Given humanity's capacity for wrongdoing, there will always be some who choose to violate nature and transgress against God's commandments. (4) Each prophet encounters opposition from those (always a majority) who persist in their rebellion against God and justify their actions through various forms of self-delusion by *kufr* (rejection of God) and *zulm* (oppression). (5) Peace is attainable only when human beings surrender to God's will and live according to God's laws. (6) Since it is unlikely that individuals or societies will ever conform fully to the precepts of Islam, Muslims must always be prepared to fight to preserve the integrity of the Muslim faith and Muslim principles (8:59, 60, 73).

These principles identified by Hashmi—particularly the first three—clearly provide a strong foundation for peace building and conflict resolution in Islam. For example, the first assumption indicates that an individual's violent behavior and perceptions can be changed because a person's nature is one of moral innocence. Humans can learn to be peaceful and abandon their wrongdoing. The second assumption sees humans as essentially peaceful by nature rather than evil. Human nature is to aspire to peace and not to war or violence. Humans seek harmony with nature and other living beings. The third and fourth principles assume that conflicts are an integral part of life and that people are enjoined to grapple with them in morally prescribed or tenable ways, a view that conforms to the core assumption of conflict resolution theories and practices. This illustrates an important principle of conflict transformation: conflict is a natural phenomenon and it will always be part of the human reality. Therefore, those who reject God and oppress others will constantly struggle with those who attained peace by surrendering to God's will. Being a good and faithful Muslim becomes the condition necessary to achieving internal and external peace and harmony. The last principle, which requires Muslims to defend the Islamic faith, is mainly a call for action and resistance to unbelief and oppression.

Hashmi, like other researchers in this category, recognizes the peaceful assumptions of Islam, but he dwells on the latter points (especially the sixth assumption) to support the argument that Islam cannot be an "absolute nonviolent" religion since it justifies acts of war and the use of force under certain strict conditions. He provides a well-developed set of conditions that should guide Muslims in the use of force. However, Hashmi's main argument is that although Islam allows the use of force, it prohibits aggression; its main objective is achieving peace through justice and the preservation of the faith and values. Like other scholars in this group, Hashmi assumes that defending Islam, and attaining justice and peace, does not take place via nonviolence; consequently, the use of limited or conditional force is permitted and under certain circumstances is a necessary step.

Kelsay (1993), examining the nature of peace from a classic Sunni perspective, notes that peace is characterized by four main features: (1) a conception of human responsibility, in which humans are endowed with knowledge and reason, which makes them responsible for their actions; (2) the possibility of human choice—humans are expected to select either the way of heedlessness or ignorance (*jahiliyah*) or the way of submission (*islam*); (3) a political outcome resulting from these choices. Kelsay sees the way of heedlessness and the way of submission as institutionalized in Islamic and non-Islamic political entities. The territory of Islam (*dar al-islam*) and the territory of war (*dar al-harb*) are viewed in this way as political institutions; whereby the fourth approach to peace involves a program of action in which jihad is employed to extend the boundaries of *dar al-islam*, the territory of Islam (peace). Kelsay concludes that "Sunni theorists understood force to be a possible and useful means of extending the territory of Islam and thus a tool in the quest for peace" (1993, 35).

Scholars in the just-war and peace category spent a great portion of their studies investigating the application of jihad in *dar al-harb*, the territory of war. In supporting the argument that Islam does not absolutely prohibit war or the use of force, scholars in this group have explored the existence and applicability of the rules of violent engagement. They often point out the following Qur'anic verses: "To those against whom war is made, permission is given (to fight), because they are wronged—and verily, Allah is Most Powerful for their aid" (22:39). "Fight in the cause of Allah those who fight you, but do not transgress limits; for Allah loveth not transgressors" (2:190).

Abdullah Yusuf Ali's commentary on these verses perfectly illustrates the principles of this group: "War is permissible in self-defense, and under well-defined limits. When undertaken, it must be pushed with vigour (but not relentlessly), but only to restore peace and freedom for the worship of Allah. In any case strict limits must not be transgressed: women, children, old and infirm men should not be molested, nor trees and crops cut down, nor peace withheld when the enemy comes to terms" (1991, 76, comm. 204).

Within this second group of scholars, there has been a great deal of discussion and research by both Muslim and non-Muslim scholars about the context and meaning of *jihad*. Many of these studies conclude that *jihad* does not mean the constant use of the sword to resolve problems among Muslims or with non-Muslim enemies. On the contrary, the highest form of *jihad* has been interpreted as by means of the Holy Book itself or "the weapon of Allah's Revelation" (Abdullah Ali 1991, 901, comm. 3110). "Therefore listen not to the Unbelievers, but strive against them with the utmost strenuousness, with the (Qur'an)" (25:52). These scholars often cite the Qur'anic verse forbidding the use of force for imposing religion: "Let there be no compulsion in religion" (2:256).

The well-known Indian Muslim reformist Moulavi Cheragh Ali (1844–1895), who defended Islam from the accusations of western scholars, stated in regard to jihad and fighting: "All the fighting injunctions in the Qur'an are, in the first place, only in self-defense, and none of them has any reference to make warfare offensively. In the second place, it is to be particularly noted that they were transitory in their nature, and are not to be considered positive injunctions for future observance or religious precepts for coming generations. Ata, a learned legist of Mecca who flourished at the end of the first century of the Hijrah [the Prophet's migration to Medina] as jurist-consult, held that *jihad* was incumbent only on the Companions of the Prophet, and was not binding on any one else after them. They were only temporary measures to meet the emergency of the aggressive circumstances."

Even the literal meaning for the word *jihad* has been misunderstood, as Moulavi Cheragh Ali explains: "The word rendered 'strenuous' is originally 'mujahid,' which in classical Arabic and throughout the Qur'an means to do one's utmost, to make efforts, to strive, to exert, to employ one's-self diligently, studiously, sedulously, earnestly, zealously, or with energy and does not mean fighting or warfare. It was subsequently applied to religious war, but was never used in the Qur'an in such a sense."[14]

Based on this and other verses, scholars in this category reflect on the possibility of both nonviolent jihad and certain restrictions on the use of violence. While self-defense does not generate much dispute among these scholars, the notion of offensive attacks has stirred great debate. However, the use of violence itself is not challenged by most Islamic scholars, and they conclude that just war is seen as permissible in Islam, as Fred Donner states: "The Qur'anic text as a whole conveys an ambivalent attitude toward violence. On the one hand, oppression of the weak is roundly condemned, and some passages state clearly that the believers are to fight only in self-defense. But a number of passages seem to provide explicit justification for the use of war or fighting to subdue unbelievers, and deciding whether the Qur'an actually condones offensive war for faith, or only defensive war, is really left to judgment of the exegete" (1991, 47).

Donner goes on to argue that "war was definitely seen as valid, indeed even necessary, means of dealing with non-Muslims, at least in the cases when non-Muslims attack Muslims, and perhaps in more general terms" (47). The dual meaning of jihad is also captured by Khadduri, in the use of jihad as a valued instrument with which Muslims sought to achieve their objectives. "But the *jihad,* though often described as a holy war, did not necessarily call for fighting, even though a state of war existed between the two *dars—dar al-salam* and *dar al-harb*—since Islam's ultimate goals might be achieved by peaceful as well as by violent means" (1984, 164).

Khadduri also recognizes jihad as a just war but, again, the only type of war permitted in Islam. Jihad is considered a collective duty in the sense that believers have a duty to participate in fighting when they are so called upon by appropriate religious authorities. Due to changes in Islamic political and territorial boundaries, particularly with the concern that internal security and Muslim unity were at risk, Islamic scholars began revising their notion of jihad. Thus emerged a conventional acceptance of jihad as a defensive war instead of a constant state of war with the unbelievers (Khadduri 1984, 169; see also Ibn Taymiyya 1949, 115–16).

Those who emphasize the legitimacy of war often find its cultural justification in pre-Islamic and Arabian cultural tradition. Sachedina (2000, 113) provides an example. In spite of a greater emphasis on forgiveness, the Qur'an justifies the use of force under specific circumstances, in keeping with pre-Islamic Arab tribal culture, which had institutionalized the military to defend tribal security. But for Sachedina, the recognition of use of force goes beyond historical justification. Sachedina argues that using limited physical force was recognized by the Qur'an as reflective of the reality of human nature underlined by alternations between peace and conflict under harsh and complex sociopolitical conditions. Instead of rejecting this reality, the Qur'an seeks to effect moral restrictions on the use of force, permitting its expression only defensively and within the context of interpersonal human conduct. However, the Qur'an was then used to justify the offensive use of force in jihad. Attacking unbelievers or converting them by force is clearly not supported by the Qur'an. What is unambiguous is that only when the Muslim community is attacked will defense be appropriate and a duty of its members. "Legitimate *Jihad* makes human relationships central for building an ideal polity. More important, *Jihad* is divinely sanctioned only as a measure for enhancing the security and integrity of the Muslim polity. Hence any *Jihad* that leads to meaningless destruction of human life and ignores concerns for peace with justice is non-Koranic *Jihad*" (Sachedina 2000, 121).

Esposito (1988), too, aptly describes the debate over jihad as one in which many Westerners have been quick to characterize Islam as a religion spread by the sword, or through holy war, whereas modern Muslim scholars are more apt to point to the defensive, deeper meaning of jihad. As Esposito puts it, "A combination of ignorance, stereotyping, history, and experience, as well as religio-cultural chauvinism, too often blind even the best-intentioned when dealing with the Arab and Muslim World" (1992, 170).[15]

In fact, the association of Muslims with jihad and violence has become so pervasive that it influences not only Muslims but non-Muslims who live among them as well. Such mischaracterization is reflected in the popular term People of the Sword.

The self-fulfilling prophecy of jihad therefore has become a phenomenon of our times. Not only are Muslim activists (violent and nonviolent alike) suffering the imagery of age-old misperceptions and misrepresentation, but the religion and its followers also sustain that labeling and stereotyping as a result. Thus, labeling and self-fulfilling prophecy are partially responsible for the Muslim people's reactions to what the West views as the rules and more of the Islamic doctrine (Abdelkader Ali 1993).

These tendencies have contributed to the lack of studies examining nonviolence, peace building, and conflict resolution in Islamic tradition and religion. Nevertheless, Esposito provides an objective definition: "In its most general sense, *jihad* in the Qur'an and in Muslim practice refers to the obligation of all Muslims to strive (*jihad*, self-exertion) or struggle to follow God's will. This includes the virtuous life and the universal mission of the Muslim community to spread God's rule and law through teaching, preaching, and, where necessary, armed conflict" (1988, 40).

The current religious interpretation of jihad as a holy war has been influenced by the role of Muslim jurists throughout history, particularly in early periods, during which they justified offensive wars and broadened the interpretation of Qur'anic jihad. Such an interpretation can be explained by political circumstances that engendered pragmatic and realistic formulations to justify the undertaking of jihads, especially if the de facto rulers were concerned with consolidating their rule from an Islamic legal basis in a Muslim public order (Sachedina 1996, 129). These arguments support the assumption that religious practices, beliefs, and values vary with political, economic, social, and cultural factors. Thus the discussion of jihad and peace building must be similarly situated in a historical context.

Researchers in peace and just-war studies have also investigated the question of whether Islam is compatible with pacifism. (Many scholars in this category have used the term *pacifism* mainly as a reference to antiwar concerns. Thus, while they are clear that war is permitted in the defense of a Muslim state and for the self, they also agree that Islam prohibits wars of aggression, expansion, or prestige.) Violence and war are the last resort that a Muslim should deploy in dealing with other people. Persuasion, verbal exchanges, and prayers are all methods preferred in Islam. Scholars in this group support just war in Islam by pointing out such verses as: "Fighting is prescribed for you, even though it be hateful to you; but it may well be that you hate something that is in fact good for you, and that you love a thing that is in fact bad for you: and God knows, whereas you do not" (2:216).

Hashmi concludes, "The Islamic discourse on war and peace begins from the a priori assumption that some types of war are permissible—indeed required by God—and that all other forms of violence are, therefore, forbidden" (1996, 151). Thus, according to the Qur'an, the use of force must ultimately be defensive and limited to the violation of interpersonal human conduct.

The approach that associates Islam with just or defensive war does not negatively value peaceful means of resolving conflict based on Islamic approaches. On the contrary, members of this group suggest that nonaggression, the pursuit of justice, and even peaceful and nonviolent means are the proper and preferred methods of propagating the Islamic faith and for uniting the Muslim community. They find warrant for peaceful means in the Qur'an and the Prophet's commitment to nonviolent resistance during his early years in Mecca. Even the Prophet's reluctant endorsement of limited warfare after his move to Medina has been taken to support the view that fighting is undesirable for Muslims and that it is permissible only if there is no other effective way to resist aggression against the faith (Nardin 1996, 249).

In fact, many of these studies can be classified as "empirical idealist" in nature (a term used by Khadduri 1984 to classify his work on justice). They recognize the peaceful nature of Islam and acknowledge the theological as well as practical legitimacy, for the conditional use of force, and most of their studies are based on evidence derived from the Qur'an and the Prophet's tradition.

Like Hashmi, K. G. Saiyidain rejects the association of Islam with the absolute prohibition of war (i.e., pacifism): "It cannot, therefore, be said that Islam does not envisage the possibility of the use of force at all or does not sharply reprimand and stand up against those who go out of their way to deprive other people of the right to follow 'Truth' as they see it" (1994, 175). Thus, he argues that for a Muslim to be denied the right of worship is a valid reason to apply force, because such a condition qualifies as *kufr* (unbelief).

Sachedina further clarifies the use of the term *pacifism*. He places greater importance on justice and rejects the type of pacifism that calls for absolute rejection of all forms of violence without concern for justice. Thus, Sachedina emphasizes that Islam's defensive strategy with regard to human violence stems from the human rejection of faith. "As such," Sachedina writes, "pacifism in the sense of rejecting all forms of violence and opposing all war and armed hostility before justice is established has no place in the Qur'anic doctrine of human faith or its inevitable projection into not only identifying with the cause of justice but working for it on earth" (Sachedina 1996, 147).

Sachedina goes on to note that "pacifist silence in the face of continuous violation of justice amounted to being an accomplice of those unjust forces, and that was regarded as a major sin of associating other beings to God" (148). These passages are examples of the qualifications associated with pacifism in Islam as a passive philosophy or strategy. A similar characterization of the need for vigilance and activity within the Islamic concept of peace is presented by Mohammed Muqtedar Khan: "If peace and nonviolence are to be conceived as instrumental values, then there must be clearly identifiable values whose intrinsic worth must be more than that of peace. . . . I wonder how many would challenge my contention that justice, equality, and freedom are values more valuable than peace? I am not willing to give up my freedom or allow myself to be treated as an inferior or be treated unjustly without a fight. Can we demand that people give up their rights and freedom and accept injustice in the interest of maintaining peace?" (1997, 6).

Peace, nonviolence, and pacifism have been seen by some scholars as a surrender to injustice and thus as incapable of defending the values of equality, freedom, and justice. In particular, these scholars point to several verses of the Qur'an to substantiate an overarching concern for justice and a rejection of this type of pacifism: "Nor slay such life as Allah has made sacred, except for just cause, nor commit fornication—and any that does this (not only) meets punishment, (but) the Penalty on the Day of Judgment will be doubled to him" (25:68–69). "Nor take life—which Allah has made sacred—except for just cause. And if anyone is slain wrongfully, we have given his heir authority (to demand Qisas [punishment] or to forgive): but let him not exceed bounds in the matter of taking life: for he is helped (by the Law)" (17:33). "Take not life, which Allah hath made sacred, except by way of justice and law" (6:151).

These Qur'anic verses have led some scholars in this category to conclude that Islam as a religion does not provide a basis for the "absolute rejection of violence" or a creed of total pacifism. Furthermore, they uphold the notion that Islam has always encouraged its followers to adopt the middle course, to follow a realistic path in solving day-to-day problems. It instructs them to keep in mind the spirit of equality, brotherhood, love, and purity of character in all social interactions. Since absolute prohibition of violence would not be a middle way, limited force is permitted under certain conditions.[16]

On the value of human life, these scholars single out the following verse: "We ordained for the Children of Israel that if anyone slew a person—unless it be for murder or for spreading mischief in the land—it would be as if he slew the whole people: and if anyone save a life, it would be as if he saved the life of the whole people" (5:32). Although scholars in this group recognize the centrality of the second part of the verse, which emphasizes the sacredness of life in Islam, they still use the entire verse to furnish evidence for the inevitable need to use force.

Kelsay (1993) has developed a specific list of situations in which armed conflict is permitted in Islam:

> A just cause, which can also be understood as the imperative to extend the boundaries of the territory of Islam; an invitation/ declaration of Muslim intentions, in which the ruler of the Muslims communicates with enemy authorities to either accept Islam or pay tribute as an acceptance of the state of Islam; the requirement of right authority to declare such war or armed conflict; conduct of war in accordance with Islamic values, because Muslims are to fight for the right cause and straight path and not for the destruction and spoils of war or personal glory.[17]

Nardin (1996) argues the constraints on the conduct of war in Islam can be traced to the pre-Islamic period, or to the "rules of the game" of intertribal warfare. These rules prohibited fighting during certain times of the year and condemned excessive destruction. These rules were established as a code of honor protecting children, the aged, prisoners, and women and reflected a view of war as a means to an end. The Qur'an and Sunnah (the prophet's sayings and actions later established as legally binding precedents) supported such rules. "If the purpose is to organize the world based on Islamic principles, then indiscriminate killings are forbidden because they neither respect nor facilitate that end" (1996, 259).

The foregoing interpretation of the rules of armed engagement has been subject to debate and disagreement not only among the various sects of Islam but also among religious and political authorities (al-Sharif al-Radi 1978, 1:77; Kishtainy 1990, 12).[18] For example, who determines the status and definition of the right ruler or authority, and how? For the purposes of this study, it is important to acknowledge the general consensus that has emerged among Islamic scholars, and religious figures agree that the use of violence and armed conflict is certainly permitted according to these teachings. But it must also be kept in mind that fighting and violence must always be defensive in Islam, permitted only under very specific conditions, such as defending one's fundamental rights or defending the oppressed and the helpless so that they may be released from the clutches of tyranny. The Qur'an asks: "And why should ye not fight in the cause of Allah and of those who, being weak, are ill-treated (and oppressed)?—men, women, and children, whose cry is: 'Our Lord! Rescue us from this town, whose people are oppressors; and raise for us from Thee one who will protect; and raise for us from Thee one who will help'" (4:75).

The discussion of just war and peace in Islam thus tends to be from the limited- or defensive-war perspective. In this tradition in Islamic studies, there is a clear recognition of the validity of war and violence as a defense mode, but not developed is the concept of violence as an offensive mode. As a result, most scholars have the term *peace* in their studies but few really relate to it in a meaningful way. Such studies tend to gloss over the notion of peace and quickly move on to address in detail the conditions upon limited force or war. This underscores the need for more Islamic studies devoted to the notions of peace and nonviolence in Islam, rather than a rehashing of existing treatises on violent jihad or defensive wars.

Ayoub (1997) and Sachedina (1996), among others, have proposed the notion of "quietism" in Islam, rather than absolute pacifism, arguing that Islam views human existence as caught up in contradictions and conflicts between darkness and light, justice and injustice, and that it enjoins a continuing moral struggle. Thus, in their views, pacifism in its pure and absolute sense, without due consideration of justice, cannot accurately reflect authentic Islamic teachings.

The above limited definition of pacifism in Islamic tradition (similar to early religious Christians, who called for absolute pacifism by withdrawing from the real world and refusing to interact with it [see Johnson 1987]) is a type of pacifism that is associated with a life of simplicity, poverty, and a prohibition on bearing arms (as described by Sachedina 1996, 147). Practitioners of nonviolence,[19] in both Muslim and non-Muslim countries, have demonstrated, however, that nonviolence is an effective way to advance justice and freedom and that pride and empowerment are significant spiritual consequences of the application of nonviolent resistance (Sharp 1973, 1989). Yet, analysts in this group never considered the Gandhian approach or other forms of nonviolent resistance, such as those identified by Yoder (1992), Johnson (1987), and Sharp (1973), which have produced profound political and social results for millions of people around the world.

Scholars in this category put primary emphasis on the notion of justice and perceive the discussion of absolute pacifism or total prohibition of force as secondary. Such an approach is best described by O. P. Jaggi: "In one form or another, the principle of nonviolence has an important place in every religion. Some religions limit its practice to human beings; others encompass the entire world of living beings. Some consider it the highest virtue, and others regard it as second only to social justice" (1974, 1).

The research and writings on this subject from both Muslim and non-Muslim scholars have indicated that Islam does not advocate violence but does not shun it altogether, and that the Qur'an opposes violence but permits it contextually (Engineer 1994, 99–101, 106).

In summary, scholars in this category (Hashmi, Sachedina, Kelsay, etc.) have rejected the notion that Islam is a pacifist religion and that characterizing it as such is a diversion from potentially fruitful knowledge and wisdom about Islamic teachings concerning violence and war. Kelsay (1993, 34) suggests, as do others in this category, that nonviolence ought to be evaluated from within the overall Islamic goal of establishing a just society. Therefore the focus should not be on whether Islam provides support for nonviolence but rather where, how, and at what point do nonviolent strategies serve the goal of establishing and maintaining the social justice that Muslims endeavor to pursue. It is important to point out that most scholars in this category do not assign a negative value to nonviolent strategies. But they do argue that theologically moral and creedal pacifism is not supported in Islam and it is therefore difficult to justify such beliefs. Nevertheless, there are several examples from Islamic history and tradition that contradict this assumption (the work of Abdul Ghaffar Khan and many of the Sufi teachings are examples of an attempt to establish a creedal, or moral absolute pacifist, approach—for more details, see the next section). Researchers in the second group propound three major lessons or principles: first, certain conditions exist in the Islamic religion under which the use of violence is permitted, and the identification of and agreement on these conditions among Muslims may reduce the possibility of war and violence; second, jihad in Islam does not always or necessarily entail the use of violence and force in dealing with others (Muslims and non-Muslims alike); and third, the absolute prohibition of war, or use of force, is not supported theologically in Islam.

Studies of Peace Building and Nonviolence

A third set of studies focuses on core Islamic values that provide the basis for articulating the essential premises of active nonviolence, such as *'adl* (justice), *ihsan* (benevolence), *rahmah* (compassion), and *hikmah* (wisdom). From the outset, the very spirit of these key concepts is inimical to violence (Engineer 1994, 106). In attempting to establish a connection between Islam and nonviolence, Abdul Ghaffar Khan has identified *'amal, yakeen,* and *mahabbah* (service, faith, and love) as primary Islamic values or principles in contradiction to stereotypical characterizations of Islam as a violent religion. For instance, scholars have examined *shurah* (mutual consultation), *ijtihad* (independent judgment), and *ijma'* (consensus) as key values in Islam, and such values have been readily applied to the study of conflict resolution and nonviolence in Islam.[20] Many of these scholars, while acknowledging justifications for limited violence in Islamic scripture, nevertheless emphasize the great potential for nonviolence in Islam. They have recognized such principles as belief in unity, supreme love of the creator, mercy, subjection of passion, and accountability for all actions. As Ahmad concludes, "There are innumerable verses in the Qur'an that command believers to be righteous and above passion in their dealings with their fellow beings. Love, kindness, affection, forgiveness, and mercy are recommended for the true faithful" (1993, 40).

Many of the scholars in the previous two categories based their research on just-war theories or theological and religious studies of scripture. Studies in this third group are conducted from within the framework of peace studies, theories of nonviolence, or an Islamic reformist approach to scripture and tradition.[21] Their outlook is aptly stated in this hypothesis: "There is no theological reason that an Islamic society could not take a lead in developing nonviolence today, and there is every reason that some of them should"(Burns 1996, 165) Supporters of this hypothesis find ample support in various interpretations of the Qur'an and Hadiths in their effort to locate principles of peace and nonviolence in Islamic tradition and religion (A. Said 1994; Abu-Nimer 1996a,b; D. Crow 1998; Easwaran 1984; Kishtainy 1990; Sai'd 1997; Sachedina 2000; Satha-Anand 1993a,b; Wahiduddin Khan 1998).

Like the studies in the second group of just war and peace, some of these studies have also justified the restricted use of violence under certain strict conditions. However, their overall project is one of reconciling the Islamic tradition with nonviolent methodologies and practices. Thus, the major distinction between scholars from the second and third group is reflected in their emphasis on the centrality of nonviolence and peace (due to their theoretical frameworks or beliefs). Members of the third group place less emphasis on the theological basis for just war or the use of violence and call for the formulation of an Islamic approach of nonviolence. For instance, Saiyidain argues: "There are circumstances in which Islam contemplates the possibility of war—for instance, to avert worse disasters like the denial of freedom to human conscience—but the essential thing in life is peace. It is towards the achievement of peace that all human efforts must be sincerely diverted" (1994, 175).

In supporting such notions, Satha-Anand lists eight theses when addressing Islam and nonviolence:

(1) For Muslims the problem of violence is an integral part of the Islamic moral sphere; (2) Violence, if any, used by Muslims must be governed by rules prescribed in the Qur'an and Hadith; (3) If violence used cannot discriminate between combatants and noncombatants, then it is unacceptable to Islam; (4) Modern technology of destruction renders discrimination virtually impossible at present; (5) In the Modern world, Muslims can not use violence; (6) Islam teaches Muslims to fight for justice with the understanding that Human lives—as all parts of God's creation—are purposive and sacred; (7) In order to be true to Islam, Muslims must utilize nonviolence as a new mode of struggle; (8) Islam itself is a fertile soil for nonviolence because of its potential for disobedience, strong discipline, sharing and social responsibility, perseverance and self-

sacrifice, and the belief in the unity of the Muslim community and the oneness of mankind. (1993b: 15)

Although in his second thesis Satha-Anand allows for the use of limited violence, in his fifth thesis he clearly prevents the use of violence in the present day. Therefore, in this study Satha-Anand and others are classified differently from the previous scholars (in war and jihad studies and in just-war and peace studies, who acknowledge the legitimacy of using violence based on Islamic scripture, focus their writing on such aspects, and argue against the concepts of pacifism and nonviolence in Islam).

Ahmad similarly states that "Islam does not rule out violence in certain situations; this violence, however, is defensive in character" (1993, 50). He focuses on values that are relevant to peace building and nonviolence. From this perspective, Islam emphasizes social justice, brotherhood, and the equality of mankind. The virtues of forgiveness and mercy, tolerance, submission to God, right means, and recognition of the rights of others are emphasized again and again both in the Holy Book and in the Hadiths. Furthermore the Prophet demolished all national and racial barriers. Islam aims for a peaceful and just social order.

In promoting this paradigm of Islamic nonviolence, these scholars rely on the following justifications:

(1) The historical context of the Qur'anic revelations has changed and so should the use of violence as a means to resolve differences. Spreading the faith is therefore no longer theologically permissible. Whatever means Muslims used to create, establish, or spread their faith fourteen hundred years ago are no longer applicable or appropriate to contemporary realities. If Muslim culture and tradition are to prosper again, Muslims (leaders and people) must adopt a nonviolent approach to settling differences, whether internal or external.

(2) The enormous changes in the status of the Muslim community in the global system and in local communities undermine the efficacy and long-term viability of violent means. For many Muslim communities who live as minorities around the world, there is a sharp contrast to their economic, social, and political status six to seven centuries ago, when they were the majority or the dominant force in their regions and outside.

(3) Global interdependencies—social, economic, and political—have rendered impracticable the use of violence, especially in the form of weapons of mass destruction, for settling conflicts.

(4) The new global realities, including advanced weaponry systems and

increasingly destructive forms of warfare, oblige Muslims—indeed, all people—to abandon violence since there can no longer be assured limits to its extent (Satha-Anand 1993a; Wahiduddin Khan 1998; Sai'd 1997; Janner 1997; Kelsay 1993; Easwaran 1984; Engineer 1994; Paige, Satha-Anand, and Gilliatt 1993).[22]

(5) As a minor element in the life of the Prophet and in the scripture, violence should be of no greater importance to Muslims today than it was then. The Hadiths and Islamic tradition are rich sources of peace-building values and if applied in Muslims' daily lives will lead only to nonviolence and peace.

An excellent pioneering study by Abdul Aziz Sachedina (2000) illustrates the use of the above arguments to promote the need for a new pluralist Islamic paradigm in dealing with the "other." Given the reality of corruption and religious manipulation, in pursuit of the goal of political change in Muslim countries, Sachedina calls for the "rediscovery of Islamic common moral concern for peace and justice" (2000, 6).

This new type of hermeneutic discourse, based on pluralism, nonviolence, and peace, is much needed for interreligious relationship building. Sachedina asserts that an "Islamic theology of the twenty-first century must communicate beyond the language of a particular tradition" (2000, 43). This is a call for a new theological approach and narrative based on pluralism and not exclusivity. Such an approach is based on two conditions: a consideration of history, and the interaction of normative tradition and sources with the social and political realities of Muslims. Only then can the Islamic interpretation be useful in facing the future and understanding the present and the past (47).

Sachedina recognizes a similar paradigm shift in international relations through the fact that Muslim states are sharing same and equal membership with non-Muslim states in global settings (2000, ch. 1).[23] These circumstances require different theological and hermeneutic discursive approaches. Therefore he states, "Past juridical decisions have become irrelevant in the modern system of international relations, and they are thus unable to shed light on the pressing task of recognizing religious pluralism as a cornerstone of interhuman relations" (49).

Muslims thus face an epistemological crisis, because there is a lack of intellectual studies and new methodological approaches to examine the adaptation of Islam to the new world. The political opportunists in Muslim countries have done this in a simple yet effective way that helps them in mobilizing the masses. The pluralists and peacemakers, however, have not systematically engaged in similar efforts.

Using an empirical idealist approach, Sachedina offers the most comprehensive study and detailed examination of pluralism and its roots in Islamic religion and tradition. Sachedina's study on pluralism (2000) is an example of emerging scholarly work that moves away from the peace and just-war group into the peace-building category. He devotes his entire research to the exploration of pluralism as a major peace-building concept in Islam. The study is an example of how to explore and regulate the relationship between politics and religion, in a way that religious pluralism and diversity are guaranteed not only by passive tolerance but also by the protection of human rights. "Religious pluralism is a fundamental resource that can be tapped by humankind to establish peace and justice in any contemporary society" (2000, 11).

Sachedina reveals the obstacles confronting scholars who take a stand in situating their work beyond just war and peace studies toward a more idealist or visionary position: "It took the crisis I faced with the Muslim religious establishment in 1998 to convince me that the time had come to state my firm belief in Koranic notions of human dignity and the inalienable right to freedom of religion and conscience. Attempts were made to silence me through religious edict [fatwah] and to stop Muslim audiences in North America from listening to my well-articulated plea for better intercommunal relationships through mutual tolerance, respect, and acceptance of the religious value in all world religions" (2000, xi).

The minority of Muslim scholars who advocate and promote the notion of Islamic pluralism and peace building are under tremendous pressure from their communities to stop their reformist efforts (the next section discusses the obstacles that face scholars and practitioners when presenting such interpretations in their communities). However, it is clear that such a path has been opened, and its expansion and discovery are needed today more than any time in Islamic history.

Sachedina, like Farid Esack (1998), identifies "a trend among Muslims who profess a strong commitment to Islam's social-ethical dimensions, but who never attend public prayers or observe prescribed rituals" (2000, 7). Millions of Muslims follow such lifestyle preferences, but they are excluded by Muslims who monopolize the moral and ethical standards of Islam (e.g., by determining that virtue can be attained only through prayer, the hajj, or other religious rituals).

In addition to the emphasis on the daily peaceful application of Islamic religion and tradition, identifying the Islamic textual justifications for shunning violence has been a major focus for scholars in this category. They emphasize Islamic sources, particularly Qur'anic verses, that condemn violence and war in any context: "Whenever they [People of the Book] kindle the fire of war, God extinguishes it. They strive to create disorder on earth and God loves not those who create disorder" (5:64). Tolerance and kindness toward all other people without exception are also emphasized: "God commands you to treat (everyone) justly, generously, and with kindness" (16:90).

Jawdat Saiʿd (1997) notes a famous Hadith that has been widely quoted in Islamic literature and is often hung as a calligraphic adornment in Muslim homes:[24] "Whenever violence enters into something, it disgraces it, and whenever "gentle-civility" enters into something it graces it. Truly, God bestows on account of gentle conduct what he does not bestow on account of violent conduct."[25] Saiʿd, like other scholars in this category, attempts to reinterpret historical symbols, stories, and other events in the Islamic tradition to foster a change in Muslims' approaches to life in general and to conflict in particular.

Members in this community of interpreters stress that there are many Hadiths and Qurʾanic verses that support nonviolence and peace in Islam. They often rely on the Meccan period of the Prophet's life (610–622 C.E.), during which the Prophet showed no inclination toward the use of force in any form, even for self-defense. He practiced a nonviolent resistance that was reflected in all his teaching during that period, when Muslims were a minority and under threat. The Prophet's teachings focused on the values of patience and steadfastness in facing oppression. "Of the twenty-three-year period of prophethood, the initial thirteen years were spent by the Prophet in Mecca. The Prophet fully adopted the way of pacifism or nonviolence during this time. There were many such issues in Mecca at the time which could have been the subject of clash and confrontation. But, by avoiding all such issues, the Prophet of Islam strictly limited his sphere to peaceful propagation of the word of God" (Wahiduddin Khan 1998, 5).

Others have also cited this period of the Prophet's life as a source of nonviolent inspiration. Although tortured, accused of blasphemy, humiliated, ostracized, he permitted himself neither violence nor even swearing. On the contrary, the Prophet's teachings centered on prayer and the hope for enlightenment and peace (Ahmad 1993).

Arab-Muslim scholars who support nonviolent struggle have revisited historical and cultural interpretations and have provided a new way to view the early period of Islam. Interpretations of events during such period are often used by Muslims to justify or legitimize certain current actions. For instance, Kishtainy (1990) argues that, contrary to the perception of the pre-Islamic and early Islamic periods as rife with militancy and brutality, they were, as compared with the history of the Greek and Roman empires, relatively noncoercive. In the pre-Islamic period, Arabs had not developed the kind of militancy, commitment, and training associated with the Spartans, Prussians, Samurai, and so on. Even the pre-Islamic "long wars" were, in fact, no more than skirmishes and raids that caused little loss of life. Kishtainy asserts that the Muslim empires spread, for the most part, through treaties and with a minimal number of battles. The two major battles (Qadisiya and Yarmuk) of this period that Muslims are proud of lasted no more than four days each (1990, 11).

Kishtainy discusses a number of seminal Islamic teachings that are conducive to nonviolent practices: tolerance, persuasion, arguing, suffering, patience, civil disobedience, withdrawal of cooperation, rejection of injustice, strikes, emigration, boycotting, diplomacy, publicity, propaganda, and special rituals (fasting, parallel lines of prayers, religious chanting) (1990). Arab-Muslim history is rich with examples of such practices in various national and religious struggles of liberation.

As mentioned earlier, many scholars in the present category argue that although the use of force is prescribed in the Qur'an under specific and strict conditions, nevertheless, Islamic values systematically give higher ground to forgiveness than to revenge or violence. "The recompense for an injury is an injury equal thereto (in degree): but if a person forgives and makes reconciliation, his reward is due from Allah: for (Allah) loveth not those who do wrong. But indeed if any do help and defend themselves after a wrong (done) to them, against such there is no cause of blame. The blame is only against those who oppress men with wrongdoing and insolently transgress beyond bounds through the land, defying right and justice: for such there will be a Penalty grievous" (Qur'an, 42:40–42).

Active nonviolent resistance and open defiance of persecution are the proper Muslim responses, according to the above verses. In fact, these actions reflect the Prophet's own practices during this period (Hashmi 1996). In this period, there were no calls for war or the use of violence, but there was a clear call for active resistance, based on the higher moral ground of forgiveness, not revenge.

The Prophet's migration to Medina in particular is viewed as a strategic act of nonviolence that enabled the Prophet to construct a powerful center of Islam that is still the model for a Muslim community (Wahiduddin Khan 1998). A similar example of migration and avoidance of confrontation appears in the Prophet's instruction to the poor family of former slaves to take refuge with a Christian king in Abyssinia (Hashmi 1996).

Many Hadiths have been identified by writers and researchers in this category to illustrate the importance of peace building and patience. For example, the story of Abel (Habil) and Cain (Qabil) is a parable of nonviolence from the Qur'an. Abel represents justice and righteousness, refusing to soil his hands with blood. Cain represents aggression and the readiness to kill on any pretext (Saiyidain 1994, 169). "Recite to them the truth of the story of the two sons of Adam. Behold! They each presented a sacrifice (to Allah): it was accepted from one, but not from the other. Said the latter: 'Be sure I will slay thee.' 'Surely,' said the former. 'Allah doth accept the sacrifice of those who are righteous. If thou dost stretch thy hand against me to slay me, it is not for me to stretch my hand against thee to slay thee: for I do fear Allah, the Cherisher of the Worlds" (5:27–28).

Sai'd (1997) best summarizes several of the sayings in an attempt to substantiate the pacifist nature of Islam:

> I don't see anyone in this world who has clearly explained when it is incumbent upon a Muslim to behave like (Abel) the son of Adam! Nor does anyone teach the Muslims that the Messenger of God said to his companion Sa'd Ibn Abi Waqqas, "*Kun ka-ibni Adam* (Be as the son of Adam)!" at the time when Muslims turn to fight one another. The Prophet said to his companion Abu Dharr al-Ghifari in a similar situation, when Abu Dharr asked him, "But what if someone entered into my home (to kill me)?" The Prophet replied: "If you fear to look upon the gleam of the sword raised to strike you, then cover your face with your robe. Thus will he bear the sin of killing you as well as his own sin." And in the same situation, the Prophet told his companion Abu Musa al-Asha'ri: "Break your bows, sever your strings, beat stones on your swords (to break the blades); and when infringed upon by one of the perpetrators, be as the best of Adam's two sons" (Abu-Dawud Ibn Sulayman 1998, bk. 35, no. 4246).

In support of the notion that Islam strongly advocates nonviolence, scholars point to several nonviolent Muslim communities. One such sect is the Maziyariyya, who dropped fasting and jihad from the pillars of the faith altogether. (The pillars of Islam include almsgiving, pilgrimage, and the belief that there is one god, Allah, and Mohammed is his prophet.) The Sufis place great emphasis on the spiritual aspects of jihad, not its physical aspects, in their emphasis on the conquest of self. Sufi communities highlight the Prophet's teaching that one's battle with oneself (*al-jihad al-akbar*) is more difficult and more compelling than jihad against the enemies of Islam (*al-jihad al-asghar*). Saiyidain observes that only love can conquer evil: "The real fight is against man's own nature—its cruelty, its desire to exploit, its denial of justice, its narrowness and stupidity" (quoted in Thompson 1988, 53). Sufi quietism is not a form of despair, disgust, or defeatism but a positive and activist promotion of justice through the purification of self (Sisk 1992, 34).

A third example is the Ahmadiyya movement, which stresses the meaning of striving, or exertion, in jihad. The spirit of jihad is reflected in every Muslim's ability and willingness to sacrifice the self in the protection of the weak and oppressed. Thus the test of jihad lies in the willingness to suffer, not in the practice of warfare (Ferguson 1978, 136).[26] In fact, the Ahmadiyya movement declared that jihad had been superseded and was no longer relevant to the modern world (Sisk 1992, 35; see also Friedmann 1989).

In supporting the peaceful nature of Islam, scholars (from both the just-war and the nonviolent studies groups) define the Arabic word *islam* as "the making of peace." A Muslim, according to the Qur'an, is he who has made peace with God and man. Peace with God implies complete submission to his will who is the source of all purity and goodness, and peace with man implies the doing of good to one's fellow man: "Nay, whoever submits himself entirely to God and is the doer of good to others, he has his reward from His Lord, and there is no fear for such, nor shall they grieve" (2:112).

A well-known illustration of the centrality of peace is reflected in the daily greetings of Muslims: *Al-salam 'alaykum,* which means, "Peace be upon you." This greeting is derived from the Qur'an: "And their greeting therein shall be Peace" (10:10). In the paradise that Islam depicts, no word shall be heard except *peace*: "They shall hear therein no vain or sinful talk, but only the saying, 'Peace, Peace'" (56:25–26). This is also evident as one of the names of God is the "Abode of peace" (*dar al-islam*), with another verse stating that "God invites to the abode of peace" (10:25). Additional support for this notion is expressed in the verse, "And the servants of (Allah) most Gracious are those who walk on the earth in humility, and when the ignorant address them, they say, 'Peace!'" (25:63).

Thus, like scholars in the second group, proponents of nonviolent studies emphasize that peacemaking and negotiation are the preferred strategies for resolving conflicts, as clearly expressed in the Qur'anic verse, "But if the enemy incline towards peace, do thou (also) incline towards peace, and trust in Allah: for He is the One that heareth and knoweth (all things)" (8:61).

In regard to conditions under which fighting is permissible in the Qur'an, scholars and researchers of nonviolence and peace building cite the following verse: "Fight in the cause of Allah those who fight you, but do not transgress limits; for Allah loveth not transgressors" (2:190). However, according to those scholars, it is true that the fight can be violent, but it can also be waged by heart and tongue (understanding and patience) (Satha-Anand 1993b). In another response to the notion of fighting or the use of force in jihad, others have argued that jihad has been interpreted as the Calling (al-da'wah). Wahiduddin Khan (1998) suggests that al-da'wah, not the sword, is the primary and true meaning of jihad. Through al-da'wah, believers will receive God's protection against the harm of adversaries, and even the direst of enemies will turn into friends. Such tangible benefits foster a positive mentality within the Ummah (Muslim community) and give evidence of the truth of Islamic teachings.[27]

Scholars in the just-war and peace category have argued that struggle against injustice is the sole justification for engaging in jihad, and that peace stems from a society in which there is an active concern for justice, and not just the absence of conflict (Sachedina 1996, 155). In addition, many scholars in the second group have argued that justice and peace cannot exist in Islam until most people accept the reality of God (Nasr 1998; Carmody and Carmody 1988). Ferguson best summarizes this notion: "Faith in God, who has created this world 'to good purpose' and ensuring justice in all personal, as well as social and national, relations are inevitable conditions for peace; those who have faith and do not let it be debased by the least injustice are the ones who shall have peace. It is they who are on the right path" (1978, 158; see Qur'an 6:82–83).

In response to the second group, studies of nonviolence in Islam argue that even if justice (not nonviolence or peace) was the ultimate goal of Islamic religious teaching, it can be argued that pursuing peace through nonviolent strategies is the more viable and effective method for achieving it, especially when such methods are used to empower the victims of injustice. The nonviolent resister does not attempt to convince the victims of oppression to adjust to an unjust reality but assumes that nonviolent methods, if applied correctly and systematically, will themselves lead to justice (Kishtainy 1998).

Supporters of peace-building approaches argue that Islamic values and principles, in both religious and daily practices, are compatible with and support the adoption of nonviolent means of achieving justice. Satha-Anand suggests the values that underlie the five pillars of Islam are the core values for Muslim nonviolent action: (1) obeying God and the

Prophet only and disobeying others if necessary; (2) practicing discipline through prayer, solidarity, and the support of the poor through a *zakah* tax; (3) self-sacrifice, suffering, and patience through fasting; (4) unity and brotherhood through pilgrimage (Satha-Anand 1993a).

In conclusion, the relationship between the studies of the two categories, peace and just war and nonviolence, in Islam can be framed similarly to Childress's characterization (1982) of the relationship between the various just-war traditions and pacifists or nonviolent resisters. The pacifists (nonviolent resisters, not the absolute pacifists described in Johnson 1987) and just war theorists are actually closer to, and more dependent on, each other than they often suppose, for they share the assumption that war is evil and in principle is not acceptable. Both agree on the moral priority of nonviolence over violence, and that "violent acts are always in need for justification, because they violate the duty to not injure or kill others, whereas only some nonviolent acts need justification" (Childress 1982, 93).

Studies of nonviolence in Islam suppose that even if Islam as a religion permits the use of force under strict conditions, a nonviolent approach can nevertheless be adopted by Muslims based on a strong set of core principles, values, and beliefs derived from their scripture and traditions. Islam as a religion and tradition privileges and embodies values, beliefs, and strategies that facilitate nonviolence and peace building. Evidence for these values are found in the Qur'an, Hadiths, and traditional cultural practices. The following chapter discusses nonviolent and conflict resolution principles inherent in Islam and explores their correspondence with the theory and practice of nonviolence and peace building.

2

Islamic Principles of Nonviolence and Peace Building

A Framework

As noted in the previous chapter, there is solid agreement among scholars, in the second and third groups (studies of just war and peace and studies of peace building and nonviolence), that Islam as a religion is built upon a foundation of peaceful values and principles. In order for practitioners and advocates of peace building to utilize an Islamic framework in the settlement of various disputes, it is necessary to address such questions as: What are the values and principles that facilitate peace-building and non-violent strategies? To what extent are those values and strategies supported by and based in Islamic religion and tradition? How, and in what context, are those values expressed? This chapter identifies a set of Islamic principles and beliefs that support the application of nonviolent and peace-building strategies. The chapter is not a comprehensive analysis of the Islamic laws or Shari'ah on peace building, nor is it an attempt to fully account for all possible sources in the Qur'an or Hadith that relate to peace in Islam. Rather, it aims to capture the basic religious and traditional peace-building principles and beliefs and their day-to-day practices on social and political levels. Discussing these values and principles would contribute to the building of a larger analytical and theoretical framework for peace building derived from Islamic religion and tradition.

The Pursuit of Justice

While this is not a theological study of Islam, whose purpose is to explore the foundational Islamic values of peace building and nonviolence, I must nevertheless rely mainly on the Qur'an and Hadith as the two most reliable and accepted religious sources in Islam. How does Islam view the relationship between peace and social justice? This question has been ignored by Western writers, in part because they tend to focus on the political relationship between Muslim and non-Muslim nations. Social justice is just one of a number of values that relate Islam to peace. Many Muslim and non-Muslim scholars have pointed to Islamic principles and values such as unity, supreme love of the creator, mercy, subjection of passion, and accountability for all actions, all of which are supported by innumerable verses in the Qur'an that command believers to be righteous and above passion in their dealings with their fellow human beings. Love, kindness, affection, forgiveness, and mercy are recommended as virtues of the true faithful (Ahmad 1993, 40). Other Islamic values directly related to peace building are *'adl* (justice), *ihsan* (beneficence), *rahmah* (compassion),[1] and *hikmah* (wisdom). Still others, discussed by Abdul Ghaffar Khan, are *'amal, yakeen,* and *muhabat* (service, faith, and love). Moreover, Islam emphasizes social justice, brotherhood, equality of mankind (abolition of slavery, and racial and ethnic barriers), tolerance, submission to God, and recognition of the rights of others. These values are repeatedly affirmed both in the Qur'an and in the Prophet's tradition.

George Hourani (1985) lists the main virtues taught by the Qur'an: "Piety, i.e., humble obedience and fear of God; honesty in dealings; justice and avoidance of all wrongdoing; and chastity. Love of God and fellow is rarely mentioned explicitly, but is really implied by the other virtues." This chapter discusses seventeen such values and principles found in the Qur'an and Hadith, values that clearly demonstrate an affinity between Islam and peace building.

A major call of Islamic religion is to establish a just social reality. Thus, any act or statement from Muslims should be evaluated in terms of its potential contribution to that end. In Islam acting for the cause of God is synonymous with pursuing *'adl,* justice. Islam calls for such action by the strong and weak alike. It is the Muslim's duty to work for justice and reject oppression on both interpersonal and structural levels. The following Qur'anic verses forcefully convey this outlook: "Allah commands justice, the doing of good, and liberality to kith and kin, and He forbids all shameful deeds, and injustice and rebellion: He instructs you, that ye may receive admonition" (16:90). "Ye who believe! Stand out firmly for justice, as witnesses to Allah, even as against yourselves, or your parents, or your kin, and whether it be (against) rich or poor: for Allah can best protect both. Follow not the lusts (of your hearts), lest ye swerve, and if ye distort (justice) or decline to do justice, verily Allah is well-acquainted with all that ye do" (4:135). "O ye who believe! Stand out firmly for Allah, as witnesses to fair dealing, and let not the hatred of others to you make you swerve to wrong and depart from justice. Be just: that is next to Piety: and fear Allah. For Allah is well-acquainted with all that ye do" (5:8).

Among the words most commonly associated with the noun 'adl, Khadduri (1984, 6) lists qist, qasd, istiqamah, wasat, nisab, hissah, and mizan. Based on such dictionaries as Ibn Manzur, Lisan al-Arab, and al-Fayruzabadi, al-Qamus al-Muhit, the verb 'adala (in its various forms) means (1) to straighten or fix; (2) to straighten up or sit straight; (3) to amend or modify; (4) to run away, depart, or deflect from one (wrong) path to the other (right) one; (5) to be equal or equivalent, to match, or to equalize; (6) to balance or counterbalance, to weigh, or to be in a state of equilibrium.

In Islam, divine justice is enshrined in the revelation and divine wisdom that was communicated by the Prophet Muhammad. Justice rooted in divine wisdom is applicable to all times and all people. However, public rulings, laws, and the opinion of scholars arrived at through human reasoning (ijtihad) necessitates adaptation and refinement to address the changing world (Khadduri 1984, 3). Thus, scholars agree on the divine nature of justice but disagree on how it should be implemented on earth.

Muslims therefore maintain the core belief that a higher standard of justice must be found, consisting of a higher set of values, norms, and virtues to be realized on earth. This belief motivated scholars to seek the criteria and expressions of justice for human life. As Ibn Khaldun argues, individuals are innately driven to seek justice and are, by their nature, just—whether this "just nature" is guided by reason, revelation, or social habit (Khadduri 1984, 227).

All the diverse schools of jurisprudence are agreed that divine justice is ideally realized Islam. Such belief indicates the following assumptions:

1. Justice is known to man through available evidence (both revelation and reason). However, knowing justice through revelation is the more dominant belief.

2. Whether justice is the embodiment of the highest human virtues or a direct emanation from God (perfection), it is an ideal notion that Muslims are obliged to pursue.

3. Those who believe in a single, just God are the subjects of divine justice, and all others are the objects of that justice. Divine justice is conceived as divine laws, eternal, perfect, and existing irrespective of time and place, as a design for universal applica-

tion to all men. Even men who do not believe in one God can
seek refuge in it.

4. The standards of justice, whether determined by revelation or
reason, indicate for men the path for right and wrong, so that
all, each according to his "light," would pursue the right and reject the wrong in order to achieve the good in this life and salvation in the next. (Khadduri 1984, 192)

This ideal and comprehensive notion of justice can facilitate the development of Islamic peace-building strategies because of an overarching
emphasis on individual responsibility and the primary moral obligation to
fight against injustice. The early caliphate was known for its emphatic
pursuit of justice, particularly the rule of 'Umar Ibn al-Khatab, a period
widely revered by Muslims that also provides models for the pursuit of
justice in society.

In tracing the Islamic notion of justice from its inception as a religion
into the modern age, Khadduri identifies two main approaches: the modernist (rationalist or reformist) and the revivalist (revelationist). The debate between them has not necessarily been negative, or mutually exclusive, but functional and complementary in achieving progress in Islamic
societies. If the modernists leap too far ahead of the mainstream in their
reforms, the revivalists force them to step back and allow time for the new
ideas to be assimilated.

In underscoring the centrality of justice in Islamic tradition, scholars
have pointed to the number of times that the term *justice* (or *injustice*) has
been mentioned in the Qur'an. For example, Khadduri states, "In the
Qur'an there are over two hundred admonitions against injustice expressed in such words as *zulm, ithm, dalal,* and others, and no less than
almost a hundred expressions embodying the notion of justice, either directly in such words as *'adl, qist, mizan,* and others as noted before, or in
a variety of indirect expressions." Except for the existence of one God, no
other religious moral principles are more emphasized in the Qur'an and
the traditions than the principles of justice, uprightness, equity, and tem-
perance (1984, 10).

In spite of this major emphasis on justice, however, there are no specific
measures in the Qur'an or traditions that spell out how to establish justice
on earth. Such responsibility was undertaken by Islamic scholars who
have attempted to derive from authoritative texts the specific elements
necessary to guide Muslims in their pursuit of justice. As a result justice is
one of the most studied concepts in Islam. Some scholars have conceptu-

alized categories of Islamic justice, while others have approached it chronologically or thematically. For example, in his comprehensive treatment of the term *justice*, Khadduri (1984) includes thematic categorical analysis of the political, theological, philosophical, ethical, legal, international, and social forms of justice. Indeed the search for specific theological understanding and application of justice in Islam is one of the most important contributions of Muslim scholars throughout the Islamic history. The most important theological approaches to justice to emerge from this effort are identified by Khadduri: the Jabarites or those who follow strict interpretation of predestination; all humans and their acts are created by God and man's life on earth is the unfolding of divine will; the Qadarites, who maintain that all human are created by God, but man alone is responsible for his action, or simply that man has choice; exponents of rational justice, who like Mu'atazila argued that the individuals are capable of deciding and carrying the responsibility of their actions, and that there are two levels of justice—human and divine (Khadduri 1984, 41); and Sufis (mystics), who articulate a notion of justice as defined through spirituality and meditation. Sufis believe that *haq* (truth) is the highest value that can be derived from "a spiritual experience gained directly from union with God and not from ordinary human action." *Haq* embodies all other values. It is expressed as the kingdom of God within every person, which can be experienced and communicated through the heart (*qalb*), spirit (*ruh*), or "inward secret" (*sirr*) (71). Divine justice is not to be gained in the hereafter, but in the present through contemplation of light, beauty, and love of God. In possession of these qualities, a person attains inward satisfaction and knows implicitly the practice and laws of divine justice.

The Qur'an repeatedly reminds Muslims of the value of justice, which it presents not merely as an option but as a divine command (see esp. verses 4:58, 5:8, 16:90, 42:15, and 57:25). Justice is an absolute and not a relative value, a duty to be pursued among the believers and with the enemies, too.[2] On this point, the Qur'an is clear: "Serve Allah, and join not any partners with Him; and do good—to parents, kinsfolk, orphans, those in need, neighbours who are near, neighbours who are strangers, the companion by your side, the wayfarer (ye meet), and what your right hands possess: for Allah loveth not the arrogant, the vainglorious" (4:36). "God does command you to render back your trust to those to whom they are due. And when you judge between people, that you judge with justice. Indeed, how excellent is the teaching that He gives you. For verily God hears and sees all things" (4:58). "O, Ye who believe, be steadfast in service of God's truth and bear witness for justice and let not hatred of a people seduce you so that you deal with them unjustly. Act justly for that is what piety demands" (5:8). "God loves those who are just" (60:8).

The Islamic tradition calls for resistance to injustice through activism, third-party intervention, and divine intervention. The interconnection and interdependence of peace building and justice are thus never far from the surface in Islam. Peace is the product of order *and* justice. The notion that peace cannot be achieved without justice is echoed in the works of numerous peace-building researchers and activists (see Lederach 1997; Burgess and Burgess 1994). The imperative to strive for peace through justice falls equally on ruler and subject and is a natural obligation for all humanity (Kelsay 1993). Muslims are thereby expected to mobilize steadfastly against injustice. Mahmoud Ayoub (1996, 43) draws on the following verse to describe the special obligation that the Muslim community has in relation to justice: "Thus have We made of you an *Ummah* justly balanced [*wasat,* on middle ground] that ye might be witnesses over the nations, and the Messenger a witness over yourselves" (2:143). Based on this and other verses (55:9, 60:8), *qist* (the notion of dealing fairly with others, equity, fair play) is social justice in its broadest sense—first in our relationship to God and second in our relationship to society. From these perspectives, Muslims find a sacred obligation to treat one another with *qist.*

Mahmoud Ayoub (1996) also emphasizes the notion of *wasat* (middle ground) and *al-nasf* (sharing the equity, to do or demand justice; *al-nasf* and *insaf* mean justice) as representing the characteristic of fairness in Islam by drawing on such verses as: "There is no god but He: that is the witness of Allah, His angels, and those endued with knowledge, standing firm on justice [*qist*]. There is no God but He the Exalted in Power, the Wise" (3:18). There is also an important distinction between *'adl* and *qist* (justice, equity, fair play). Justice also has a legal meaning in terms of just laws. Shari'ah is the norm by which Muslims seek to administer and supervise a just order. The lack of codified law in the Shari'ah is not seen as a weakness but rather as a stronger method of procedural justice, since Islamic social and ethical codes were intended to remain flexible to allow for changes in space, time, circumstances, and variations (Ayoub 1996, 43). Scholars agree that such injunctions as *al-zakah,* the levy to purify wealth for the welfare of the poor, and *al-awqaf,* the estates in mortmain and their usage to assist the poor, are central to insure the realization of justice.[3]

Raquibuz Zaman (1996) further elaborates on specific Islamic precepts that promote economic justice: (1) *al-zakah,* one of the five pillars of Islam. This operates under the assumption that anyone who has both the basic necessities and comforts of life possesses *nisab* (taxable wealth).

Such people should pay *zakah,* which should be used exclusively for the support of the poor (those whose hearts have been reconciled to Islam), for the ransoming of slaves, and for wayfarers. (2) While voluntary charities are *zakah* (for those who have taxable wealth), the Qur'an urges all people to give generously to charity from whatever wealth God has bestowed on them. Such giving is known as *sadaqah.* (3) *Waqf* is another form of voluntary charity. Individuals with wealth may leave part of their inheritance for *waqf,* which will be used to assist needy Muslims. (4) Other measures to provide for the poor include the 'Id al Adha (the feast of immolation), an expiatory animal sacrifice. (5) Through *al-wasiyah* (will), Muslims leave a third of their estate to charity.

In addition, Zaman (1996, 55) notes that other methods of promoting economic justice and equity are implemented through various Islamic laws that encourage mutual support and cooperation. For example: (1) *al-musa'adah* (the law of mutual aid); (2) *bayt al-mal* (the public treasury); (3) *diyah* (blood money), in which the family of the offender is obligated to pay money to the victim's family; (4) *al-diyafah* (law of hospitality), which is based on the prophetic tradition outlining the social obligation to treat guests graciously;[4] (5) *al-musharakah* (the law of sharing), which obligates Muslims to share their harvest of crops with those who cannot afford to buy them. This law also encourages heirs to remember the needy when they divide their inheritance (4:80); (6) *al-ma'un* (the law of acting in kindness), which requires that Muslims not only give to charity but also lend their tools and equipment to the needy, who can not afford them; (7) *al-irth* (the Islamic law of inheritance), which promotes economic justice and equality by distributing an estate equitably among all members of the family (based on Zaman 1996). While some of these laws are more central than others, Islamic tradition clearly places a high priority on communal solidarity through inculcating a strong ethic of shared socioeconomic responsibility, as reflected in distributive and procedural approaches to justice. These laws and principles reflect a strong moral and institutional foundation and resource for the grassroots peace-building ethos in Muslim society.

Islamic principles and teachings are clearly compatible with contemporary notions of nonviolent activism that mobilize communities to resist social injustice. Contrary to the popular misperceptions among the opponents of this method of resolving conflicts, this approach does not mean submission or passivity in the face of aggression and injustice, as has been argued by militants in struggles in areas such as Palestine, Northern Ireland, and South Africa. Instead, the practices of Gandhi and Martin

Luther King, among others, clearly demonstrate the uncompromising militancy of nonviolent techniques. Nonviolent strategies can dissolve the structural violence embedded in certain social conflicts, thus going beyond superficial tinkering or temporary solutions, which may defuse tensions while preserving an unjust system. The primary goal of theories and concepts of conflict transformation and nonviolence is to overcome the underlying bases of structurally violent systems (Galtung 1969), on both the micro and macro level, as a prerequisite for the realization of a just society.[5]

Social Empowerment by Doing Good (*Khayr* and *Ihsan*)

Empowerment through *ihsan* and *khayr* (doing good) is also an important path to justice in the Islamic tradition. Islam's rapid growth was in a large measure a response to its deep commitment to empower the weak, and it remains a religion of dynamic social activism in terms of individual duties and sense of social responsibility. Struggling against oppression (*zulm*), assisting the poor, and pursuing equality among all humans are core religious values throughout the Qur'an and Hadith.[6]

One should do good (*ihsan*—grace, beneficence, kindness) not only to one's parents and relations but also to orphans and the impoverished (Qur'an, 17:24–26). The emphasis in Islam is on doing good (*khayr*), not on power and force (*quwwah*), and good deeds are associated with *al-sirat al-mustaqim* (the straight path) and with all the virtues of the Prophet: "Let there arise out of you a band of people inviting to all that is good, enjoining what is right, and forbidding what is wrong: they are the ones to attain felicity" (3:104). "Those who believe (in the Qur'an), and those who follow the Jewish (scriptures), and the Christians and the Sabians— any who believe in Allah and the Last Day, and work for righteousness, shall have their reward with their Lord; on them shall be no fear, nor shall they grieve" (2:62).

There is an abundance of teachings in Islam concerning both social justice (distributive, administrative, or restorative) and empowerment. Acts of social and economic justice are so important in Islam that they are even elevated to the practice of worshipping God (Saiyidain 1994; see Qur'an 4:36–37). As mentioned, the value of *zakah* (almsgiving) and *sadaqah* (voluntary charity) relates to individual and collective responsibility, specifically directed toward helping and protecting the poor, women (through inheritance laws), children, and commanding the just treatment of debtors, widows, orphans (90:13–16), and slaves (24:33).[7] Charity is a good deed incumbent upon every Muslim. The Prophet said: "There is a *sadaqah* to be given for every joint of the human body; and for every day on which the sun rises there is a reward of *sadaqah* for the one who establishes justice among people" (Sahih al-Bukhari 1992, vol. 3, bk. 49, no. 870). Charity is prescribed in at least twenty-five Qur'anic verses. All encourage Muslims to take more responsibility for redressing social injustice in their communities. For example, "It is not righteousness that ye turn your faces towards East or West; but it is righteousness to believe in Allah and the Last Day, and the Angels, and the Book, and the Messengers; to spend your substance, out of love for Him, for your kin, for orphans, for the needy, for the wayfarer, for those who ask, and for the ransom of slaves; to be steadfast in prayer, and practise regular charity, to fulfill the contracts which ye have made; and to be firm and patient, in pain (or suffering) and adversity" (2:177).

Muslims have obligations toward the underprivileged in their community: "Did He not find thee an orphan and give thee shelter (and care)? And He found thee wandering, and He gave thee guidance. And He found thee in need, and made thee independent [in a financial sense]" (93:6–8).

The Prophet's compassion for the weak and impoverished was as much the result of his own experience as from Qur'anic teaching. As the Prophet said: "I and the person who looks after an orphan and provides for him, will be in paradise like this, putting his index and middle fingers together" (Sahih al-Bukhari 1992, vol. 7, bk. 53, no. 224). But there is no shortage of such teachings in the Qur'an: "Therefore treat not the orphan with harshness, nor repulse the petitioner (unheard)" (93:9–10). Caring for and helping the underprivileged is a central mechanism for social empowerment and for maintaining a sense of community. The abolition of slavery was a clear example of the ethical principles that guided Muslims in addressing issues of oppression, poverty, and human suffering.[8]

Muslims are further expected to maintain good and honorable interpersonal relationships. "No Muslim can become a Mu'min (genuine believer) unless he likes for all others (not only Muslims) what he likes for himself and makes friends with them for God's sake" (al-Tirmidhi 1965, bk. 39, ch. 19; bk. 45, ch. 98). "Allah commands justice, the doing of good, and liberality to kith and kin, and He forbids all shameful deeds, and injustice and rebellion: He instructs you, that ye may receive admonition" (16:90). "Be good and kind to others even as God is to you" (28:77). Abdullah Yusuf Ali's commentary on this last Qur'anic verse captures the need to do good: "Spend your wealth in charity and good works. It is Allah who has given it to you, and you should spend it in Allah's cause [such as helping the poor and needy which is one of the important elements of Allah's cause]" (A. Ali 1991, 982, comm. 3407).

Doing good, however, does not stop there; it encompasses duties to the community as well. According to Islam, a nation cannot survive without making fair and adequate arrangements for the sustenance and welfare of all the poor, underprivileged, and destitute members of every community. The ultimate goal would be the elimination of their suffering and poverty.

In short, for Muslims justice and doing good, to both Muslims and non-Muslims, are essential features of their religious practice. The commitment to justice and its attendant virtues, upheld by both the Prophet and the Qur'an, lends itself to mobilization for sympathy and a shared ethos among contemporary Muslims for achieving peaceful social and economic development. Understanding these complementary religious principles is helpful for achieving the effective resolution of conflict. Nonviolent mechanisms (the outcome and process) of conflict resolution are designed to empower the parties involved in a conflict by providing equal access to decision making and by establishing an ownership of conflict among the parties. Many mediators therefore emphasize the need for equal access for the parties around the negotiating table, since nonviolent strategies are based on empowering, mobilizing, and engaging people in the process of resolving their conflicts.

The Universality and Dignity of Humanity

The universality of humanity is a central precept in Islam, amply affirmed throughout the Qur'an and Hadith and conveyed through the belief in the equality of origins and rights and the essential solidarity of all people. Humans are regarded as the most dignified and exalted of all creatures, with the potential for knowledge and moral action. All humans are born with knowledge of God, and the Qur'an is intended to be a way for humans to remember their origin and cultivate their connection with God. Humanity is God's vicegerent on earth. The Qur'an states, "Behold, thy Lord said to the angels: 'I will create a vicegerent [khalifah] on earth.' [The angels] said: 'Wilt Thou place therein one who will make mischief therein and shed blood?—Whilst we do celebrate Thy praises and glorify Thy holy (name)?' He said: 'I Know what ye know not'" (2:30). Human beings are a manifestation of God's will on earth and part of a larger, divine plan. Thus, protecting human life and respecting human dignity is sacred in Islam. The Qur'an also stresses the honor bestowed on humans: "We have honoured the sons of Adam; provided them with transport on land and sea; given them for sustenance things good and pure; and conferred on them special favours, above a great part of Our Creation" (17:70). Thus, the life of a person should be aimed at preserving human dignity and pride. Islamic scholars have cited several Qur'anic verses to establish the importance of human dignity and pride: "We have indeed created man in the best of moulds" (95:4). "It is We Who created you and gave you shape; then We bade the angels bow down to Adam, and they bowed down; not so Iblis [Satan]; he refused to be of those who bow down" (7:11).

It is considered a good deed to intervene or act to protect the basic dignity and pride of the person, as a divinely created being deserving of respect and protection. "In Islam, every person has human sacredness and he is under a protection [that is] sacrosanct until he violates his own sanctuary. By committing a crime, the person with his own hands removes such blanket of protection and immunity. Due to this human dignity, Islam protects its enemies, as well as its children and elders. God blessed humans with such dignity, as the base for all human relationships" (Daraz n.d., 164, cited in Howeidy 1993, 27). Thus, when addressing conflicts based on Islamic values, promoting and preserving the dignity of the parties involved becomes an important motivation in resolving the conflict.

The foundational idea in the Qur'an is that people are one community. It reflects the universality and inclusivity of Islam in dealing with all mankind. Accounting for the diversity of cultures and faiths in the world, the Qur'an notes that human differences are also intended as God's will so that "you may know one another" (49:13). Thus Muslims repeat: God is the creator of all people.

Equality

Islamic teachings point beyond the settlement of short-term disputes; they aspire to unite humanity in a single family based on the equality of all members. This precept is based on the idea of the oneness and common origin of all people: "O mankind! We created you from a single (pair) of a male and a female, and made you into nations and tribes, that ye may know each other (not that ye may despise each other). Verily the most honoured of you in the sight of Allah is (he who is) the most righteous of you. And Allah has full knowledge and is well acquainted (with all things)" (49:13).

In Islam there is no privilege granted based on race, ethnicity, or tribal association. The only two criteria for judging human worth are faith (*iman*) and good deeds (*'aml al-salih*). The Qur'an emphasizes repeatedly that there are no differences whatsoever between people except in their devotion to Allah, the creator of all humans. A well-known Hadith confirms this principle of equality: "All people are equal, as equal as the teeth of a comb. There is no claim of merit of an Arab over a Persian (non-Arab), or of a white over a black person, or of a male over female. Only God-Fearing people merit a preference with God" (M. Ali, 1944).

The Prophet acknowledges the common origin and universal equality of humans: Ibn Taymiyya, a well-known Muslim scholar (1263–1328), argued in these terms: "The desire to be above other people is injustice because all people are of the same species. A man's desire to put himself higher and reduce the others lower is unjust" (al-Sharif al-Radi 1978, 1:77; also see Kishtainy 1990, 12). Islam underscores that all people are the children of Adam and Eve, a point often cited by traditional mediators and arbitrators as a reminder of the brotherhood of the contending parties.

The Sacredness of Human Life

Peace-building approaches assume that human life is valuable and must be protected and that resources should be used to preserve life and prevent violence. The Qur'an clearly affirms the sacredness of human life: "And if any one saved a life, it would be as if he saved the life of the whole people"(5:32). "Not for (idle) sport did We create the heavens and the earth and all that is between!" (21:16; see also 44:38). "Nor take life—which Allah has made sacred—except for just cause" (17:33). Human actions have consequences, and life is an integral part of the great cosmic purpose (Saiyidain 1994, 29).

Islam also prohibits the destruction or waste of resources that serve human life. Even when Muslims launched an armed conflict in the early period, their rulers instructed them to avoid gratuitous destruction. When the first caliph, Abu Bakr, dispatched his army on an expedition to the Syrian borders, he declared: "Stop, O people, that I may give you ten rules for your guidance on the battlefield. Do not commit treachery or deviate from the right path. You must not mutilate dead bodies. Neither kill a child, nor a woman or an aged man. Bring no harm to the trees, nor burn them with fire, especially those which are fruitful. Slay not any of the enemy's flock, save for your food. You are likely to pass by people who have devoted their lives to monastic services; leave them alone" (Sahih Muslim, vol. 3, bk. 19, no. 4456; also in al-Tabari 1969, 3:226–27).

Under pressure from his followers to go to war, Caliph Imam Ali uttered the following words: "If I order you to march on them [the enemy] on warm days, you say, 'This is the fire of summer. Give us time until the heat is over.' If I ask you to march on them in winter, you say, 'This is the bite of the frost. Give us time until the cold is over.' All this and you fleeing from the heat and the cold, but, by God, you are more in flight from the sword" (al-Sharif al-Radi 1978, 1:77; Kishtainy 1990, 12). Saving lives, exhibiting patience, and avoiding violence are values that are implicit in the Imam's remarks.

Peace-building initiatives in Islam enhance the protection of human rights and dignity and promote equality among all people, regardless of their race, ethnicity, or religious affiliation.

A Quest for Peace

Peace in Islam is understood as a state of physical, mental, spiritual, and social harmony, living at peace with God through submission, and living at peace with one's fellow human beings by avoiding wrongdoing. Islam obligates its believers to seek peace in all life's domains. The ultimate purpose of Qur'anic revelation for Muslims is to create a peaceful and just social order. But, as mentioned earlier, there are certain conditions in which Muslims are allowed to use limited defensive force. "There are circumstances in which Islam contemplates the possibility of war—for instance, to avert worse disasters like the denial of freedom to human conscience—but the essential thing in life is peace. It is towards the achievement of peace that all human efforts must be sincerely diverted" (Saiyidain 1994, 164). Peace is viewed as an outcome to be achieved only after full submission to the will of God. Thus, peace has internal, personal, and social applications, and God is the source and sustainer of such peace. Accordingly, Muslims trust that the best way to insure peace is by total submission to God's will and to Islam (Kelsay 1993).

Shunning violence and aggression in all its forms has been another primary focus of Islamic values and tradition. Many Qur'anic verses stress this principle, among them: "Whenever they kindle the fire of war, God extinguishes it. They strive to create disorder on earth and God loves not those who create disorder" (5:64). "God commands you to treat (everyone) justly, generously, and with kindness" (16:90). "Repel evil with that which is best [not with evil]: We are well acquainted with the things they say" (23: 96). Thus when evil is done to you it is better not to reply with evil, "but to do what best repels the evil. Two evils do not make a good" (A. Ali 1991, 859, comm. 2934). (It is best to use forgiveness and amnesty.) Even in conflict, Islamic doctrine prefers peace to war or violence: "But if the enemy incline towards peace, do thou (also) incline towards peace, and trust in Allah: for He is the One that heareth and knoweth (all things)" (8:61).

The quest for peace is also clear in the Prophet's tradition and life. The Prophet's tradition also supports the shunning of violence and calls for restraint. Such teaching is clear in the Hadith: "The Jews came to the Prophet and said, 'Death overtake you!' 'Aishah said, 'And you, may Allah curse you and may Allah's wrath descend on you.' He [the Prophet] said: 'Gently, O 'Aishah! Be courteous, and keep yourself away from roughness'" (Sahih al-Bukhari 1998, vol. 8, bk. 73, no. 57). Forgiveness and amnesty are also viewed as the best reaction to anger and conflict.[9] The use of violence as a means to address conflict was discouraged in the Prophet's life and Qur'an and always framed in terms of a means of last resort. During the Meccan period of the Prophet's life (610–622 C.E.) he showed no inclination to use force in any form, even for self-defense. Instead, he waged nonviolent campaigns of resistance, through all his teachings in that period, during which Muslims were a minority. The Prophet's teachings at this time in particular were focused on the value of patience and steadfastness in facing oppression. For thirteen years the Prophet fully adopted nonviolent methods, relying on his spiritual preaching in dealing with aggression and confrontation. During this time, though he was tortured, accused of blasphemy, and humiliated, and his family and supporters were ostracized, he neither cursed his enemies nor encouraged violence. On the contrary, his teachings were centered around prayer and the hope for enlightenment and peace. Ibn Umar relates that someone asked the Prophet, "Who is the best Muslim?" He replied, "The one whose hand and tongue leave other Muslims in peace" (Sahih al-Bukhari 1998, vol. 1, bk. 2, no. 10).[10]

In Islam the quest for peace extends to both interpersonal and community quarrels and disagreements. Muslims should not use violence to settle their differences but rely on arbitration or other forms of intervention; several Qur'anic verses instruct believers to refer disputes to God and to His Prophet (see 40:12, 5:95; 40:47–48; 2:13; 3:55). "And obey Allah and His Messenger; and fall into no disputes, lest ye lose heart and your power depart; and be patient and persevering: for Allah is with those who patiently persevere" (8:46).

The various Islamic principles and values of peace cannot be fully identified without revisiting the concept and understanding the value of jihad. Esposito (1988, 40) has noted that the concept of jihad is commonly seized upon by Westerners in characterizing Islam as a religion spread by the sword, or through holy war, whereas modern Muslim scholars are more apt to explain jihad as simply defensive in nature.

Scholars agree that there are conditions that permit the use of force, but they have remained sharply divided on the nature of jihad. Many studies conclude that jihad does not mean the constant use of the sword to resolve problems with a non-Muslim enemy or among Muslims. In addition to the Qur'anic verses that indicate the possibility of peaceful and nonviolent jihad, various Islamic sects have argued that there are several levels of jihad and that the jihad against self-desires, temptations, and selfishness is the most difficult to achieve.[11]

Peacemaking

In the peace-building field, in general, open, face-to-face communication about problems and conflicts is deemed more productive than avoidance or violence, reducing the cost of conflict by addressing all the grievances of the conflicting parties. A third party plays an integral part in peace-building intervention by facilitating communication, reducing tension, and assisting in rebuilding relationships. Islam encourages such active intervention, particularly among Muslims themselves. "If two parties among the Believers fall into a quarrel, make ye peace between them: but if one of them transgresses beyond bounds against the other, then fight ye (all) against the one that transgresses until it complies with the command of Allah; but if it complies then make peace between them with justice, and be fair: for Allah loves those who are fair (and just). The Believers are but a single Brotherhood: so make peace and reconciliation between your two (contending) brothers; and fear Allah, that ye may receive Mercy" (49:9–10).

These verses have been cited by scholars searching for a legitimate basis for the use of violence in Islam and thus to refute the pacifist hypothesis. Nevertheless, the passage clearly supports the concept of mediation and fair and just third-party intervention. In addition, it reflects as a core Islamic value the shunning of aggression, exemplified in the following passage: "[A]nd let not the hatred of some people in (once) shutting you out of the Sacred Mosque lead you to transgression (and hostility on your part). Help ye one another in righteousness and piety, but help ye not one another in sin and rancour" (5:2). In other words, hatred and lack of tolerance should not lead you to become an aggressor or be hostile to the other disputant, even if you have been shut out of the house of God, which is considered an act of violence. According to both the Qur'an and the Prophet's tradition, Muslims have to settle their conflicts peacefully. "[S]hould they (two) reconcile with each other . . . [this] reconciliation is best" (4:128). Another clear call for peacemaking and reconciliation is:

"In most of their secret talks, save (in) him who orders charity or kindness, or conciliation between mankind and he who does this seeking the good pleasure of Allah, we shall give him great reward" (4:114).

Peacemaking and reconciliation of differences and conflict are preferred and highlighted by the Prophet's tradition. He instructed his followers: "He who makes peace between the people is not a liar" (Sahih al-Bukhari 1992, vol. 3, bk. 49, no. 857). The Prophet's intervention in resolving the problem of the Black Stone in Mecca is based on a well-known Hadith—as a classic example of peace building (Ibn Hisham 1992, 192–99). It illustrates the creativity of a peaceful problem-solving approach conducted by a third party (in this case, the Prophet himself). The clans of Mecca had a dispute over the Ka'bah's building and the lifting of the Black Stone to its higher location. The clans asked for the Prophet's advice and intervention, due to his reputation as a trustworthy and faithful person. The Prophet proposed a simple yet creative method to resolve the dispute. He placed the stone on a cloak and asked each clan to hold one side of the cloak and jointly lift the stone to the desired height. Then he placed the Black Stone in its new location.[12]

This type of arbitration in Islam was also explored by other researchers (e.g., Khadduri 1955). He identified several occasions in which the Prophet acted as arbitrator before and after prophethood. For example, in the incident of the Aws and Khazraj tribes of Medina, the Prophet acted as mediator according to the Arab tradition and ended their enmity; in arbitration between the Prophet and the Banu Qurayza (a Jewish tribe), both agreed to submit their dispute to a person chosen by the tribes. Khadduri concludes that third-party intervention was an acceptable option to end fighting. The decision of the third-party member is binding if their decision is not affected by their relatives. Khadduri also mentions the arbitration case between Ali and Mu'awiya, which was initiated to end their fighting.

In short, Islamic values shun aggression, violent confrontation, and bigotry and favor the methods of peace building and nonviolence for resolving conflicts. Such values correspond to those identified by contemporary practitioners and scholars in peace building (conflict resolution and peace studies) as foundational strategies in the field of conflict resolution (see, e.g., Laue 1978; Burgess and Burgess 1994).

Knowledge and Reason

Rationality, reason, and cost-benefit calculations are presumed to be prerequisites for successful dialogue and most conflict resolution processes.

Conflict resolution and peace-building methods tend to assume that a rational approach to problems is more effective in reaching peaceful agreements and reducing the potential damage ensuing from conflicts.

Hikma (wisdom) and *'aql* (rationality) are two major Islamic virtues, repeatedly cited in the Qur'an and Hadith. "Invite (all) to the Way of thy Lord with wisdom and beautiful preaching; and argue with them in ways that are best and most gracious" (16:125). This verse clearly encourages the faith-based use of reason, dialogue, and courtesy in dealing with others.[13]

Like Khadduri, George Hourani (1985) traces the history and centrality of rationalism within the Mu'atazilite [path of unity and justice] school of the ethics of reason.[14] Sachedina (2000, 21) also conceptualizes the relationship between God and humanity from a rationalist perspective dependent on revelation that connects divine justice with human interaction. However, God grants humans free choice over, and responsibility for, their actions. This stream in Islamic philosophical and theological thought is most associated with the Mu'atazilite and different Shi'ite schools. The Mu'atazilite rationalists believed in natural human reason, which allows them to discover and decide on the ethical choices available to them. From this perspective, humans are autonomous sources of ethical knowledge. God created humans to be capable of knowing good and evil objectively. God's justice then depends on the objective knowledge of good and evil as determined by reason. The Ash'ari, or revelationists, believed that discovering the God-human relationship and scope of divine justice is beyond human logic. Thus, without justification or explanation, and strictly on the basis of trust and faith, Muslims should accept divine will and its creation of everything around them, including human knowledge. In this view, God alone is the source of all actions and provides humans with some voluntary choice. Values have no guidance; it is the will of God that reveals and imposes upon actions. As Sachedina explains, "God-Human relations are founded on individual autonomy as regulated by divine jurisdiction; interhuman relations are within the jurisdiction of human institutions founded on political consensus with the purpose of furthering social justice and equity" (2000, 5).

Thinking and pursuing knowledge are two central virtues in Islamic tradition and scripture. Many traditional sayings support these virtues: "The acquisition of knowledge is compulsory for every Muslim, whether male of female." "The best form of worship is the pursuit of knowledge" (Sunan Ibn Majah n.d., bk. 19, no. 108, 22–23). "Worship without knowledge has no goodness in it, and knowledge without understanding has no goodness in it, and the recitation of the Qur'an which is not thoughtful has no goodness in it" (Abu Dawud 1998, bk. 20, ch. 1; al-Tirmidhi 1965, bk. 19). "Thinking deep for one hour [with sincerity] is better than seventy years of [mechanical] worship" (Ibn Majah cited by al-Albani 1988).

A number of Qur'anic verses encourage the use of the mind: "And He hath constrained the night and the day and the sun and the moon to be of service to you and the stars are made subservient to you by His command. Lo! Herein are portents for people who use their mind" (16:12). Reason and reflection are viewed as paths to spiritual wisdom: "Do not be like those who say we hear and they hear not. Lo! The worst of beasts in God's sight are the deaf and dumb, who understand not" (8:21–22).

The story of creation in the Qur'an teaches us that when the angels claimed that Adam was going to do evil things on the earth, God told them: "I know what you do not know" (2:30). However, God granted Adam knowledge of the names of things, a power the angels did not possess. Thus, humans are endowed with a creative power for knowledge.

Several nineteenth-century Islamic reformists emphasized the elements of knowledge and reason in Islam. For instance, Jamal al-Din al-Qasimi and Taher al-Jaza'iri elaborated on reformist Islamic views similar to those being spread by Abduh, Rida, and Kwakibi in Egypt. Like Abduh, Qasimi endeavored to reconcile reason and revelation in Islam. He argued that "Islam is a rational religion: Islam calls on man to use reason; and whoever employs reason to study the natural world will grow stronger in faith" (Commins 1986, 406). Similarly, Hussein Nasr (1998) has argued that knowledge is one of the most important principles characterizing Islam.

The above appreciation of reason and pursuit of new information and knowledge in Islam can be a central theme in resolving conflicts and reducing enmity and misperceptions between enemies. For example, the various approaches of problem solving in the field of conflict resolution are based on the control of emotions and rational thinking. Such an approach of rational problem solving can be easily developed utilizing Islamic teachings of knowledge and rational thinking.

Creativity and Innovation

Nonviolent strategies encourage creativity and innovation in dealing with conflicts and relationships by generating new options that do not compromise the sense of justice. *Ijtihad* (independent judgment) is a notion that has been advanced not only among the 'ulama (religious scholars) but also among other Muslims as a powerful tool of nonviolent conflict resolution for Muslims. In the 1930s, Muhammed Iqbal (1875–1938), one of the major figures in modern and modernist Islam, called for "the transfer of the power of *ijtihad* from individual representatives of schools to a Muslim legislative assembly" (Iqbal 1930). *Ijtihad* is the intellectual effort to interpret divine will for human implementation, the basic outlines for which were considered fully defined and codified in the eleventh and twelfth centuries, when the "door of itjihad" was proclaimed closed. Iqbal called for the reopening of ijtihad for Muslims. He argued that the closing of the door of *ijtihad* is a pure fiction, prompted partly by the crystallization of legal thought in Islam and partly by an intellectual laziness that turns great thinkers into idols, especially in a period of spiritual decay. He predicted that "modern Islam is not bound by this voluntary surrender of intellectual independence" (Iqbal 1930).

According to Khurshid Ahmad, vice president of the Jami'at al-Islami (Islamic association) in Pakistan, "God has revealed only broad principles and has endowed man with the freedom to apply them in every age in the way suited to the spirit and conditions of that age. It is through *ijtihad* that people of every age try to implement and apply divine guidance to the problem of their age" (in Voll and Esposito 1994, 12).

The notion that there are multiple interpretations for Islamic religious sources is also acknowledged by Sachedina (2000), who argues that there are various and subtle possibilities for interpretation. He echoes the repeated claim by Muslim reformists that individual *ijtihad* is a duty that can be practiced by any Muslim as long as the methods and the weighing of the argument are vigorous and drawn from authoritative texts. But the fact that such scholars offer an interpretation of Qur'anic passages immediately places them in conflict with traditionalists, who have closed the doors of *ijtihad*.

Closing the door of *ijtihad* has been viewed as a great obstacle in the revival of virtually every aspect of Islamic civilization. Thus when exploring the Islamic roots of pluralism, Sachedina (2000, 133–34) calls for opening the process of reasoning and inferring the decisions from the revelation, and encourages scholars not to regard existing historical interpretation as sacrosanct. Most of the judicial decisions regarding the autonomy and treatment of non-Muslims have become irrelevant in the pluralist, increasingly interdependent reality of the modern days.[15] Muslim jurists issued their teachings either under circumstances of domination or in efforts to curry favor with leaders, conveniently overlooking the essential Islamic premises of inclusivity and pluralism, in addition to the basic principle that being "the community sent by God" means the preservation of the rights of the other and creating socially and politically just societies rather than looking for political expansion or consolidation (138).

Having said that, it is important to point out that *ijtihad* requires creativity, flexibility, and the ability to abandon old perceptions and meet new challenges. These traits are also core requirements for many peacebuilding efforts (dialogue, mediation, nonviolent mobilization, and protest movements). Farid Esack (1998) maintains that Muslims cannot stop thinking and rethinking their environment or accept the notion that the door of creative juristic thinking (*ijtihad*) is closed. He asks, "How does one fast from dawn to dusk when you end up in a place where the sun does not set for six months?" (10). Muslims will always be confronted with new dilemmas and challenges based on new knowledge and deeper awareness.[16]

In the case of the Black Stone, the Prophet proposed a simple yet creative means of resolving the dispute: He had the quarreling clans join together to lift the stone to the desired height. The resolution of this problem implies a repudiation of violence and competition, and an appreciation of the creative possibilities of joint problem solving. In fact, there are many accounts of interventions by the Prophet in which he utilized such skills and principles in arbitrating or mediating disputes; these examples serve as powerful referents and resources for conflict resolution efforts.

Forgiveness

The forgiveness that vanquishes hatred and anger is a prized virtue in Islam, greater even than justice (42:40, 24:43). In fact, believers are urged to forgive even when they are angry. The Prophet said, "God fills with peace and faith the heart of one who swallows his anger, even though he is in a position to give vent to it" (42:37, see also verse 42:37 on forgiveness and control of anger). The Prophet himself, when he entered Mecca with the first Muslim followers, set an example of great forgiveness toward the Meccans, who had fought him by declaring the whole place as a sanctuary (Sahih al-Bukhari 1992, vol. 5, bk. 59, no. 603).[17] The Prophet always prayed when he was persecuted during the Mecca period, saying, "Forgive them, Lord, for they know not what they do."[18]

Forgiveness also figures prominently in the Qur'an as the way people should interact with each other: "Keep to forgiveness [O Muhammad] and enjoin kindness, and turn away from the ignorant" (7:199). An interpretive text says, "The most gracious act of forgiving an enemy is his who has the power to take revenge" (Saiyidain 1994, 93).

Mercy is another quality or behavior expected from a Muslim and is one of the most frequently cited and revered attributes of God. God has mercy upon those who are merciful to others (7:151). Mercy is an important step in the process of forgiveness and reconciliation. The value of forgiveness and its relationship to mercy is similarly supported by a story about some of the Prophet's followers who asked him to invoke the wrath of God upon the Meccans because of their persecution of Muslims. His reply to them was: "I have not been sent to curse anyone but to be a source of *rahmah* [compassion and mercy] to all" (al-Bukhari, 4:175, 9:141; cited in Nurbakhsh 1983, 2:81). When applying these principles of forgiveness to current realities, it is clear that instead of vengeance, there is a need to rediscover the processes and values of restoration through forgiveness and compassion in Muslim political society.

Individuals' responsibility for their actions and the process of gaining forgiveness is clearly prescribed in the following verses: "When those come to thee who believe in Our Signs, say: 'peace be on you;' Your Lord hath inscribed for Himself (the rule of) Mercy: verily, if any of you did evil in ignorance, and thereafter repented, and amended (his conduct), lo! He is Oft-Forgiving, Most Merciful. Thus do We explain the signs in detail: that the way of the sinners may be shown up" (6:54–55). To "service of the divine" is the way to implement repentance (*tawbah*), through which the "arrogant and jealous self, melted in the furnace of self-reproach, reforms in remorse and turning toward God by seeking the forgiveness of one's fellow humans" (Sachedina 2000, 111). The cycle of revenge must be broken by Muslims because "restoration is a source of life" (see Qur'an, 2:179) not revenge or vengeance (112). In this context—the use of jihad in the Qur'an as a means for restoration rather than retribution—individuals can use jihad to demonstrate a moral resolve to work for peace and justice. Thus, humans are expected to initiate a process of restoring their relationships as part of their nature and their place in God's order, and must act responsibly toward each other to gain God's forgiveness.

Retribution is usually attached to the principle of forgiveness in Islamic tradition. In general, retribution tempered with pardon leads to restoration in Muslim culture community. Acknowledgment is considered the first step, as a "turn to god," an act of asking forgiveness (*ghufran*). Acknowledgment means quickly humbling oneself and then asking for forgiveness (Sachedina 2000, 103). In pre-Islamic society, primarily retributive measures were used to resolve conflicts, which caused tremendous fratricidal suffering, division, and destruction. The excessive nature of these retributions and the continuing reach of the conflicts over generations needed to be curbed. The Qur'an provided clear guidance for the Arab tribes on how exactly they should implement the law of fair retribution (2:178).[19]

Deeds and Actions

In Islam the real test is in action. Lip service is not enough. God judges kindly those who have faith and have done good deeds: "On those who believe and work deeds of righteousness, will (Allah) Most Gracious bestow Love" (19:96). "If you do good, it will be for your own self; if you do evil, it will react on you" (17:7). An individual is responsible for his or her deeds; no one else can guide him or bear the responsibility of others' actions: "He that doeth good shall have ten times as much to his credit: He that doeth evil shall only be recompensed according to his evil: no wrong shall be done unto (any of) them" (6:160). "It was not We that wronged them: they wronged their own souls: the deities, other than Allah, whom they invoked, profited them no whit when there issued the decree of thy Lord: nor did they add aught (to their lot) but perdition!" (11:101). "Whoever works righteousness, man or woman, and has Faith, verily, to him will We give a new Life, and life that is good and pure, and We will bestow on such their reward according to the best of their actions" (16:97).

According to Islam a person bears three major types of responsibilities, in the execution or avoidance of which he or she will be judged by God: (1) responsibility toward Allah, to be fulfilled through the performance of religious duties faithfully; (2) responsibility toward oneself, by living in harmony with oneself; (3) responsibility toward other humans, by living in harmony and peace with them.[20]

Involvement through Individual Responsibility and Choice

Moral choice and rational persuasion are important Islamic principles that emphasize responsibility for one's own actions. Even the Prophet himself was not responsible for the decisions of others: "But if they turn away, Say: 'Allah sufficeth me: there is no god but He: on Him is my trust—He the Lord of the Throne (of Glory) Supreme!'" (9:129). If others do not accept God's message, it is their choice, their responsibility. Allah is the sole arbiter of humans' choices. Individual responsibility, choice, and God's arbitration on Judgment Day are also reflected in verses 18:29, 34:28, 88:21–22, and 109:6.

"Now then, for that (reason), call (them to the Faith), and stand steadfast as thou art commanded, nor follow thou their vain desires, but say: 'I believe in the Book which Allah has sent down; and I am commanded to judge justly between you. Allah is our Lord and your Lord: For us (is the responsibility for) our deeds, and for you for your deeds. There is no contention between us and you'" (42:15).

The sense of individual choice and the call for involvement extends to the political system, in which the ruler expects his followers to take full responsibility for fighting injustice.[21] Abu Bakr told his people, "I am no better than you. . . . I am just like any one of you. If you see that I am pursuing a proper course, then follow me; and if you see me err, then set me straight" (al-Tirmidhi 1959, ch. 53). Persuasion thus not only puts humans in charge of their own fate, it also supports individual actions.

Persuasion is a major strategy in the Qur'an, underscoring the privileged position of reason and intellect, and reflected in the numerous verses that present the arguments of those who opposed the Prophet, as well as the systematic refutations of those arguments through rational proof and evidence (Howeidy 1993).

Syed Nawab Naqvi (1994) establishes the importance of "free will" and choice in Islam by deducing basic axioms supporting these precepts: "in the Islamic ethical scheme, man is the best of God's creation"[22] (cited by al-Bukhari, ch. 53; also cited by Muhammad Ali 1944). Man is God's vicegerent (khalifah) on earth: "It is He Who hath made you (His) agents, inheritors of the earth: He hath raised you in ranks, some above others: that He may try you in the gifts He hath given you: for thy Lord is quick in punishment: yet he is indeed Oft-Forgiving, most Merciful" (6:165). Hence, the purpose of human life is to realize one's status as a moral agent invested with free will and able to make choices between good and evil, right and wrong. By virtue of his or her freedom, a person can either realize the truth of being God's vicegerent on earth or deny him- or herself this exalted role by making wrong choices. In other words, humans will be held accountable for the choices they make (Naqvi 1994, 25). Thus according to Islam, every human is endowed by creation with a natural ability (*fitrah*) for knowledge and justice. Thus it is up to individuals to discover their role in life and how they are going to serve humanity. *Fitrah* provides moral direction. There are certain responsibilities and actions which will guide this *fitrah* to be achieved or revealed. *Fitrah* does not judge the wrong or right of human faith but rather evaluates the moral righteousness of the actions. *Fitrah* has the capacity to relate and integrate individual responsibility with spiritual and moral awareness (as described by *taqwah*—a keen spiritual and moral perception and motivation) (Sachedina 2000, 82–86). Thus, it is the individual responsibility for human choice that leads to going astray (away from the straight path) and not utilizing the innate universal gift of divine justice given by the Creator to every human. Everyone has the autonomy and capacity to discover divine justice (3:86, 3:90).

Since deeds and individual responsibility are so central to Islam, involvement in community life becomes the most visible channel for meaningful deeds. Therefore, Muslims are urged to improve their communal life, to support one other, and to combat poverty. Such goals can be attained only through actions, the doing or shirking of which is the criterion by which God judges humans. Peace building in Islam is thus based on a framework of deeply embedded religious beliefs regarding individuals' responsibility for their actions and their active participation in a larger social context.

Patience (*Sabr*)

Muslims are encouraged to be patient and to suspend their judgment of others, whether Muslim or non-Muslim. Sabr (patience) is a virtue of believers, who are expected to endure enormous difficulties and still maintain a strong belief in God. It should be pointed out that in Arabic, "*Sabr* implies many shades of meaning, which it is impossible to express in one English word. It implies (1) patience in the sense of being thorough, not hasty; (2) patient perseverance, constancy, steadfastness, firmness of purpose; (3) systematic as opposed to spasmodic or chance action; (4) a cheerful attitude of resignation and understanding in sorrow, defeat, or suffering, as opposed to murmuring or rebellion, but saved from mere passivity or listlessness, by the element of constancy or steadfastness."[23]

The Qur'an elaborates on this idea in the following passages: "Nay, seek (Allah's) help with patient perseverance and prayer: it is indeed hard, except to those who bring a lowly spirit" (2:45). "O ye who believe! seek help with patient Perseverance and Prayer: for Allah is with those who patiently persevere" (2:153). "But if ye persevere patiently, and guard against evil—then that will be a determining factor in all affairs" (3:186). "O ye who believe! Persevere in patience and constancy; vie in such perseverance; strengthen each other; and fear Allah; that ye may prosper" (3:200).

There are at least fifteen additional Qur'anic verses that encourage Muslims to be patient and steadfast in their daily lives and in their pursuit of a just life.[24] Patience is a key virtue in peace-building and socioeconomic development projects, whose benefits are often more apparent in the long term than in the short term.

Patience is also associated with making a personal and individual sacrifice. "Be sure we shall test you with something of fear and hunger, some loss in goods or lives or the fruits (of your toil), but give glad tidings to those who patiently persevere" (2:155). Patience and perseverance, as interpreted by Yusuf Ali, are not mere passivity (A. Ali 1991, 62, comm. 158). "It is active striving in the way of truth, which is the way of Allah." Thus, oppression and persecution can be resisted and overcome with praying and active patience (a believer continues to fulfill his/her duties as a Muslim and practices patience as a form of resistance). Patience and restraint are better than revenge. The Prophet said, "Power resides not in being able to strike another, but in being able to keep the self under control when anger arises" (Sahih al-Bukhari 1998, vol. 8, bk. 73, no. 135). Even when arguing or engaging in a conflict, the Prophet said: "Whoever has (these) four qualities is a hypocrite, and whoever has any one of them has one quality of hypocrisy until he gives it up. These are: whenever he talks, he tells a lie; whenever he makes a promise, he breaks it; whenever he makes a covenant, he proves treacherous, and whenever he quarrels, he behaves impudently in an evil-insulting manner" (vol. 3, bk. 43:18). "And if ye do catch them out, catch them out no worse than they catch you out: but if ye show patience, that is indeed the best (course) for those who are patient. And do thou be patient, for thy patience is but from Allah; nor grieve over them: and distress not thyself because of their plots. For Allah is with those who restrain themselves. And those who do good" (16:126–28).

In commenting on these verses, Yusuf Ali says:

In the context this passage refers to controversies and discussions, but the words are wide enough to cover all human struggles, disputes, and fights. In strictest equity you are not entitled to give a worse blow than is given to you. But those who have reached a higher spiritual standard do not even do that. . . . Lest you should think that such patience only gives an advantage to the adversary, you are told that the contrary is the case: the advantage is with the patient, the self-possessed, those who do not lose their temper or forget their own principles of conduct (A. Ali 1991, 670, comm. 2163).

This strong command instructs Muslims on how to use patience and self-restraint in reacting to conflicts, a type of patience that will give them the advantage. Sabr is an important quality of believers as agents of change in Islam. The same characteristic is required of peace builders and those engaged in sustainable development. Assisting people and promoting peaceful coexistence in conflict areas requires patience among both the interveners and the beneficiaries.

Collaborative Actions and Solidarity

Peace-building approaches assume that collaborative efforts to resolve a problem are more productive than competitive efforts by individuals. A well-known saying in the Islamic tradition is "God's hand is with the group (*jama'ah*)," which is often cited to motivate disputants to reach an agreement and gain strength by working together. It also contains the pragmatic idea of reducing costs and damages that might be incurred in a conflict. This idea is also used to forge unified support against an outside enemy and to motivate people to avoid political and social rivalries (*fitnah*). In general, the saying encourages the collaborative approach to life's challenges, including, potentially, collective undertakings for social or economic development or peace building.

In Islam the basis for solidarity is wider than the Muslim community alone; all humans have a common origin in God, who created them all equal. Therefore, they should assist one another and not neglect one another's needs. "O mankind! Reverence your Guardian-Lord, Who created you from a single Person, created, of like nature, his mate, and from them twain scattered (like seeds) countless men and women—fear Allah, through Whom ye demand your mutual (rights) and (reverence) the wombs (that bore you): for Allah ever watches over you" (4:1).

Solidarity among Muslims is a central value too, reflected in another well-known traditional Hadith: "Help your brother, whether he is an oppressor or he is an oppressed one. People asked: 'O, Allah's Apostle! It is all right to help him if he is oppressed, but how should we help him if he is an oppressor?' The prophet said: 'By preventing him from oppressing others'" (Sahih al-Bukhari 1992, vol. 3, bk. 43, no. 623). The Prophet also declared: "None among you has faith until you desire for your fellow Muslims what he/she desires for him/herself" (Sahih al-Bukhari 1992, vol. 1, bk. 2, no. 12).

This is a clear summons to avoid the use of violence and prevent aggression by Muslims against other Muslims and non-Muslims. Solidarity in this context is different from mere tribal solidarity, or 'asabiyah—assisting members of the same tribe, clan, or family against outsiders regardless of the conditions.[25] Nonviolent strategies in Islam are most effective if they are based on collective approaches and political and social solidarity.

The Ummah

The concept of the Ummah has been a foundation for collective action since the time of the Prophet. During the early period of Islam in Mecca, the Prophet propagated such values of collaboration and collectivism to mobilize his followers and to respond nonviolently to the accusations and attacks of his opponents. Brotherhood and equality are the founding principles of the concept of the Ummah (Khadduri 1984, 143).

Some argue that the concept of Ummah has vanished because of the contending political regimes in Muslim world, that it applied only when Muslims were all under the same political authority. But Farid Esack argues that "the notion of Ummah has not only survived but continues to give Muslims a deep sense of belonging." The Ummah has even expanded to include non-Muslims. All those who believe in God are members of this community too. Esack adds, "The universal community under God has always been a significant element in Muslim discourse against tribalism and racism" (Esack 1998, 10).[26] In supporting this argument, other scholars stress that the People of the Book (i.e., Christians, Jews, and Muslims), as recipients of the divine revelation, were recognized as part of the Ummah, based on the following Qur'anic verse: "And surely this, your community (Ummah), is a single community" (23:52). The charter of the Medina—the first constitution created by the Prophet—is another proof of such an inclusive and religiously diverse community.[27]

The Prophet instructed his followers on many occasions on the importance of solidarity between the believers and Muslims. He compared their relationship to the organs of the body, which communicate pain if one part is ill, or to a building, which is strengthened by the coherence of its parts. "The believer to another believer is like a building whose different parts enforce each other. The Prophet then clasped his hands with fingers interlaced (while saying that)" (Sahih al-Bukhari 1992, vol. 3, bk. 43, no. 626).

Islam has been considered a religion of structural transformation and change, particularly in its impact on pre-Islamic civilizations. In this context, the principle of Ummah, in both its specific and general meanings, has emerged in Muslim history as a powerful mechanism of social and political transformation (Wahid 1993).

Peace-building initiatives can preserve a community's structure and identity throughout the planning, implementation, and follow-up stages of social change. Communal solidarity can thus contribute to the success of the overall process. The idea of Muslim community has proved a powerful tool of social mobilization and selflessness and thus has enormous potential for contributing to peaceful conflict resolution.

Nonviolence and peace building are based on collective and collaborative approaches that aim to respond to the needs and interests of the parties; they seek to create future bonds, relationships, and agreements between disputing parties. Collective approaches allow victims of injustice to exert influence and power over the other side. The purpose of the collective mobilization of power is to create a change in the behavior and perception of the other side. Such methods have been used by many leaders of nonviolent movements on various political and social levels. Practitioners of conflict resolution use this method to assist a party in realizing its power base. It is clear that the Ummah offers a powerful mobilizing tool for various Muslim communities to pursue justice and assert themselves nonviolently to redress structural injustices.

Inclusivity and Participatory Processes

Peace building endeavors to encourage participatory forums and inclusive procedures, deeming them more productive and effective than authoritarian, hierarchical, and exclusionary decision-making approaches. Peace-building strategies are based on assisting parties in negotiation based on joint interests, or bringing in a third party to facilitate such a process.

The Qur'an clearly embraces inclusiveness over exclusiveness in the quest for justice, and the *mujahidin* (followers who strive for Islam) are considered more important than the leaders (Esack 1998). These principles are best reflected in the Muslim tradition of mutual consultation (*shurah*) in the governing process. Through public and private consultation, the governor, or leader, should seek active advice and input from his followers before making a decision. Leaders are "[t]hose who harken to their Lord, and establish regular prayer; who (conduct) their affairs by mutual Consultation; who spend out of what We bestow on them for Sustenance" (42: 38). Shurah has been widely discussed by Islamic scholars, particularly those who support the notion that democracy is not antithetical to Islam. For these scholars, shurah (1) is not merely a consultation by the rulers but is an inclusive process in which all Ummah members are asked to provide input in the decision-making process. Shurah, unlike consultation, is obligatory; (2) it involves all matters of concerning the Ummah; (3) it represents all segments of society, regardless of how their position of power (parties, religious groups, Muslim and non-Muslim, and so on) differs from the people of *ijtihad,* who are the Islamic jurisprudents (*fuqaha'*; sing. *faqih*); and (4) holds freedom of expression at its core. If freedom of expression for all people is not guaranteed, then shurah is not realized. The meaning of *shurah* is solidarity in society based on the principle of free consultation and genuine dialogue, reflecting equality in thought and the expression of opinion (al-Shawi 1992; cited in Howeidy 1993, 117). Not only is the ruler or governor obligated to consult with his advisors, but he is also enjoined to involve the populace in the process. The people of the shurah represent all the segments of the society, unlike the people of *ijtihad,* who are the experts in Islamic jurisprudence.[28] The Prophet encouraged Muslims to consult both with each other and with experts. He repeatedly consulted with other Muslims and followed their advice, even when he disagreed with them.[29]

The principle of inclusivity thus conduces to democratic decision making. Some of the Islamic principles that are consonant with democratic and inclusive decision making are the following:

(1) The Islamic governance is for the Ummah: its approval is a sine qua non for the continuation of rulers. Thus, the legitimacy of governance is based on the Ummah's satisfaction and approval rather than the caliph's (M. Musa 1967).[30]

(2) The community as a whole—not the ruler alone—is obligated to pursue religious injunctions, build a good life, and look after the public interest. The Qur'anic verses supporting the principle of almsgiving (*zakah*) offer evidence for the mutual responsibility of members of the community. Helping others and sharing part of one's wealth are part of a Muslim's basic rights and duties (al-Ghazali 2:306; cited in Howeidy 1993, 106).

(3) Freedom is a right for all. Freedom is the other side of monotheism. By acknowledging his loyalty to God alone, a person is free from all other loyalties.[31] Individual freedom of decision is expected and favored by the Prophet, who says, "Do not be a conformist, who says I am with the people, if they do good I do good, and if they do harm, I do harm" ('Awwa 1983, 215). If freedom of expression for all people is not guaranteed, then shurah is not being practiced.

(4) All people are equal in their origin; they originate from the same God and partake equally of the same divine soul. "O Mankind! We created you from a single (pair) of a male and a female, and made you into nations and tribes, that ye may know each other (not that ye may despise (each other)" (49:13). In his last speech, the Prophet said, "You all have one father and one God" (Ibn Hisham 1992, 361).

(5) The other, the non-Muslim, who also partakes of his common human heritage and commands the respect that flows from it, is accorded societal legitimacy. The Prophet stood to respect a funeral, and when it was mentioned to him that it was a Jewish funeral, implying that such respect was not necessary, he replied, "Is not that a soul?" (Sahih al-Bukhari, vol. 2, bk. 23, no. 399).[32] In addition, the Qur'an stresses the legitimacy of human differences in several other verses (e.g., 11:118–19, 30:22, 49:13).

(6) Oppression is prohibited, and opposing it is a duty. *Zulm* (unjust treatment) is one of the gravest transgressions—it contradicts the main goal and value of the Prophet's message of justice (4:148, 42:42, 46:12).

(7) The law stands supreme: Islamic laws are to be followed by both the rulers and the people. Observance of this principle is designed to protect the people from tyranny (Howeidy 1993, 13).

In addition to shurah, *ijma'* (consensus building) is an important mechanism of decision making in Islam. The two principles, grounded in the Prophet's own practice, support collaborative and consensus-building processes rather than authoritative, competitive, or confrontational procedures.

These principles in the Islamic tradition and religion encourage popular involvement and responsibility in society and politics, not passive endurance in the face of oppression. In fact, it is the duty of the Muslim to resist *zulm* and work against it. The Prophet said, "Best of the *jihad* is a word of truth (*Haq*) to an oppressing sultan." Moreover, regardless of the level or nature of the conflict (community-interpersonal or political-social), consensus and inclusivity are more effective than authoritarianism in resolving conflicts or implementing projects.

Pluralism and Diversity

Pluralism and diversity are among the core values of the Islamic religious and cultural tradition. The Qur'an recognizes diversity and the tolerance of differences based on gender (49:13; 53:45), skin color, language (30:23), belief, and rank (64:2, 6:165). Harmony between the different social groupings and communities is praised, and competition and control of one by the other is condemned (2:213, 10:19, 7:38, 13:30, 16:63, 29:18, 35:42, 41:42, 64:18). The Qur'an asserts that differences are inherent in human life and part of God's plan for humanity. Thus ethnic, tribal, and national differences have no real bearing on closeness to God. The extent and degree of faith is the sole criterion by which different groups will be judged. The existence of difference among people is a basic assumption in Islam. Scholars cite the Prophet's saying, "My Ummah's differences are a mercy"(Howeidy 1993, 23).[33]

To protect such diversity among people, the Qur'an repeatedly emphasizes the respect and protection of People of the Book, and the Prophet stressed that "on the day of Judgment I myself will act as the accuser of any person who oppresses a person under protection (*dhimma*) of Islam, and lays excessive [financial or other social] burdens on him" (al-Baladhuri 1866, 162; cited in Sachedina 2000). The Prophet also supported of the unity and harmony of Islam with other religions: "We the prophets are brothers and our religions are one and the same" (Ibn Hisham 1992, 501–4).[34]

Thus, differences among people are an inevitable and integral feature of humanity. "If thy Lord had so willed, He could have made mankind one People: But they will not cease to dispute" (11:118). These differences are integrally related to the free will that God has bestowed on humanity, for people should be expected to be diverse not only in nationality and affiliation, but also in the expression of their faith and the path that they choose to follow (also see Qur'an, 10:99). Such a principle of free will and an individual's responsibility for all his or her actions is reflected in the Qur'an: "If Allah so willed, He could make you all one People: but He leaves straying whom He pleases, and He guides whom He pleases: but ye shall certainly be called to account for all your actions" (16:93).

Tolerance of the "other," or non-Muslim, believers (People of the Book) is repeatedly accepted and emphasized in Islam. The equality of the followers of different religions is reiterated in both the Qur'an and Hadith. Muslims are asked to remember that there is no difference in the treatment of people of different religions except in their faith and deeds (3:113–14, 2:62, 5:68). The Qur'an calls on Muslims to abandon fighting and to coexist peacefully with people of other religions. It reaffirms the validity of the traditions of other faiths and requires its followers to respect their scriptures. In fact, the expansion of Islam through al-da'awah in Asia and Africa or the Pacific region took place mainly among non-Muslims. Under such circumstances Islam could not have survived or prospered without having been strongly pluralistic and tolerant of diversity (Esack 1998).

There are many Qur'anic verses supporting this strong notion of pluralism in Islam. Some of these verses follow:

Say, "O People of the Book! come to common terms as between us and you: that we worship none but Allah; that we associate no partners with Him; that we erect not, from among ourselves, lords and patrons other than Allah." If then they turn their back, say ye: "Bear witness that we (at least) are Muslims (bowing to Allah's Will)." (3:64)

Say, "O People of the Book, you have no ground to stand upon unless you stand fast by the Torah and the Bible and all that has been revealed to you from your Lord. . . . Those who believe (in the Qur'an), those who follow the Jewish scriptures and Sabians and the Christians—any people who believe in God, the Day of Judgment, and do good deeds, on them shall be no fear nor shall they grieve." (5:68–69)

Pluralism prevailed in the early Muslim community. There was no single Islamic law or constitution, no standardization of the Islamic law. The Sunni tradition yielded four legitimate schools of thought, none of which were limited to purely legal precepts (Esack 1998). In fact, the Qur'an is used to legitimize the validity of difference (*ikhtilaf*). Several interpretations of the Qur'an coexisted simultaneously in several areas. On the other hand, Islam has been intolerant of unbelievers, or infidels (*kafir*; pl. *kuffar*). Throughout history those who were cast as infidels were persecuted and punished by rulers and other followers.

The Medina charter, which was contracted between the Prophet and the various tribes, is an example of the high level of tolerance and respect of diversity assumed by Islam. Under the charter, all Muslims and Jewish tribes (apparently, no Christians were involved at that time, but it was used as a guiding principle in dealing with Christian tribes later) are considered one community, but each tribe retains its identity, customs, and internal relations. The charter was supplemented by a set of rules derived from the Qur'an and Sunnah to protect the rights of each group. Freedom of religion and the right not to be guilty because of the deed of an ally were among the protected rights.

Pluralism in Islam is reflected in the belief that the people are one community (Ummah), bound by a moral and spiritual identity and not by any other categories (such as race, birth, or gender). Sachedina even goes further, rejecting a narrow interpretation of the Qur'an verses that suggest salvation to Muslims only. He refutes the notion that the principle of "only my religion is genuine" exists in the Qur'an or the belief that only Islam rests on truths received in revelation, only Islam possesses the intrinsic values necessary for attaining religious perfection. In refuting these three principles of antipluralism he reinterprets the Qur'an verses that historically have been used to support such principles (2000, 37–40). For example, he explains that when commentators and interpreters explain the term Islam they restrict it to the Muslim community instead of explaining it as an act of surrender and submission to God, usually including all the *mu'ahidin* (people who believe in one God and are in peaceful relations with Muslims). Another example of change in interpretation is the use of the term *unbeliever*. Historically it referred to the pagan Arabs, whom the Muslim attempted to convert. However, with time, interpreters began expanding the term to include Christians and Jews. This tendency contradicts both the Prophet's teachings and the Qur'an's equal recognition of the People of the Book.

The Qur'an emphasizes repeatedly that "humankind is one community." Among the principles Sachedina (2000, 23–25) identifies as the basis for religious pluralism in Islam are: (1) the unity of humankind under one God; (2) the particularity of religions brought by the prophets; and (3) the role of revelation (the Qur'an). As Sachedina asserts, these principles do not deny the contradictions that might exist among religions, and they recognize the oneness of humanity and the need to work for better understanding among people of faith. The notion of freedom of conscience in matters of faith is the cornerstone of the Qur'an's notion of religious pluralism, both at the interreligious and intrareligious levels. Such principles constitute a strong base for Islamic approaches to interfaith dialogue and understanding.

Of critical importance to peace-building strategies and conflict resolution practices are seven main principles (*usul*) derived from the Qur'an that support coexistence and tolerance (Howeidy 1993, 202):

(1) Human dignity deserves absolute recognition, regardless of a person's religion, ethnicity, or creed (see verse 17:70). This dignity is an immunity for the individual given by God.

(2) All humans are related and spring from a common origin (4:1, 5:32, 6:98).

(3) The differences among people are designated by God and are part of his plan for humanity. Differences in ethnicity, race, culture, and so on, are a factual and integral part of life (10:99, 11:188, 199, 30:22).

(4) Islam acknowledges other religions and asserts their unified origin (2:136, 42:13).

(5) Muslims have the freedom of choice and decision after the calling for submission or the message of Islam has been delivered (see verses 2:256, 17:107, 18:29, 109:4–6)

(6) Judgment belongs to God alone and only on Judgment Day (16:124, 31:23, 42:48, 88:25–26).

(7) Muslims should practice good deeds, justice, and equity in their dealings with all human beings (4:135, 5:8, 60:8).

Differences are a given in Islam. Therefore there is no justification for violating people's rights to existential or identity rights based on their religious affiliation (42:15). This outlook explains why Islam was not consumed or corrupted by the many cultures it confronted as it spread across civilizations. Instead, it created a new civilization. Islam has been both multicultural and pluralist in theory and practice. The diverse Muslim cultures of Asia, Africa, and Europe are expected to tolerate one another's differences as well as those of the non-Muslims in their communities. Unfortunately, a more "centralist and narrow" view of the world, as defined by many minority social and political movements in Islamic societies, has often eclipsed this tolerant vision in the contemporary Muslim world (Kadi 1998).

Muslim scholars are still grappling with Islam's relationship to the ideas of tolerance and difference. For example, Farid Esack expresses skepticism in regard to diversity and its consequences for the Muslim community. He cautions against an automatic acceptance of all differences without discernment based on the logic of Islamic precepts and practices. He suggests that the primary theological challenge for Muslims resides in understanding where to set the limits on diversity and acceptance of changes (e.g., women leading Friday prayers). In essence, he argues that Western values and cultures underlie pluralism, which he views as an extension of Western hegemony over the so-called underdeveloped world. He proposes that the acceptance of diversity not be the mere willingness to entertain every novel idea and practice. Instead, it should be geared toward specific objectives, such as freeing humankind from injustice and servitude to other human beings, so that people are free to worship God in their own way (Esack 1998).

In peace building, diversity and tolerance of differences are core principles. Peace builders hope to bring people to the realization that they are different and that such differences should not constitute a basis for discrimination or bias. Moreover, it is harmful and unjust to deprive people of their rights because of their nation, race, religion, or creed. These values have been made integral parts of Islam since its inception. In short, for Muslims diversity and tolerance of differences are God's wish, since He created a diverse rather than a uniform human race.

Conclusion

The preceding assumptions and principles constitute only a portion of the bases for conflict resolution and nonviolence in Islam. All these precepts are well grounded in Islamic texts and traditions (Qur'an and Hadith). Satha-Anand reveals Islam's connectedness to nonviolence and peacemaking: "Islam itself is a fertile soil for nonviolence because of its potential for disobedience, strong discipline, sharing and social responsibility, perseverance and self-sacrifice, and the belief in the unity of the Muslim community and the oneness of mankind" (1993b, 14).

An Islamic peace-building framework, applied to a context of community socioeconomic development, can promote objectives such as an increase of solidarity among members of the community; bridging the gap of social and economic injustice; relieving the suffering of people and spare human lives; empowering people through participation and inclusivity;

promoting equality among all members of the community; and encouraging the values of diversity and tolerance.

Initiatives for peace building, and social and economic development, in an Islamic community would benefit greatly if the above Islamic principles were integrated into the planning, implementation, and evaluation phases. At present these are ideals, not actual practices. The reality in most Muslim communities today is far from the realization of such principles. Contemporary Muslim scholars have often argued that many of today's Muslims seem not to follow them in their daily lives.[35] Nevertheless, these ideals persist and are being transmitted to successive generations through cultural and religious beliefs. In fact, much of the frustration among many Muslims stems from the failure to apply these values in their communities.

In this chapter and the one preceding we have seen the significant gap between Islam's possibilities for nonviolent practice and its perception among Westerners as a warlike religion. This divide evinces the need for a stronger and more solid "community of interpreters" in studying Islam and peace building, as well as scholars who will attempt to contextualize Islamic religious and traditional values in the framework of peace building and nonviolence rather than war. The effort to reconstruct legitimate nonviolent alternatives—social, religious, and political—in resolving internal and external conflicts in Muslim societies is a starting point for socioeconomic strategies.

The evidence clearly shows that Islam as a religion is conducive to nonviolent and peace-building methods through its various rituals and traditions. For instance, the weekly Friday prayer is a natural place for gathering that has been used by many political leaders and movements (Satha-Anand 1998). Scholars such as Satha-Anand (1993a,b), Robert Johansen (1997), and Ralph Crow, Philip Grant, and Saad Ibrahim (1990) have begun examining Islamic traditions and religion to identify other rituals and traditions that can be an effective source for nonviolent actions, such as (1) fasting rituals, which are excellent training for hunger strikes; (2) ritualistic prayers, for the habituated formation of worshipers into parallel lines to prepare people for engagement in disciplined actions; and (3) religious chanting, which can become an outlet for peaceful marches, meetings, and sit-ins. These correspondences support the assumption that peace-building strategies, combined with economic and social development initiatives, can and should be based on local and indigenous traditions and beliefs. For concrete examples of such an application, see the three case studies of peace building in Muslim communities in part 2.

Finally, two main challenges face Muslims today: identifying the obstacles that prevent their economic, social, and political development and designing and implementing effective strategies and intervention within the above framework of values and principles to overcome such obstacles. Having identified the principles and values of peace building in the Islamic tradition, the question of their mere existence becomes irrelevant. Thus, we can move on to an examination of the application of such principles in day-to-day contexts and identify the obstacles that prevent their application.

II

Social, Political, and Cultural Applications
of Nonviolent Strategies in Muslim Communities

Peace-Building Initiatives in Muslim Communities

There are many individual, local, and regional examples of the application of the values of peace building and nonviolence in Muslim communities. In these instances the role of Islamic tradition and values is often reflected in one of two ways: first, in a direct religious framework in which interveners and participants are observant Muslims. In these contexts, peace building values are invoked in resolving the disputes. Traditional dispute resolution (based on Shariʿah) is a classic example of a framework in which the arbitrator-mediator is a religious person who can knowledgeably draw on authoritative scripture for guidance and facilitation. Another example of the direct use of Islamic values is a form of traditional dispute resolution conducted in the Muslim and Arab worlds that is based on tribal and traditional norms and values (ʿurf). In this process, interveners apply Islamic and Arab cultural values and principles using explicit religious references. It should be noted that in the day-to-day life of Arab Muslims, there are no firm borders between those types of dispute resolutions. Religious and cultural values and norms exist in all interactions.

Second, the use of Islamic tradition is reflected in a cultural, social, professional, or political framework in which the third party or disputants directly and indirectly use Islamic values to resolve their conflicts. The peace-building and conflict resolution programs (training workshops) conducted by various local and foreign organizations in Muslim communities are good examples of this framework. The values of peace building and nonviolence are the core of these training programs, where the participants are usually Muslims.

For the purpose of this study, peace-building values and principles in Muslim communities are categorized in three levels of intervention: traditional (sociocultural), professional, and political. For sociocultural dispute resolution, peace-building and nonviolent values are conceptualized as an important part of the fabric of daily life in Muslim communities. The social and cultural institutions of mediation (*wisatah*), arbitration (*tahkim*), and reconciliation (*sulh*) are integral components of the structure of Muslim communities, traceable to Bedouin traditions, tribal laws, and society, even before the spread of Islam. Many tribes in the Middle East still use these mechanisms in resolving their disputes.

An example of the use of such traditional methods in tribal society was provided by the deputy mayor, along with three of the local traditional leaders, who participated in a conflict resolution training workshop for Egyptian diplomats in the fall of 1994 in Marsa Matruh (a seaside resort city about 125 miles from the Libyan border). The purpose of this conference was a search for common ground and an introduction to conflict training. Its organizers had been mediating and arbitrating disputes among their tribes since the 1960s. They were, in their own words, "aiming to maintain harmony and stability in the tribe." They described the use of noncoercive methods by the weaker parties to influence the decision of the leaders on certain issues. Fasting and boycotting (social, political, and economic) were among the techniques identified by the leaders as effective means in handling the power imbalance that often constitutes a major obstacle for conflict settlement. In resolving such tribal conflicts, mediators and arbitrators follow a tribal tradition that includes invoking many verses from the Qur'an and sayings from the Hadith to support their claims, decisions, and strategies. Chapter 3 will further explore the role, dynamics, and objectives of traditional dispute resolution processes in Arab-Muslim communities and highlight the role of Islamic religious and cultural values in such communities.

Professional training workshops in peace building and conflict resolution have proliferated in non-Western countries since the end of the cold war (Abu-Nimer 1996b).[1] There are reports on hundreds of training workshops in peace building attended by thousands from countries such as Jordan, Egypt, Turkey, Morocco, Lebanon, Philippines, Indonesia, and Palestine. Most participants in these training workshops did not perceive conflict resolution and nonviolence concepts to be incompatible with Islam as a faith or as a cultural tradition.[2] On the contrary, in every workshop I conducted between 1993 and 2001, Muslim participants cited the scripture and the Prophet's tradition to support the validity and applicability of these principles in their own Islamic cultural contexts.[3]

In a conflict resolution workshop in the city of Gaza, some trainers expected a professor from the Islamic University there to resist the idea of conflict resolution and nonviolence more than other participants. He, however, turned out to be among the most enthusiastic participants. He argued that "those values are often repeated in the weekly preaching in the mosque. Your training workshop is only a way of systematically operationalizing those skills, so they become accessible to all segments of the society."[4]

In those workshops, particularly in Jordan and Palestine, participants suggested the use of the local imams (prayer leaders), mukhtars (community leaders who are often the heads of the largest clan in the community and usually are associated with Syria, Lebanon, Palestine, and Jordan), and 'umdahs (the Egyptian equivalent of mukhtars) in the conflict resolution process. These local leaders were suggested because of their credibility, derived—especially among the imams—from their strong faith and observance of Islam. In fact, these leaders have been conducting mediation and arbitration and helping to resolve conflicts peacefully every day for hundreds of years (Abu-Nimer 1996a,b).

Nonviolent political movements in Islamic contexts: As indicated earlier, most studies of nonviolence, peace, and democracy in Islam often assume the political incompatibility of Islam with these values, usually because of conflict between Western interests and Islamic cultures, with all the attendant threats, stereotypes, and mistrust.[5] Participants in these debates often ask for examples to show that nonviolence and peace building methods have been successfully applied by Muslims. Failure to supply any examples is usually considered proof that Islam as both a religion and a tradition is inimical to nonviolence. It is thus important to identify those Islamic social and political movements that have used methods of nonviolence and peace building.

There are several documented examples of nonviolent campaigns and movements in Muslim communities. The volume edited by Crow, Grant, and Ibrahim (1990) briefly reviews many recent cases: for example, the mass protest against the British in Egypt in 1919; the revolt of Muslims of Peshawar Pathans in Pakistan in 1930; the Palestinian general strike of 1936; the 1948 Iraqi uprising; the Iran Revolution of 1978–79; the Golan Druze resistance movement in 1981–82; the activities in defense of al-Aqsa Mosque in Jerusalem since the 1970s; the Sudanese insurrection of

…and the first Palestinian Intifadah, which began in 1987. Other …ples of nonviolence and peacemaking have been reviewed by authors …h as Kishtainy (1990), Satha-Anand (1993b), and Johansen (1997).

Only a few of those examples, however, have been thoroughly investigated to extract or analyze the nonviolent and peace-building principles used by the Muslim communities in these cases. Abdul Ghaffar Khan's movement in the Pashtun region is a well-known and well-documented political resistance movement in which Muslims adopted nonviolent principles and strategies based on Islamic principles and precedents in confronting injustice and in dealing with their enemies. Many studies have documented this effort (see, for example, Easwaran 1984; Tendulkar 1967; Pyarelal 1966; Korejo 1993). Abdul Ghaffar Khan's "Army of God" in the Pashtun-controlled northwest Indian subcontinent (currently Pakistan) was a nonviolent resistance movement of a hundred thousand people who fought against the British for twenty years. According to Easwaran, the strategies and principles of Ghaffar Khan's movement were based on the Qur'an: "There is nothing surprising in a Muslim or a Pashtun like me subscribing to the creed of nonviolence. It is not a new creed. It was followed fourteen hundred years ago by the Prophet all the time he was in Mecca, and it has since been followed by all those who wanted to throw off an oppressor's yoke. But we had . . . forgotten it" (quoted in Easwaran 1984, 103). After Pakistan achieved independence, the movement vanished because of policies adopted by the Pakistani president. Nevertheless, the nonviolent movement of Abdul Ghaffar Khan was a solid and regionally influential political resistance movement that spanned two decades and directly contributed to the liberation of the region from British colonial control.[6]

The strong commitment to the principles and practices of nonviolence was evident in the level of discipline exhibited in Ghaffar Khan's followers in their struggle against the British and in their efforts to provide social services and implement reforms in their society. When recruited, the Servants of God had to sign a ten-point pledge in which they swore to serve God, sacrifice their life and wealth for their people, oppose hatred, live by nonviolent principles, not expect or desire reward for their service, and please God in all their undertakings (Johansen 1997).

Ghaffar Khan's philosophy and approach to nonviolence was deeply rooted in Islamic religion. Korejo comments, "He rooted his beliefs and actions in his own understanding of the Qur'an. Although he had no formal higher education, he had a strong sense of confidence in his own ability, through study, meditation, prayer, to find the most faithful path for him and others who might follow his lead. His independent mind, devout faith in God, and understanding of the Qur'an posed a challenge to the authority of Muslim clergy and their traditional religious interpretations"(1993, 81). Johansen writes, "Of all traditional strands of Islam, his views seem most congenial to Sufi mystic traditions, but there is no evidence that they may have influenced his thought. He apparently did not rely on the institutionalized roles of the mullahs, the educated clergy ('Ulama), or those of holy descent (Sayyid)" (1997, 61).

The main Islamic value that Ghaffar Khan preached and practiced was *sabr* (patience or endurance). In his teaching and philosophy of nonviolence, he relied on the teachings and actions of the Prophet during the early Meccan period. Through these interpretations he managed to prohibit forcible retaliation and the use of violence among his followers. "I am going to give you such a weapon that the police and the army will not be able to stand against. It is the weapon of the Prophet, but you are not aware of it. That weapon is patience and righteousness. No power on earth can stand against it. . . . When you go back to your villages, tell your brethren that there is an army of God and its weapon is patience. Ask your brethren to join the army of God. Endure hardship. If you exercise patience, victory will be yours" (quoted in Tendulkar 1967, 129).

In another recent report on a Muslim community using nonviolent methods and strategies of mobilization and resistance, Satha-Anand (1998) describes the struggle of Thai Muslim fishermen to gain their fishing rights, the Muslims in Bangkok preventing the routing of a highway through their neighborhood, and another Thai Muslim community that organized and successfully regained control of its streets from drug dealers. These three cases are on a middle communal level involving conflicts that could have escalated into ethnic and religious conflicts. However, the strategies of nonviolence deployed by these communities prevented such escalation and contributed to the attainment of their objectives.

Satha-Anand identifies several factors that allowed those Muslim communities to successfully adopt such nonviolent strategies: (1) The participants were all minorities in a non-Muslim majority. (2) They fought for a just cause that was perceived by the whole society as legitimate and just. (3) Their nonviolent actions were tactical and pragmatic, and strategic rather than ideological—they knew that it was safer for them to use nonviolent tactics under prevailing conditions. (4) The communities were well organized (as Muslim minorities, the nature of the Muslim communities made the actual organization and mobilization much easier than other ethnic groups; by utilizing the central local meeting place [mosque] as well clear religious ceremonies that bring people together [funerals, weddings, religious feasts, etc.]). (5) The leadership of the movements was horizontal: there were always several influential voices within the groups, those of ordinary people rather than the leaders. (6) Nonviolence became a voice for the voiceless, who were empowered by communicating their messages in powerful ways. Based on his analysis of these cases, Satha-Anand concludes, "Muslims are 'naturally' prepared for nonviolence, with their emphasis on fighting or engaging in action for just cause with discipline, empathy, patience, and solidarity. All those qualities are crucial for getting organized and voicing their claims for justice" (1998, 22).

Studies that focus on middle-range community analysis and activity are most valuable for the study of peace building in Islamic contexts. This level is often neglected by policymakers and researchers, but it offers the potential of replicating such experiences in day-to-day activities in many other Muslim communities.

Another well-known example of a nonviolent political movement in an Islamic context is the Palestinian Intifada. At least during this popular uprising's first two years, Palestinian Muslims and Christians coalesced in a nonviolent struggle against the Israeli occupation (Sharp 1989; McDowall 1989; Lockman and Beinin 1989). The civil disobedience and organized nonviolent protests were deliberately planned, justified, and implemented within a sociocultural and religious framework.

Most of the strategies used by the Intifada's young leaders and activists were nonviolent: massive public marches, strikes, boycotts of Israeli products, giving up Israeli identity cards, mobilizing community cooperative associations, underground schooling, and meetings with Israeli representatives. In order to mobilize such massive political and social movements, the political and communal leadership of the Intifada, including Hamas, Islamic Jihad (at early stages), and secular leaders, had to draw on values of solidarity, brotherhood, sacrifice, and discipline. These values did not arise from a vacuum but were rooted in a cultural, religious, and social Islamic context.

Since most of the analysis of the first Palestinian Intifadah has been conducted by social scientists or sociologists, there has been no examination of its strategies and activities from a cultural-religious peace-building perspective. There is, then, a need to investigate the role of the Islamic cultural traditions that facilitated the effective application of nonviolent strategies in the Intifadah. Chapter 5 in this study is an attempt to address that need.

3

Peace Building and Nonviolence in a Sociocultural Context

Traditional Arab-Muslim Mechanisms for Dispute Resolution

Peace-building strategies and values are reflected in common daily practices in Muslim communities. The dispute resolution practices are fully functional and widespread in traditional rural, tribal Bedouin and urban Muslim communities. They are applied by well-trained local interveners who are respected by their communities. Those traditional peacemakers use and depend on traditional local values and beliefs. This chapter focuses on community and interpersonal practices for dispute resolution as a case study to illustrate and identify Islamic values in peace-building mechanisms. The primary emphasis is on how certain Islamic religious and cultural values and tradition influence those peacemaking practices. This chapter discusses dispute resolution processes, values, the role of a third party, outcomes, and rituals, mainly among Arab communities with a Muslim majority (especially within Palestinian, Egyptian, Lebanese, and Jordanian communities).

Frameworks of Dispute Resolution in Arab-Muslim Communities

Dispute resolution processes and techniques have been studied by anthropologists in various Islamic and non-Islamic traditional communities in Africa, Hawaii, Latin America, China, Japan, the Middle East, and among Native Americans (see Wolfe and Yang 1996). Cathy Witty (1980) describes daily dispute resolution mechanisms in a Lebanese Sunni village, echoing John Rothenberger's earlier study (1978) of traditional dispute resolution mechanisms among Lebanese villagers. Lawrence Rosen (1984) captures the role the *qadi* (religious judge) plays in resolving disputes in a Moroccan community, and Abu-Nimer (1996a) details the use of religious stories and rituals in settling community disputes in a Palestin-ian village, comparing them with Western dispute resolution mechanisms. Daniel Smith (1989) focuses on the symbolic and ritualistic aspects of reconciliation, or *sulh,* providing a detailed description by interviewing traditional mediators among Arabs in Galilee. (Some regions use the term *sulhah,* which refers to the event or ritual of reconciliation rather than the process.) However, Smith drew no conclusions about the social and politi-cal implications of such process in bringing about harmony or control. George Irani (1998) briefly discusses the potential relations and applica-tions of traditional dispute resolution rituals to the political interactions and conflicts in the Middle East.

In general, three types of dispute resolution have been identified in Muslim Arab communities: resolution based on tribal laws; resolution based on Islamic law (Shariʿah), generally delivered by a judge (*qadi*); and resolution based on cultural and traditional practices (*ʿurf,* or customary law influenced by Shariʿah) as applied in both rural and urban settings (but different in its rituals and stipulations from the often rigid Bedouin tribal methods).

These three sets of procedures are not mutually exclusive. Interveners in one context (urban, rural, or Bedouin) might use, intentionally or unin-tentionally, values and norms from the others. For example, traditional mediators in a rural setting often draw on Islamic values and beliefs, while the Shariʿah arbitrators often rely on traditional and cultural norms when settling a community or interpersonal dispute. The tribal leader as arbitra-tor-mediator might rely on both the Islamic laws and the *ʿurf.* Regardless of the setting, Islamic values, beliefs, and tradition constitute an important source in the application of dispute resolution in the Arab world.

Dispute resolution mechanisms in Arab society date back to pre-Is-lamic times, when tribal laws and traditions were the norms that governed mediation and arbitration procedures (Zinati 1992). The Prophet himself was called upon to mediate or arbitrate on many occasions because of his reputation and credibility as an honest and unbiased intervener. He peace-fully settled a dispute between two rival tribes (the Awus and Khazraj), who in turn gave him protection and assistance when he and his support-ers migrated to Medina to escape the persecution of the Meccans.

These tribal traditions of dispute resolution have survived to this day. But Islamic tradition and religion have deeply influenced and reshaped such procedures, providing uniform moral codes and social responsibili-ties. Qurʾanic verses and stories from the early and later periods of Islamic history have been integrated into tribal arbitration processes. In many tribes the Shariʿah is now a primary source of laws that govern arbitration and mediation procedures.[1]

For example, among the Awlad Ali in North Africa and western Egypt, the arbitration process is based on a tribal constitution that has been passed from one generation to the next. The tribal constitution (called *daray'ib* by the Awlad Ali) determines the decisions that ought to be issued, depending on the nature of the specific conflict (Ismaʿil 1986).[2]

Customary law in these communities functions as a mechanism for social control and cohesiveness, bringing the tribe's members together into a unified community. The dispute resolution procedures employed by the elders help maintain social control and in many cases increase the gap of power and control that separates the tribe's members (Ismaʿil 1986; Abu-Nimer 1996a). These customary laws typically begin as a behavior or decision that an elder or tribal leader initiated in a given situation. When repeated, it becomes a norm. The action or belief is then adopted by members of the tribe and transformed into obligatory behavior that is consolidated over subsequent generations into customary law (Zinati 1992).

Administering an oath and offering testimony and evidence are still important methods of customary law. Islamic values and beliefs are central to these procedures. Tribal leaders (or a third party) use the Qur'an to conduct the oath for both the accused and the group of elders from his tribe, who are usually nominated by the accused to take the oath in support of his innocence (*zakayyi,* or according to Islamic law *tazkiya,* purification or the attestation of honorable record). Refusal to take the oath is in itself a proof of culpability. A false oath is believed to affect the person himself as well as his relatives, which may have catastrophic consequences for the person and his social network. The phrasing of the oath usually varies with the nature of the case involved (rape, homicide, etc.).[3]

The dispute resolution method among the Awlad Ali in Egypt is mainly a process of arbitration based on traditional laws. The Sinai Bedouin tribes have a similar council structure and framework, but they have evolved somewhat different negotiation and mediation techniques. These include the development of a tribal party that specializes in thirteen types of disputes or problems. Among them are: *sulh,* judges of peace and war; *munshid* or *masaʿudi,* who deal with issues of honor; *zaiadi,* who judge issues related to camels; and judges of women's issues (Ismaʿil 1986).

The application of these dispute resolution methods is not unique to Sunni Muslims but are also drawn upon by Shiʿites. Nizar Hamzeh (1997) describes a complex system of dispute resolution mechanisms applied by Hizbullah (Party of God) in southern and northern Lebanon. Although

Hizbullah is an Islamic resistance group primarily known in the West for its struggle against the Israeli occupation of southern Lebanon, they have deployed a set of nonviolent dispute mechanisms—arbitration, mediation, and reconciliation—aimed at bringing order and stability to their own communities.

The collapse of socioeconomic and political institutions in Lebanon after the civil war erupted in 1975 left a power vacuum that Hizbullah filled by establishing Islamic-based conflict resolution systems. Hizbullah soon adopted a complex mediating role in the Muslim community's day-to-day conflicts. Through judicial settlements in Shari'ah courts they settled cases in municipal, regional, and high court. The decisions of the courts were binding, particularly if the disputants were Hizbullah members.

The great challenge for these courts has been to cope with long-standing vendettas, which created spiraling cycles of violence in an already destabilized society. Hizbullah moved to create an alternative system of justice for heading off these tribal practices by involving its own mediators in disputes between clans. The Hizbullah mediators would provide the disputants with two choices: enter into negotiation or submit to the Shari'ah court. The mediators are reported to have resolved two-thirds of the two hundred cases they have adjudicated in two years, with most disputants having selected negotiation rather than court. There have been several types of intervention, depending on the complexity of the case. Simple cases have been settled through mediation and arbitration, whereas complex ones have gone to court in accordance with the Shari'ah (Hamzeh 1997).

Like the urban and rural dispute resolution mechanisms in place in Palestine, but differing slightly from the tribal Bedouin dispute resolution of 'urf, the settlement procedures practiced by the Hizbullah typically followed six steps, identified by Hamzeh (1997): (1) Hizbullah is invited to mediate or intervene, and the family of the victim decides on the court or negotiation option. (2) Hizbullah actively prohibits vendettas. (3) Hizbullah uses its own military strength to hold the accused in custody and protect him from vendetta. (4) Once tensions are reduced, Hizbullah conducts an extensive process of separate consultations among both parties to determine and negotiate the fate of the accused and appropriate restitution, or financial compensation (*diyah*). Such a process can take from one to three years. In most cases the victim's family demands both exile for the murderer and financial compensation.

Depending on the case, conciliation (*musalahah*) might take place, where symbolic actions or gestures are emphasized, such as the son of the deceased dressing the accused in an *'abayah* (caftan), representing forgiveness in tribal tradition (Hamzeh 1997, 113). (5) Mediators visit every member of the families affected by the dispute to reestablish order, restore the previous relationships where possible, and elicit commitment to the agreement. (6) Hizbullah holds a *musalahah*—a gala event aimed at peace building among the tribal communities. The first public, face-to-face communication between the disputants takes place in this ceremony. A variety of unifying or solidarity-oriented speeches are typically given by the highest-ranking community members in attendance, reinforcing social and communal ties and signifying recognition of the social status and honor of the newly reconciled participants. (During the 1980s and 1990s, many of the top regional leaders of all parties gave speeches attacking Israel and the Western world and criticizing the Lebanese government for its neglect of the region.) Customarily the disputants waive their demands for compensation or certain conditions as a sign of forgiveness as well as to reestablish their honor and status within the community, and the ceremony ends with a meal for all parties involved (Hamzeh 1997, 115). According to Hamzeh, Hizbullah has used these mediation techniques chiefly in intergroup community conflicts. In intragroup disputes, arbitration is usually applied.

Mediation has been used in clan and tribal conflicts in Lebanon, particularly in the Biqa'a (Bekaa) valley in northeastern Lebanon. These mediation efforts by Hizbullah usually complement the traditional tribal practices, which still predominate. In Jordan similar patterns prevail in rural areas, particularly in small communities where institutional mechanisms exist, such as assigning specific spaces for dispute resolution. Richard Antoun (1997, 144) describes the ceremonial meal (during *sulh* among Jordanian rural communities) in a guest-house in a small village that seals the negotiated agreement. Everyone is invited to witness this process, based on tribal law and village custom. The social and cultural values that operate and are reinforced in the guesthouse where the reconciliation takes place are hospitality, generosity, dignity, and pride in one's own clan. The delegation (*jahah*) may refuse to drink coffee or eat, indicating their disappointment in the host's refusal to accept their suggestions or positions. Such ritual is a form of pressure, a tactic to gain concessions, since the failure to produce an outcome may humiliate or disappoint the *jahah* (respected third parties), thus damaging the disputants and their clans' social status.

Mediators often use their kinship connections as a tool to exert pressure and gain access when they negotiate with certain parties to the conflict. They also use their assistants as committee members (Antoun 1997, 158). The third party (*mukhtar*) is effective because of the presence of respected elders who are entrusted to discern the underlying causes of conflict and balance the longer-term interests of the community with the weight, motives, and contexts of the conflict. They can hash out the matter between or on behalf of the disputants. These third parties uphold traditions and social values. They know and appreciate the norms and etiquette of the guesthouse. The third party shoulders and delegates responsibility, coordinates activities, and exercises decision making and foresight in often volatile, dynamic situations (160).

The essential process of dispute resolution in traditional Arab society, as described by Antoun and others, entails the negotiation of goods and symbolic gestures to restore certain sociocultural norms. Antoun states, "An essential principle of achieving conflict resolution in this and other disputes I witnessed in the Jordanian countryside is the trading of moral condemnation and symbolic goods in return for substantive concessions" (1997, 162). Many of the cases subjected to the tribal/village mode of mediation/arbitration involved the balance of honor. It is necessary to deal with the imbalance of honor before compromises on substantive issues can be worked out. Some of the assumptions behind the process of *Sulh* in general (associated with *jaha*, or *Wasta*, the intermediary) are as follows: (1) The disputants have to be convinced that harmony is better than victory. (2) Third-party intervention is essential in most disputes. (3) The *Sulh* process, if controlled and conducted appropriately, is intended to lead to reconciliation and social harmony; and is preferable to the civil court or the Islamic court since it restores order to the community. It may not remove the root causes of the problem, nor does it have the objective of reforming the society or addressing the structural arrangements that generated the conflict (Abu-Nimer 1996b, 35). As Antoun puts it, "Thus its function remains as its moral weight. 'You have done the right thing,' says the community/society" (Antoun 1997, 163).

Even though Antoun suggests that the social, economic, and educational changes that took place in the specific case study in Jordan demonstrates the resilience of Islamic institutions, newer institutional and legal institutional approaches to conflict resolution have also weakened tribal and clan affiliation. Traditional methods of dispute resolution evolved as pan-societal and cultural. They reinforce personal dignity in a world of fraying clan and close kinship norms, a world increasingly differentiated and stratified by wealth and education. Similar to Zinati's analysis (1992) of dispute resolution mechanisms in northern Egypt, Antoun identifies three court systems in Jordan, too: the tribal court, the Islamic court, and the civil court. These three "cultural brokers" are important in settling disputes in contemporary Jordanian rural communities.

The framework of dispute resolution among Palestinians in general (rural and urban areas) is historically influenced by Bedouin tribes from the Sinai and Negev deserts. This is particularly evident in the approach typically taken in murder cases. Negotiation begins immediately through a third party, who is often called on by a family member of the offender. The third party at this point protects the offender from violence and prevents escalation. The third party also suggests three names of judges or interveners. The offender's family and the victim's family each can reject one nominee. If they agree, then the selected nominees proceed with a meeting of the council, which includes a judge, a neutral third party, the litigants, and their *kafil* (guarantor)—a relative of the victim or offender. The *kafil* is often an elder who has influence in the tribe or community and is thus able to guarantee the implementation of all decisions. The negotiation or arbitration then takes place among the elders from both sides, with the assumption that they are capable of reaching a peaceful, just, and wise resolution. The guarantors have to take an oath to carry the responsibility faithfully before they can begin representing their relatives.[4]

Traditional dispute resolution mechanisms among Palestinians have been described in several studies. Joseph Ginat (1996) identifies traditional dispute resolution procedures in an Arab Bedouin tribal community in the Negev Desert, in southern Israel. His study focuses mainly on blood feuds and ways in which these tribes have settled them. Elias Jabbour (1997), with the help of an American researcher, is the only traditional dispute practitioner who has actually attempted to describe his own work. His report includes certain cases he has settled and identifies basic values and procedures he employed among Palestinian Arabs in Galilee. Tribal methods of dispute resolution in a Palestinian community (*atwah* or *sulh asha'iri*) have also been described by Ali Qleibo. The giving of *atwah* (the amount of money or compensation given to the victim's family as an initial sum to guarantee their temporary acceptance of the truce and their withholding of revenge) is one such tribal method of resolving social conflicts. Its collective aspect makes it socially binding by crystallizing intratribal alliances and promoting social solidarity. The application of these dispute resolution mechanisms in the Fertile Crescent regions (using the same principles but different names and rituals) illustrates the strong impact of the tribal factor in both rural and urban Arab settings.

The practices of dispute resolution through *atwah* (*diyah*) coexist with both Islamic Shari'ah and the legal court system. The traditional dispute resolution through *atwah* exists not only in nomadic and seminomadic areas, as claimed by Qleibo, but also, to a limited extent, in some rural and urban areas. The *hamulah* (extended family) is the core kinship unit that employs, preserves, and supports tribal codes of dispute resolution. The *hamulah* is a patronymic extended family composed of five generations descended from a single grandfather. It is the functional equivalent of a close-knit extended family (Qleibo 1990).

Various researchers have identified a set of values associated with tribal dispute resolution, including: honor (*sharaf* or *a'rd*),[5] saving face (*karamah*), valor (*muru'ah*), wisdom (*hikmah* or *hilm*), generosity (*karam*), respect (*ihtiram*), dignity, and forgiveness (*'afu*). Many dispute resolution practices in such communities are aimed at preventing shame, restoring respect, and saving face. Such communities have been described as "shame-oriented" (Augsburger 1992).[6]

All acts and statements initiated by parties involved in dispute resolution are centered on and motivated by these values. For instance, when the parties negotiate the material compensation that the offender is expected to pay to the victim's family, the third party asks the victim's family to make concessions for the sake of the respected elders around the circle. By accepting this request, reducing the amount of payment, or even waiving the payment entirely, the victim's family members publicly restore their honor and save face. One of the important events of the negotiation occurs during the *sulh* ceremony, when the victim's family decides to forgive the offender and accepts no payment in exchange. Such an act is aimed at reflecting all the above values in public.[7]

Both victims and offenders can seek dispute resolution through the form of *atwah* (giving money as a guarantee for the application of dispute resolution procedures) or *sulh* (conciliation). There are three main phases in these tribal procedures:

(1) *Atwah:* providing a sum of money to the family of the victim. When accepted, it indicates an agreement that revenge will not take place for the period of the dispute resolution.

(2) *Hudnah* (truce): a period or phase, which starts after the acceptance of the *atwah*. The mediation or investigation takes place during this truce period.

(3) *Sulh:* the process of reconciliation. Some regions use the term

sulhah, which refers to the event or ritual of reconciliation rather than the process. During this phase, the parties agree upon the outcome of arbitration or mediation efforts. If they publicly accept the outcome, then often there is an amount of compensation (*diyah*) that has been determined before the public ceremony. In some cases, one party may reject the *sulh* and its terms. Different communities employ different rituals and festivities to eventually restore harmony, peace, and order to the small ruptured community.

In the summer of 1998, I witnessed a rural community mediation that took place between two clans in a Palestinian village. Members of the offender's clan were allowed to return to their village after seven years of exile following the murder of two people. Having reached a settlement, the two clans agreed to conduct a *sulhah*, or reconciliation session, to make the agreement public, to prepare for the return of the offender's family to the village, and to normalize the lives of the two clans in the town. On the assigned day of the *sulhah*, hundreds of villagers gathered in the town's main square and awaited the arrival of the mediating committee. The process began with the reading of three Qur'anic verses that supported the mediation efforts.[8]

The head of the reconciliation committee gave the main speech. He recited a story from the Hadith that supported the negotiation and called for the prevention of blood feud or violence. Two other respected members of the committee (one associated with the victim's clan and one from the offender's clan) continued the reconciliation process. They delivered speeches in which they told stories from the Hadith and the Qur'an encouraging parties to maintain peace and harmony among all believers. A representative of the offender's family read his prepared notes in which he offered his remorse and his clan's request for forgiveness. Those two messages were delivered through Qur'anic passages, such as: "But indeed if any show patience and forgive, that would truly be an exercise of courageous will and resolution in the conduct of affairs" (42:43).

Similarly, the representative of the victim's clan accepted the agreement and declared his clan's sincere intention to work to attain peace and resolve the differences peacefully. He ended his speech with a story whose central theme assured the audience that forgiveness does not mean weakness; on the contrary, it is a sign of strength: "Forgive when you are able" (*al-a'fu 'inda al-makderah*).[9] "Those who avoid the greater crimes and shameful deeds, and, when they are angry even then forgive" (42:37). "Tell those who believe, to forgive those who do not look forward to the Days of Allah: it is for Him to recompense" (45:14).

Another value that is often recalled at these speeches is *sabr* (patience). Participants repeatedly cite the Qur'anic, saying, "God is with those who are patient" (*Inna Allah ma'a al-sabirin*). Both Muslims and non-Muslims were reciting such invocations in a recent *sulhah* in an Arab village in Palestine. *Sabrun jamil* (patience is beautiful) is another Qur'anic saying recited on these occasions.[10]

Traditional dispute resolution methods in Arab-Muslim communities are deeply influenced by Islam. Dispute resolution procedures based on Shari'ah rely almost entirely on Islamic values and traditions. A Muslim Palestinian local leader in Gaza, who specializes in resolving disputes based on *shar'a* (derived from *shari'ah*), stressed that arbitration and intervention are better than continuing a dispute. He stated that arbitration is supported and mentioned in the Qur'an at least on two occasions: "If ye fear a breach between them twain [husband and wife], appoint (two) arbiters, one from his family, and the other from hers; if they wish for peace, Allah will cause their reconciliation: for Allah hath full knowledge, and is acquainted with all things" (4:35). "Allah doth command you to render back your Trusts to those to whom they are due; and when ye judge between man and man, that ye judge with justice: verily how excellent is the teaching which He giveth you! For Allah is He Who heareth and seeth all things" (4:58). Regardless of whether the arbitration is binding or not, it is clear that using an arbitrator to settle disputes is socially and culturally preferable to using violence, force, or even imposition.

In describing the values and principles he uses in the process, the Gazan intervener relied on several of the Prophet's sayings and on shared spiritual beliefs by stating the following:

> We remind the parties about God and that faith in God is the basis for all behavior. We remind them of death and of the futility of earthly life. Therefore, how can they quarrel about worthless worldly things? We remind them of the following: destiny and fate; that Islam is the religion of justice, it treats justly both victim and offender; the neutrality of *shar'a* and its encompassing blessing; that a person who refuses *shari'ah* is placing himself in the circle of *kufr;* that *sulh* is *khayr* (reconciliation is good); that you should "be to people like trees, when a stone is thrown at them, fruit is thrown

back" (Hadith); that returning aggression with *ihsan* (doing good) will bring good and reconciliation; and that by doing good to people, you will own their hearts, as often a human has been owned by his own good doing (*ihsan*).[11]

The intervener makes clear to those involved in conflict that forgiveness and reconciliation are superior to revenge and violence, again citing from the Qur'an: "The recompense for an injury is an injury equal thereto (in degree): but if a person forgives and makes reconciliation, his reward is due from Allah: for (Allah) loveth not those who do wrong" (42:40).

There is a larger repertoire of sayings, statements, and stories that warn people against lies, aggression, false oaths, and doing harm to others: "We remind the person that on the day of judgment, every aggressor will pay the price for the aggression [*a 'la al-baghi tadur al-dwa'i 'r*]; God gives time but does not neglect [*yomhil wla yohmil*]; a mistake is not a reason for another mistake; and all people will lose by fighting."[12]

The intervener aims to have the parties propose and accept a resolution by appealing to the good that resides in all parties. He avoids articulating any form of resolution until three days after the first consultation, when the disputants return to consider the intervener's instructions.

The intervener uses the Prophet's tradition and an accompanying set of traditional and cultural sayings that call for good actions. For example: A believer bought a piece of land and, after paying the price, found a pot of gold. He took it back to the man who sold him the land and told him: I bought the land and not the gold. But the man said: I sold you the land and everything in it. They went to Solomon, who said: Marry the boy and girl from each family and give them the gold.

Another story shared by the arbitrator illustrates the importance of justice in Islam: "When Caliph Ali had a dispute with a Jew over a shield, they took the case to a well-known Muslim judge. He asked for evidence [*bayyinah*] based on the Prophet's sayings. The Jew then admitted that he wanted to test the religion of Islam."[13] Using oaths is also part of the procedure employed by the Gazan intervener. He explained that "a false oath places the person in fire." If the person lies, God is his only judge. To support the dramatic consequences of a false oath, the intervener told a story about a Palestinian in the 1940s who accused another man of taking one Egyptian pound. For his day in court, the accused came well dressed and had money in his pocket. He placed his hand on the Qur'an and lied. His clothes were burned, as was his ten pounds. The victim said: "I leave you to God, and I do not want any money." Later, after disasters continued to plague the accuser, he threatened to kill the victim if he did not accept the mediation and end the case.[14]

In the Shari'ah there is no need for *tazkiyah*--an act in which five relatives of the accused take an oath to testify that he is innocent or telling the truth. *Tazkiyah* arises frequently in traditional tribal law ('*urf*) in Palestine, Egypt, Jordan, and Lebanon.

In explaining the religious basis for the oath, the Prophet was quoted to the effect that "providing evidence is the responsibility of accusers and the oath is the responsibility of the person who denies" (*al-bayyinah 'ala man ida'a, wa al-yamin 'ala man ankr*). This procedure is used by the intervener in Shari'ah and it is similar to the Bedouin tribal tradition.

Another Hadith is used when the intervener reminds the witness that he or she should bear witness only if they saw events very clearly and have no doubt about what they saw. Thus, the intervener recalls the Prophet saying to a witness, "Do you see the sun?" The witness replied, "Yes." The Prophet said, "Witness like the sun."[15]

From these examples we see that whether dispute resolution mechanisms are implemented by rural, urban, or tribal communities, there are certain common values and principles that characterize the process. It is also clear that Islamic religious values play a central role in both rural and tribal approaches.

Assumptions of Traditional Dispute Resolution

Regardless of the nature of a dispute, there are certain assumptions that underlie the process and outcome of dispute resolution in Arab-Muslim communities. First, conflict is regarded as negative, something to be avoided. To support such an assumption, mediators and arbitrators often declare, "God does not love the aggressor." Therefore, the natural and ordinary goal of people is to establish harmony or avoid being in conflict with others.

Second, the goal of dispute resolution mechanisms is to restore order and the disrupted balance of power rather than to change power relationships or the status quo. To reach a settlement, the third party often says, "Let us put an end to evil (*sharr*) and agree upon the suggested terms." The third party focuses on the destructive forces of the conflict, calling attention to all the hurt and loss it engenders for the individual, the family, and the larger community.

In most settings, the role of the third party is to reach an agreement that the conflicting parties can accept without necessarily addressing the structural injustices or institutional arrangements underlying the conflict. When a party raises the issue of an institutional or structural injustice (for example, the relationship between the police or military and the community, the inadequate distribution of resources in the country, or urban development that harms the poor), the third party might ask, "Are you going to change the world through this case? Accept what has been offered, because you will not get better compensation."[16]

Third, community, clan, tribe, and family ties initially contribute to escalation and subsequently to de-escalation of conflicts. Although a conflict might begin between individuals, it typically escalates and widens to include the nuclear and extended families, the clan, and, eventually, the entire community. Third parties rely on the community and clan influence to restrain the behavior of individuals and ultimately to settle the conflict. The individual in a dispute will obey his or her elders, community leaders, fathers, and so on, in accepting or rejecting a settlement. Community leaders and the clans' interests may pressure their members to settle a case even though initially they were not ready or willing to do so. In addition, the community and clan are the primary guarantors of the implementation of an agreement, because often violation of the accord may harm the clan's interest, image, or status.

Fourth, the initiation and implementation of intervention are based on social norms and customs, which are usually derived from an Arab Islamic tradition and culture. These codes can be used to establish individual status and to press for an agreement between two groups (families or communities). These negotiation techniques are based on social and cultural codes, which are in turn shaped by values, norms, and belief systems that constitute the individual's worldview. Some of those values include restoring lost honor; avoiding shame upon one's family, religion, or community; and preserving the dignity of a person's family, elders, religion, and national group. The dispute mechanisms are designed to restore such values through a specific set of procedures, rituals, and negotiated settlements. For instance, while land and money can be traded for a physical attack on an elder, they often are accompanied by a form of public apology, which becomes the main focus of the process, a process that is described by Antoun as "the trade of goods and symbols" (1997, 160).

Fifth, an emphasis on relationships is the main characteristic of these negotiations and third-party interventions. Parties present their grievances in terms of relationship and status in the community or the perceptions of "others." Thus, a dispute over a parking space in a small refugee camp entails considerations like the following: "If I give up or compromise, how will I be perceived by the others in the neighborhood?" Or "I am accepting this settlement because I care about the community and the relationship with my neighbors." Such statements reflect the importance of restoring relationships and saving face in the community. There is a particular emphasis on past, future, and dependent relationships that underline the social network in these communities and as a result influence the nature of the resolution. Interdependency is greater in pastoral and agricultural communities than in urban neighborhoods, but it can leverage a settlement in both contexts.[17]

Sixth, face-to-face negotiations are not always the third party's first option. In fact, in many disputes the parties meet only at the end, when settlement has been reached through shuttle diplomacy conducted by the third party. In the words of a Gazan Muslim arbitrator, "Anger clouds people's judgment." He argues that by not letting the parties meet, he guarantees his control of the process. He can save the parties potential humiliation or commitment to intractable positions in their interaction. He conducts the inquiry by transmitting messages that will bring the parties closer to each other; eventually he ends up preaching to every party about the necessity of agreement from a religious perspective. The contending parties are thus relieved of their anger, brought closer to their faith through careful, gradual guidance, and reassured that self-sacrifice is ultimately rewarded in the longer term.

The Third Party's Role in Traditional Dispute Resolution

In traditional processes of dispute resolution, a third party often volunteers to intervene. However, it is not unusual for parties to come to them for help. The nature of the conflict and the makeup of the parties determine the size and composition of the third-party group and intensity of the arbitration process. For instance, in a community conflict that has escalated to involve two ethnic or religious groups, the third party would likely include the highest level of regional and maybe even national leaders of the contending communities. However, for a dispute involving two small families or individuals, a group of two or three local leaders is sufficient.

For example, in Gaza the dispute resolution system includes three levels of third parties: (1) family elders, who intervene to settle internal issues among family members; (2) local community leaders, who settle disputes that involve the local communities within the refugee camp or its vicinity; and (3) regional leaders, who are the most respected and best known in Gaza, and who settle disputes involving parties from different cities in the region.

When the third-party committee is formed, it often includes outsiders or people who have no direct interest in the outcome of the dispute. However, some have a connection to the disputants (same religious sect, political party, etc.). This connection is used as a way of persuading the disputants to accept the implementation of a settlement. Knowledge of the parties and their tradition, history, and relatives is another source of influence used by the third party.

The age of the third-party members also plays a role. They are usually older men who, according to local social and cultural standards, are classified as elders who command the communities' respect. For example, a tribal intervener among the Awlad Ali in Egypt is called ʿaqilah (wise man). Such a title is granted only to older men and elders.[18]

Members of the third-party panel may have no direct power to sanction the parties economically or politically. Nevertheless, their cultural, religious, and social status gives them the influence needed to pressure the parties into accepting a specific settlement. Since all disputants are members of the community, they are interested in maintaining good relationships with the respected leaders or avoiding their anger or disapproval. According to a Gazan who participated in a dispute resolution process, "If you accept the settlement for the sake of the panel members, or as a good gesture toward them, you need to make concessions in your demands to reach an agreement, even though justice is on your side. By doing this, you are earning respect and honor from the panel. This credit might be of assistance in future circumstances."[19]

The composition of the third-party group is heavily influenced by religion. In an Arab-Muslim community, most third-party panel members observe either Islam or some other religion. Imams (religious persons who lead prayer in the community) and qadis (Shariʿah judges) are often involved in the mediation and arbitration of disputes (Rosen 1984). Their credibility derives from their chosen sect and the intensity of their faith or their religious status. For instance, a local leader in Gaza was described to me as the most trusted person in the community because of his strict observance of Islamic values and traditions. He was the local imam. Several community members said, "He does not tolerate wrongdoing; he will tell you to your face if you have done anything wrong."

Processes of Dispute Resolution

There are several stages in which a community or interpersonal dispute is handled in a Palestinian community. First, one of the direct or indirect parties (stakeholders) requests the help of a third party by appealing to a respected leader who is known for his role in successful intervention in the community. In other cases, particularly if there is a violent escalation in the dispute and the entire community is involved, third parties—often regional leaders—visit each disputing party, requesting permission to intervene. Second, a fact-finding phase begins, with the third party shuttling between the sides, listening to their stories. Through these visits to the parties and to other witnesses, conflicting narratives regarding the issues emerge. Having gathered sufficient information, the third-party members begin a series of consultations and caucuses with the disputing parties. The negotiation phase becomes clearer as the third-party members attempt to arrive at an appropriate settlement for the case. If the third party is acting as an arbitration panel, then they issue their decision and justify it through traditional and religious norms and values. The head of the group provides the Qur'anic verses supporting the notion of justice, harmony, and *amanah* (integrity). If the third party is following the mediation-arbitration path, he then coaxes concessions from both parties to reach a settlement range, relying on religious and cultural values to persuade the parties of the importance of concessions and the restoration of justice and harmony to the community.

The third-party panel members further invoke values and norms accepted by and known to the parties involved. They propagate these values throughout the entire process of mediation-arbitration. For example, in a dispute involving two ethnic groups in a small village in Galilee during the summer of 1998, the members of the third-party panel spoke of the historical dependence between the two communities. They told stories about the period when cooperation and harmony prevailed in that village.

These religious and cultural values and norms are used by the third party to influence, persuade, and resocialize the disputants. Through their speeches and conversations, they appeal to the following values: (1) preserving the unity of the family, community, religious group, clan, or nation. Fighting must stop to allow reconciliation to take place; otherwise, the community will be weak and divided in facing outside threats or challenges; (2) protecting and preserving the honor of the family, person, faith, or community, since if these are violated shame will be brought on all members; (3) protecting future generations; (4) observing the religious duties of tolerance, compromise, respect, coexistence, and nonviolence by the third party. The third party conveys the message that to be a good Muslim, one must follow such values in practice. Forgiveness and dignity are two other cultural and religious values discussed by the third party during the reconciliation process.

In a family dispute that involved a husband and wife in Gaza, a mediator-arbitrator relied on the Prophet's Hadith that instructs men to care for their wife and family. He cited the Qur'anic verses that the husband recited as a sign of agreement and knowledge. The local mediator mentioned family harmony, protection of a woman's rights, and a sense of justice in dealing with children in an attempt to reconcile the two parties.[20]

Dealing with a power imbalance in a dispute is a challenge for interveners in all conflicts. The same Gazan intervener argued that the process provides the disputants with an equal chance to express themselves, and the Shari'ah, or Islamic laws, that govern this process do not distinguish between rich or poor, powerful or weak. Several interviewees claimed that power imbalances do not affect the process or the outcome, particularly if the third party is honest and fair. However, such faith in the process was not shared as strongly by some participants. Research indicates that power imbalances do affect the process of dispute resolution and that the system continues to function primarily as a social-control mechanism (Abu-Nimer 1996b; Zinati 1992).

A Gazan participant who was critical of the process argued that when one of the parties is poor and his opponent wealthy or influential, the process and outcome will be biased: "You can be certain that the outcome is not going to be in favor of the poor, even if justice requires it."[21] Mediators and arbitrators themselves are subject to social pressure from the influential members of the community, since the entire process is aimed at preserving the status quo. Another disparity is evident in marital disputes, in which the wife is at a severe disadvantage—often the father, brother, or elder son functions as a spokesman in dealing with the third party.

Agreements and Rituals

The signing of an agreement takes place in a public setting, allowing the entire community to witness the procedure (whereas in Western conflict resolution procedures, the signing is conducted under the supervision of a legal authority). There are diverse signing rituals throughout the Middle East, but they all encompass the following basic functions: (1) to publicly sign the agreement so community members know that harmony and order will be restored to their life; (2) to increase the obligation of the parties to implement their share of the settlement—otherwise they will bring dishonor and shame on themselves from the community; and (3) to restore honor and respect for one party—for example, the offending party will publicly apologize and ask for forgiveness from the victim. Such an apology in itself restores the victim's respect and brings shame on the offender, while at the same time reintegrating the offender through his or her affirmation of the community's social order and traditional values.

In certain areas of North Africa inhabited by the Awlad Ali tribes, there is a special ritual for cases of murder. The offender agrees to surrender and lie on the ground beside a sheep. A member of the victim's family approaches the offender and has the choice of killing him or the sheep. Obviously, the victim's family representative will choose the sheep. However, the fact that the victim has had the opportunity to take revenge (but decided to kill the sheep) restores the respect, dignity, and the honor of the victim's family. Thus, they will not be socially stigmatized as weak or unable to revenge their victim.[22] In another public ritual practiced in *sulhah* (conciliation ritual) in Galilee and in other parts of Palestine, the offender ties a knot around a long stick using the Arab *kaffiyah* (head cover) or a white cloth symbolizing truce and peace. Then members of the third party and the victim's family each tie a knot around the stick using the same cloth. This public ritual is designed to convey the obligation and commitment of the parties to the settlement and to the restoration of peace and harmony among the community members (see Jabbour 1996). In a ritual in one of the villages in Galilee in 1996, the offender had to walk approximately two miles around town without his *kaffiyah*. Such an act, for an old man, is a great humiliation and sends a clear message of contrition and powerlessness. The ritual symbolizes the ability of the victim's family to take revenge; however, they chose this public ritual to restore their dignity and respect in the community.

Restoring respect and honor is important for future relationships, too. The party that does not restore its honor is perceived as weak and subject to future exploitation. In social networks based on relationships of power and status, respect and honor are the primary criteria for judging human worth. During their speeches, members of the third party in these rituals explain why the parties have reached and accepted a specific agreement. Religious and cultural values suffuse their narratives. For instance, a Gazan intervener explained that the parties accepted the outcome because "God will love you for such compromise; God will compensate you for this *ihsan; ihsan* for God's sake [*ihsan li wajh Allah*]. We begin the intervention by the name of God as we appeal to you for reconciliation. We are all members of the same faith." If they practice different religions, they emphasize that they are all children of God.

Conclusion

There is no doubt that Islamic values strongly impact the dispute resolution strategies, outcomes, third-party roles, and rituals. Every day, in rural, urban, and tribal Muslim communities, Islamic values are applied to resolving conflicts, preventing violence, restoring order and harmony, and creating cohesiveness and unity among rival communities. These cultural norms and values need to be fully and systematically considered when outside interveners attempt to work in a Muslim community. For instance, a development project initiated by a foreign organization must incorporate these norms and values into the planning, design, implementation, and evaluation of their projects. Inclusion of those values can benefit both the interveners and the local community.

Often the resistance to peace-building initiatives in Muslim communities is related to the fear (or threat) that some of their indigenous values and norms might be not only violated but also entirely undermined. A successful strategy would factor in those values before implementation by engaging the local community members. Similarly, a peace-building project that relies solely on Western conflict resolution methods would not be effective in settling disputes. The development of local peace-building initiatives will have to be conducted with intimate knowledge of the community members' worldview, a view that some local people will be able to articulate and integrate in the course of their application of the principles of peace building.

Considering the context is a crucial step in understanding the impact, process, and function of traditional dispute resolution mechanisms in a Muslim community. Each event has social and cultural functions rooted in the historical context of the dispute. Thus, understanding culture and religious beliefs is central to the efficacy of third-party panels.

The application of peace-building and nonviolent values in the sociocultural practices and political movements in various Muslim communities helps to preserve the communities' order and stability. Nevertheless, all peace-building efforts in such communities face obstacles and challenges. The next chapter focuses on the types of challenges that confront political activists, educators, trainers, and interveners conducting peace-building workshops and projects in Muslim communities.

4

Nonviolent Peace-Building Initiatives in Arab-Muslim Communities

Myths and Obstacles in a Training Framework

This chapter focuses on ways to overcome the political, social, and cultural obstacles to the acceptance of peace building. By examining obstacles facing practitioners in an Islamic context, I hope to offer some constructive suggestions toward an active and systematic integration of peace-building ideas into the lives of both Muslims and non-Muslims, whether they live in separate or shared communities.

Sociocultural analysis and the contexualization of obstacles are essential tools in applying nonviolent methods in day-to-day interaction in diverse circumstances (Avruch 1998). The specific reasons for Islamic reluctance to adopt more widespread and consistent nonviolent methods have to be examined case by case. While much of the literature has mainly focused on external factors—colonialism, Zionism, imperialism, and other factors that result from Western policies—this analysis concentrates on the internal environment of Muslim communities.[1] An informed analysis must first begin with the internal sociocultural and political forces that face peace builders in the Muslim communities.[2]

The obstacles to peace building in Muslim communities are often equally daunting to non-Muslim residents. In fact, minorities—mostly Christian—in Arab-Muslim societies are typically not regarded as full-fledged members of the community (Salem 1994, 146; Peretz 1994).[3] This reality doubles their sense of powerlessness and thus underscores the need for nonviolent processes. At the same time, non-Muslim communities have acquired and shared many Muslim cultural and social values and norms. A good example of such integration is the Coptic Christians in Egypt, who have embraced many of the values and norms of Egyptian Arab-Muslim culture.[4]

The discussion of obstacles and strategies for overcoming them is here divided into two parts: the macro social and cultural factors and values that shape many traditional Muslim nonindustrial societies; and the challenges that face peace builders (trainers, educators, and others) working in Muslim communities.[5]

Like others, Muslim communities employ both violent and nonviolent norms and strategies when dealing with interpersonal, community, ethnic, national, and international conflicts. As shown in the previous chapters, nonviolent and peace-building approaches have been applied in such communities around the world on various social, political, and interpersonal levels. These studies provide compelling evidence that peace building and nonviolent norms and values are integral to the daily life of Muslims. Therefore the assumption that all, or most, interactions in the Muslim community are violent is not valid.

Peace-Building Programs in Muslim Communities

Despite the deeply entrenched mechanisms for peaceful conflict resolution in Muslim cultures, some Islamic political groups in the Mideast have grown increasingly prone to violent responses to internal social and political conflicts. Since the beginning of the 1990s, tens of thousands of Algerians have been killed in a brutal civil war.[6] In Egypt, militant opposition groups have been threatening the country's economic and political systems for the past twenty years.[7] In Jordan, King Hussein intervened militarily to control the opposition in 1998, and his son deployed special forces to control protesters in Maʿan in 2002.[8] In Iraq, Saddam Hussein used his exclusive weaponry in suppressing the Kurds and the Shiʿite communities. Indonesia, the country with the largest Muslim population, is experiencing economic and political upheaval involving its non-Muslim minorities (the attacks on the Chinese minority are only one indicator of a deteriorating situation).[9] In short, political violence is spreading in Muslim societies from Iraq to Indonesia, creating a pressing need to rethink the role of force and violence in these communities and the legitimacy and applicability of nonviolent strategies in the Islamic cultural and religious tradition.

The fact that a new field of study—conflict resolution and peace studies—is emerging and being applied in many areas of the world is another motivation for developing Islamic peace-building approaches. Since the end of the cold war, many nongovernmental organizations (NGOs) and official government offices have conducted peace-building training workshops that aim to educate and assist various communities in adopting nonviolent methods. Hundreds of schools and colleges are giving degrees in the field of conflict resolution and peace building. Thousands of schools around the world have adopted such themes as part of their core curriculum (Scimecca 1991; Fisher 1997). The proliferation of peace-building programs on all levels reflects a paradigm shift in people's perceptions and interactions worldwide (Burton 1990; McDonald 1987; Sandole and Merwe 1993; Lederach 1997).

Muslim communities cannot stand by as passive observers of these changes, which are gradually influencing economic, academic, and political practices throughout the world. There is a significant contribution that can be made by Muslim communities and Muslim tradition in shaping and implementing peace-building strategies.

Global changes in technology, particularly in communication, have created new realities for all Muslims regardless of their social and regional identities, obliging them to confront new issues and challenges such as strong emphasis on consumerism, cultural lags (advance technology but slow change in the social and cultural values), and values and norms (for instance, difficulties in maintaining strong family and tribal connections and solidarity, practicing the traditional hospitality norms, codes of violation and protection of honor and dignity, etc.). They also face challenges related to traditional definition of Islamic identity by processes of secularization, rapid nationalization, or feminization. These new global realities are likely to generate more conflict and tension in the world. Peace-building methods can be effective tools in coping with the social and cultural impact of such changes, especially in areas like the status of ethnic and religious minorities, who are becoming increasingly aware of their status because of their exposure to other minorities in the world (see Ibrahim 1994b, 1995).

Training in peace building is an educational and political process that enhances the participants' awareness of their contextual relationships, particularly in dealing with social and political authorities. It represents an intentional response to the selective nature of global communication. It empowers participants through a self-examination process that promotes awareness of social and political conditions. It includes a set of tools for participants to question their basic assumptions about conflicts and settlement methods used by the authorities to maintain the status quo. Thus, peace-building training can bring about constructive changes in communities' and individuals' self-confidence. In many Muslim communities, both the traditional and the current systems of power distribution create great inequalities based on individuals' ethnicity, religion, gender, age, clan, race, and so on.[10] Most of the groups and subgroups in Muslim societies can benefit from such training programs—within their societies as well as between their societies and others (for the most part Western in nature).

The primary motivation for peace-building activism in Muslim communities is to change the current reality by fostering socioeconomic development and fulfilling basic human needs and the rights of groups and individuals (security, self-determination, identity, growth and development, etc.). These desired changes can be facilitated through self-examination and an in-depth critique of internal social and cultural realities. All peace-building strategies (nonviolent mobilization methods, conflict analysis, negotiation, mediation, reconciliation, etc.) presuppose such processes of self-examination and analysis, which often lead to the realization that individuals have the ability and responsibility to act in their own interests.

Applying Peace-Building Strategies in Muslim Communities: Macro Sociocultural and Political Obstacles

There are a variety of obstacles—political, cultural, religious, and professional—to a wider application of peace-building strategies in Muslim societies. Although such obstacles are based on the dominant cultural and social values in Muslim communities, they should not be treated as fixed rules. The application of peace-building strategies is adjustable to specific economic, social, educational, and geographical contexts.

These strategies also relate to systems of technocracy and bureaucracy: although there have been several nonviolent Muslim political movements in this century, most Muslim countries are afflicted with acute technocratic, political stagnation. Johansen (1997) writes that this lack of imaginative and creative political leadership is one of the chief props of the status quo.

Many of the Muslim leaders in political organizations and governments operate in systems of "mediocre" technocracy.[11] Those at the top select subordinates more for their loyalty than their competence. Most Muslim Arab participants in conflict resolution workshops have identified bureaucratic recruitment policies as an impediment to social and political progress (Barakat 1993; Salem 1994; Tschirgi 1994; Ibrahim 1994a).[12]

Young participants in peace-building training workshops (particularly diplomats and foreign service officers) have expressed frustration over their supervisors' resistance to the application of peace-building skills. Participants reported that their leaders often oppose the application of highly effective conflict resolution skills to internal managerial relations and to conflicts related to daily work.

This state of affairs results in the co-optation of religious leaders by political regimes, particularly the mainstream religious leadership that has begun to operate as an extension of the political leadership. In most Muslim countries, the religious clergy has been associated with the ruling regime and as a result has benefited materially:

> The states' policies are aimed at denying Islamic organization and giving the 'Ulama an autonomous political role. The policies ranged from "nationalization" and the appropriation of religion as an instrument of the state to exclusion, marginalization, and suppression. The relationship between Islamic institutions and governments in most Islamic states can be analyzed in terms of two processes: the increasing subordination and loss of autonomy of religious institutions, and the provision of religious legitimization to the policies of the state. (Dessouki 1998, 6)

In these cases the official religious leadership is being used as a tool to maintain the status quo and prevent political and social change. In many cases, the mainstream religious leadership is called upon by the political elite to intervene on behalf of the regime to rally the masses and establish support for certain policies. For example, religious leaders issue *fatwah*s on matters that might embarrass or challenge the political elite's legitimacy in Egypt, Jordan, Palestine, Lebanon, Syria, Iraq, Saudi Arabia, and other Muslim countries. For example, during the Gulf War the Egyptian religious establishment sided with the government's position to preempt opposition to government policy on religious grounds. The same was true for religious leadership in other Arab countries during the Camp David initiative.[13]

One of the consequences of this alliance between religious leaders and the political elite has been the emergence of radical Islamist political groups who utilize religion to call for rebellion against political oppression and poverty. In addition, such groups provide certain religious interpretation to deal with the social and cultural identity crises currently facing most Muslim communities.[14] The rapid exposure of Muslim societies to industrial and urban lifestyles is often cited as another factor that contributes to anomalies in cultural values and to a great deal of confusion and inability to handle the enormous amount of changes confronting such societies (Hudson 1977, 129).[15] In response to this reality of rapid change and based on a literal interpretation of Islamic teachings, there are revivalist movements calling vociferously for a return to the way of life prevailing in the days of the Prophet, without consideration for the technological and other changes that have taken place over the past fourteen centuries.[16]

Corrupt political systems: Postcolonial corruption—political, economic, and military—has contributed to a worsening of poverty and the depletion of scarce resources in many Muslim communities,[17] thus reinforcing the dominant power paradigm of competition and force.[18] Communities in the precolonial system or in traditional and pastoral cultures were less exposed to systematic violence.

Traditional values of nonviolence, patience, and steadfastness lose their resonance in the context of systematic exposure to the new cultural values of consumerism, speed, efficiency, and immediate gratification of needs. In this environment, it becomes increasingly difficult for any Muslim to practice the following verse: "O ye who believe! seek help with patient Perseverance and Prayer: for Allah is with those who patiently persevere" (2:153). The notion of charity as a form of social justice may feel increasingly anachronistic. "It is not righteousness that ye turn your faces towards east or west; but it is righteousness—to believe in Allah and the Last Day, and the Angels, and the Book, and the Messengers; to spend your substance, out of love for Him, for your kin, for orphans, for the needy, for the wayfarer, for those who ask, and for the ransom of slaves; to be steadfast in prayer, and practice regular charity, to fulfill the contracts which ye have made; and to be firm and patient, in pain (or suffering) and adversity" (2:177).

In short, a major obstacle to the application of peace-building strategies is the struggle for physical survival, which becomes the chief priority of life in the face of persistent poverty and a widening gap between rich and poor.[19] Muslim countries in the Middle East and North Africa have on average $1,780 in per capita income (Kuwait, Qatar, Saudi Arabia, and the United Arab Emirates are the exceptions), as opposed to $24,930 for high-income countries and $1,090 in low income-countries (Korany, Brynen, and Noble 1998). In many Muslim societies, economic changes and a fast-growing economic elite tied to economic globalization have left a large portion of the population behind and have created a lagging economic infrastructure.[20] It is extremely difficult to implement grassroots peace-building strategies where day-to-day survival is the major concern (Lederach 1997). Unfortunately, this has been the reality in all too many Muslim communities.

Patriarchal social structure: Islamic social systems are based on male dominance in all social and political spheres (Moghadam 1993, 114; Barakat 1993, 106), a tradition that limits the crucial role that women can and do play in peace-building activities. Modernization processes in industrial societies have contributed to a substantial weakening of the patriarchal system. Yet, particularly in the Middle East, patriarchy has managed to survive and even adapt in what Hisham Sharabi calls the "hybrid of dependent modernization,"[21] a development that places men at the top of political and social institutions to the exclusion of women.[22] Little attention is paid to women's status and issues. The concept of gender equality is absent from schools, hospitals, governments, and other institutions.[23] This discrimination extends to public and formal peace-building initiatives or projects, which remain largely a male preserve. Women are invited only if an issue pertains to them alone. With few exceptions—for example, in the Palestinian Intifada—women's potential contribution to social and political movements is lost.

Patriarchal values run counter to peace-building concepts and strategies, which are based on principles of equality, freedom, respect for group and individual rights, and empowerment of powerless communities and individuals. In many male-dominated peace-building training workshops the issues of gender relations and the patriarchal system have been defined as taboos that are often dismissed with ironic and cynical remarks. Those who insist on raising the issue are usually given a brief chance to air their concerns, but often this issue is not recognized as an obstacle to a peaceful environment. Given the lack of awareness regarding the substantive role of women in society, patriarchal values inhibit the comprehensive application of peace-building methods and values in Muslim societies.

Obedience to and respect for hierarchy: Hierarchy is a strong value in Muslim communities. Social and cultural relations are highly stratified, based on criteria such as age, gender, clan, tribe, religion, ethnicity, race, and region. Fuad Khuri explains the implications and nature of such structures through *'asabiyyah* (social and individual solidarity) and *"Al-usuliyyah"* in which "endogamy (i.e., marriage within the same clan) becomes a mechanism for preserving a caste system. In such systems the person is seen as a link in a chain (*silsila*), and the chain . . . [is] formulated on the basis of genealogy, descent, or lineality. Thus a person is distinguished not by individuality but by the solidarity thus formulated." The value of the person lies in the way he links to others, which leaves a curious effect on the question of freedom and the definition of being free (1997, 134).

Michael Hudson (1977) and Halim Barakat (1993, 38) describe the importance of kinship and tribal and clan linkages in establishing and managing political authority in Arab-Muslim communities, particularly in rural areas. These factors penetrate social, economic, and political institutions. Arab-Muslim regimes such as those in Jordan, Saudi Arabia, and Yemen still rely on tribalism as a major source of legitimacy for their authority.[24] These systems of stratification were highlighted by an Egyptian workshop participant, who emphasized, "We run our society as an army."[25]

Like patriarchy, hierarchical values are in conflict with egalitarian peace-building methods and values. Peace-building strategies encourage the individual to take independent initiative and to transcend social and cultural boundaries. Creativity is a core principle in all peace-building models and strategies. Unreflective obedience to traditional hierarchies thus impedes the implementation of peace-building strategies and remains in conflict with Islamic egalitarian principles.

It can be argued that the absence or inhibition of certain values in Arab societies prevents the development of a democratic culture. Fatima Mernissi (1992, 43) identifies sovereignty of the individual as a major value lacking in Arab culture. In her opinion Arab reformists and the nationalists have sacrificed both reason and individualism on the altar of unity.

In peace-building workshops, role playing and simulations have often had to be adapted to hierarchical relationships among the participants. In other cases, entrenched traditions have entirely scuttled such activities. Some participants have expressed frustration about executing their action plans in the post-workshop reentry phase. When asked what they would do with the workshop's experience or lessons, participants often indicated that, whatever their ideas, they would first need the approval of their managers, officers, teachers, or husbands (in the case of female participants).

Most political regimes and elites in Muslim communities continue to derive and maintain their legitimacy mainly through extensive authoritarian control systems. Through strong security and military arrangements, these political and social elites thwart any participatory movements by the mass of the population,[26] prohibiting the free expression of opinion on political, economic, or social issues.[27] Although there have been some concessions to modern liberalism in the Arab-Muslim states in the last twenty years, the regimes remain largely authoritarian and perpetuate a nondemocratic political culture (Korany, Brynen, and Noble 1998, 276;

Garnham and Tessler 1995; Ajami 1981).[28] As Korany, Brynen, and Noble put it, "In most of these countries, political elites are reluctant to release much power, or to allow too much energy or autonomy in civil society. The state remains strong enough to revert to more authoritarian measures if required. A degree of ambiguity between the 'carrot' of limited pluralism and the 'stick' of authoritarianism is purposefully cultivated: repression if necessary, but not necessarily repression" (1998, 276).

In this coercive and authoritative atmosphere, the introduction of participatory peace-building strategies confronts numerous challenges,[29] especially true when the emphasis is placed on resource mobilization and empowerment of local communities, a process that can threaten the power of local and national officials.[30]

Discouraging self-examination: These political and social institutions discourage self-criticism and internal examination. Community members do not recognize the internal obstacles to development and change. Instead of examining the shortcomings and internal problems of schools, factories, government institutions, and family and tribal structures, the masses, at the prodding of the elites, focus on external factors such as colonialism, imperialism, Zionism, and, more recently, globalization.

A full explanation and discussion of the factors that lead to the use of violence and force in Arab-Muslim communities is beyond the scope of this study, but clearly internal factors (lack of democratic or participatory frameworks, authoritarian regimes, and failure of past ideologies to resolve economic and social problems) and external factors (globalization and dependency on the West) have perpetuated stagnation in the Arab-Muslim world. This long-term lack of change invites radical and militant solutions to day-to-day problems.[31]

Integrating and analyzing these obstacles in designing peace-building initiatives in Muslim communities would be an effective strategy of intervention and a significant contribution to the process of political and social change in Muslim communities. The following section discusses those challenges that face practitioners in such a context and identifies some strategies to overcome, or in some cases avoid, such obstacles.

Myths and Challenges in Applying Peace Building in an Islamic Context: A Micro Perspective

Not all the myths and obstacles that face peace-building trainers are peculiar to Islamic contexts.[32] Some of them crop up with great frequency among a variety of groups and nationalities. American college students,

World Bank officers, or other participants from Western communities may face some of the same apprehensions and concerns when participating in peace-building training. On the other hand, there are specific concerns that are unique to participants from Muslim and Arab communities. For the purpose of this study, it is essential to discuss such obstacles, recognizing that they might extend beyond the Muslim community.

The nature of peace: In peace-building training workshops in Arab-Muslim communities, participants often question the nature or long-term goal of the peace being promoted. They often ask, Is this peace that you are preaching or preparing us for similar to the type of peace that exists between Israel and Egypt, or Israel and the Palestinians? Obviously, such participants suspect that the proposed peace might result in a disadvantageous or unjust settlement, especially when the trainers do not clarify the components of peace in their intervention model. In some cases trainers do not address the question, Does peace include equality, freedom, and justice, or is it simply a state in which parties commit themselves not to use violence against each other, regardless of the outcome or reality of the conflict?[33] This argument reflects an Islamic perspective, or positive approach, to peace.

Participants expressed satisfaction when the trainers defined their approach as including representation, inclusivity, justice, freedom, and equality. Community organizers, students, and scholars have often accepted these values as a set of basic guidelines and desired outcomes. Emphasizing justice, inclusivity, and equality as part of the intervention model defuses concerns that peace building and conflict resolution approaches might lead to the mere absence of violence without justice.

Violence can terminate conflicts: A widespread myth in the Middle East has it that violence can eliminate or terminate conflicts: the more violence is applied in handling internal and external differences, the more likely it is that "we" (Arab-Muslims) will favorably resolve such conflicts. "What was taken by force can only be returned with force" is an old Arabic saying that was often cited in response to the Israeli-Arab conflict. A similar misconception is identified by Crow, Grant, and Ibrahim (1990). Violent struggle is perceived as a necessary means to establish dignity and strength among the oppressed. This concept is especially rooted in the cultural and historical context of the Arab-Muslim regions, a context characterized by internal antagonistic relationships as external antagonistic relations with the postcolonial powers and Israel. It is this tension between the cultural (patriarchal and masculine) inclination toward vengeance and retribution and Islamic principles of peace and resolution that third parties must carefully navigate to achieve a just outcome among stakeholders. Hassan Hanafi's (1988) characterization of violence and nonviolence captures the above assumption. He argues that violence and nonviolence are two sides of the same coin, correlative terms whose certification depends on who holds more power. Those who are deprived of their human rights and dignity often pursue violent methods to defend themselves, while the state's use of violence and force to pursue its own objectives is usually ignored and legitimized. Violence should not always be viewed negatively, he holds, but should be judged in terms of target, objective, size, and the relationship between victim and oppressor. Hanafi acknowledges that there should be no dialogue between slave and master as long as the social and political oppression exists. He calls for a third way of nonviolent struggle to remove the causes of the violence (i.e., the social and political arrangements that resulted in violence). Such use of violence for national liberation would be different from oppressive violence, a distinction proposed by many participants in peace-building training workshops in the Middle East.

Conflictless society is achievable: The common belief among participants in such workshops is that conflict could be eliminated from their society and that people could live in total harmony. This assumption originates from the notion that conflict is a disease or illness that should be eradicated. This understanding often led workshop participants to conclude that the most effective conflict strategies are avoidance or competition. Violence is perceived as a tool that would insure their victory and terminate the conflict.

Contrary to the above perception, peace-building approaches are based on assumptions such as: (1) conflicts are an integral part of life; (2) "we" ought to learn how to live with the reality of conflict; (3) the goal is to find constructive rather than destructive outcomes of conflicts; (4) conflict brings change, and change is an opportunity to strengthen relationships between parties, potentially fostering a higher level of trust, cooperation, and understanding (Abu-Nimer 1999; Bush and Folger 1995). In this environment, the first day of a workshop often becomes a context for negotiation of the opposing assumptions held by trainers and participants.

Nonviolence is not an effective method: In some workshops, a number of participants have argued that Islam prescribes violence or force as an effective method to deal with enemies, especially non-Muslim enemies, by drawing on instances where the Prophet was forced to engage in defensive wars. (This point comes up most often in conferences dealing specifically with the relationship between Islam and nonviolence.)[34] Therefore, as true

Muslims, they should not import contrary concepts and strategies into their tradition and religion. Crow, Grant, and Ibrahim (1990) describe how Muslim Arabs tend to characterize nonviolent struggle as an imperialist strategy that aims to mollify the just indignation of Muslims and deflect revolutionary struggle against neocolonialism and imperialism.

The rejection of nonviolent methods is also related to the threat associated with the global invasion of Islamic communities by modernization, including industrial and urban lifestyles. Unfortunately, in the minds of many Muslims and non-Muslims, nonviolence is associated with Western Christian philosophy. As a result, they assume that a "de-authentication" of Islamic culture and tradition will ensue from a Muslim embrace of nonviolence. Underlying such an approach is a misconception that conflates nonviolence with Christianity and modernization. Some scholars sympathetic to this view have argued against the integration of pacifism and nonviolence into the Islamic tradition (see discussion in part 1 of this study). This highlights the importance of reminding participants of the considerable experience of the Prophet in waging nonviolent campaigns against his oppressors, acts of resistance that have garnered considerably less attention or publicity among Muslims today.

The dominance of politics: Political interactions, debates, and conflicts are the most important aspects of Muslims' lives. Therefore, the effectiveness of nonviolent methods can be measured only in terms of these political conflicts. The view of Crow, Grant, and Ibrahim (1990) that "nonviolent struggle is inefficient" in dealing with political conflicts reflects this obstacle. This assumption often arises in training workshops on the validity of the conflict resolution methods. Acknowledging this belief can lead a workshop dynamic into the trap of focusing on political issues alone rather than encompassing broader or underlying social, interpersonal, and economic problems as well. Participants challenge the trainers to provide successful cases in which conflict resolution and nonviolent methods have justly resolved political conflicts. The relative paucity of such examples from a Muslim context can breed skepticism about the entire approach. When some Palestinians and other Arab participants demand such political examples, many of them cynically (or ironically) would argue that the Israeli-Palestinian problem is the best example of the failure of peace-building approaches. Others cite the failure of the Arab and Muslim countries to negotiate peacefully among themselves.

By focusing on the political conflicts only, participants and trainers implicitly endorse the assumption that if change does not occur on the political level, then it is not going to happen in community relations, interpersonal interactions, labor management, or educational institutions. This conclusion or strategy hinders change by mechanically separating social, economic, religious, and political factors from group, community, and individual issues. It also indicates the level of control that the political leadership possesses over the daily lives of such communities, which are often disinclined to exercise initiative in bringing change to society.

The manipulation of the Israeli-Palestinian conflict by Arab political elites to suppress Arab and Muslim domestic social and communal issues contributes to the tendency to focus entirely on elite political interactions. This trend is rooted in (1) the nature of governance systems in the Muslim world; (2) the modern national movements and their role in producing such regimes in the postcolonial era as well; and (3) authoritarian and hierarchical cultural values.

The hierarchical framework fosters the notion that change does not spring from the bottom up, from the grass roots, but descends from the top (the political elite). Some typical sentiments are: "We individuals cannot do anything to change the political reality." "Most of the people are occupied with their daily survival and care little about such changes." "If the political elite changes, then the changes will filter down." Therefore, the answer to the questions, What is my role? and What can be done? is often, in effect, Nothing. This cynicism, one of the major obstacles in peace-building training workshops, is at loggerheads with the assumptions of community and grassroots empowerment, which calls for activism and involvement at the grassroots level and for the inclusion of all parties in the decision-making process.

Another form of resistance to peace-building concepts is usually expressed in the initial phase of the training by rejecting the Western approach. At this initial stage of the training, Palestinian or Egyptian participants in workshops (conducted between 1994 and 1996) often used to say, "These are Western approaches that do not work in our context. We have a different reality." In most cases trainers respond by emphasizing the power and potential influence of one person's initiative. Though this individualism is seemingly unfamiliar (or less accepted) in rural and traditional contexts, it does not prevent many participants from adopting these approaches and principles in community, labor-management, or interpersonal conflicts. In these transitional communities, there is a steady process of change taking place, particularly in urban areas, where the nuclear family and the individual are gaining more influence and importance in the social structures. These changes are apparent in the sensibility of young people, especially those with more education.[35] Thus, the change in the value system of the transitional Muslim community gives an edge to individual peace-building initiatives as alternatives to the more traditional collective and authoritarian approaches (Antoun 1979; Abu-Nimer 1996b).

Whether the political situation is complex or whether change emerges from political leadership exclusively, many of the participants still think that their community's social problems are unimportant or that such problems are connected to larger political issues and therefore should have lower priority in their agendas. As a result, poverty, abuse of women and children, violence among teenagers, and inter-and intrareligious conflicts do not seem worth addressing in peace-building terms. A Palestinian participant disagreed with the notion that grassroots groups can have any impact: "This argument—that grassroots activities have no impact—is often a defense mechanism used by those who refuse to change, take individual responsibility for their immediate environment, or pay the price when taking a risk."[36]

Trainers and some participants agreed that change can occur on various levels (interpersonal, school, community, city, etc.) and that individual responsibility is critical. For example, in Gaza in 1994, after the Oslo euphoria had evaporated, many Palestinians realized that their dream of statehood had gone aglimmer, at least for the time being. They also saw that their economic and political rights were deteriorating under the new peace agreement. During the training many of those participants refused to deal with any social, cultural, or internal issues. They insisted that the only problem deserving their attention was relations with Israel. The training team spent one full day listening to and identifying problems. After the participants had identified 113 different problem categories, the training team posed these questions: On which of those problems do the Israelis have the least impact? Can those problems be dealt with? In which areas can you as an individual make an immediate impact? After arranging their priorities, the participants realized their potential range of influence as individuals and agreed to act on that basis.

However, there were some other participants who argued that such techniques or approaches are dangerous, that they underestimate the power and impact of the Israelis on the situation, and that they will train Palestinians to avoid dealing with the Israelis. Others responded that reducing violence in the family and community and increasing communication among various Palestinian factions would not harm the Palestinian cause, that on the contrary, it would assist all Palestinians in dealing with Israel. These workshops illustrate ways of addressing valid concerns that may have disempowered participants in a context of conflict.

Action versus diagnosis: Participants often defend the position that debates are valuable even if they do not lead to action or practical remedies. Such argument is raised often by academicians who debate the best ways to revive the Arab-Muslim culture. One panelist in a 1995 Cairo conference announced, "Such issues of revival of Muslim and Arab culture and power should be resolved through intellectual debates before we initiate any actions." Participants who shared this belief often refused to take part in new initiatives or projects, believing that the theoretical debate was more important and had yet to be fully explored. Other participants declared that they did not perceive themselves as agents of change, willing to apply their knowledge and experience. This perspective was expressed by some academics and intellectuals, too, when they were invited to attend some of those peace-building training workshops.[37]

Stagnation in Muslim reality: The belief that Muslim societies or communities have not made any significant progress since 1200 C.E. constitutes an obstacle to internalizing peace-building values; it ignores positive adaptation to modernity and changes in the Islamic world over the last few centuries (Voll 1994).[38] This viewpoint is often based on a comparison of every aspect of the contemporary Muslim world (economic, social, technological, and even cultural and religious) to that of the Islamic empires of 640–1200 C.E.. In addition to idealizing these periods without critical examination of the social and political realities, this approach does not consider the external or internal historical factors that influenced the processes of change that occurred since the collapse of the Islamic empires.

Belittling the achievements of all Muslims since 1200 C.E. precludes an examination of Islam's role in the processes of change and places the blame for current circumstances on external factors only. This approach contributes to the "internalization of oppression" (when members of a community believe that they are unable to effect change or that they are inferior to the outsiders), and to a sense of helplessness. These dynamics are evident in the following arguments: "If we were as strong and powerful as we were during the Islamic empire, we would not need to look for methods of nonviolence to resolve our problems." "When we lost power and stopped using our forces, we became subject to colonial oppression." Participants who constantly compare their current reality with their image of the great Muslim historical empires are typically the most adamantly opposed to peace-building and conflict resolution methods.

Peace building is not justice: Another common perception is that non-violent and peace-building methods do not produce justice, and that these methods are tantamount to surrender. Participants who believe this often argue that the assumptions of conflict resolution and nonviolence mainly promote compromise rather justice. Crow, Grant, and Ibrahim (1990) also identify this belief with the argument that "nonviolent struggle prevents legitimate self-defense." The misperception is that through nonviolence the person gives up his or her rights and sense of justice by rejecting violence as a method to achieve them.

A Palestinian participant who resisted the notion of conflict resolution gave the clearest voice to this notion: "When we accept your methods we are accepting the notion that we are not going to get our full rights and that comprehensive justice will not take place. We will have to recognize the rights and the interests of the other side. They become legitimate. If we do so, then what power do we have? We will lose our rights and claims. If the problem is converted from just cause to a process of negotiation and mediation, then we start from a certain position and will end in a totally different place."[39]

Another Arab participant, from Jordan, suggested, "Muslims are not violent; they are the victims. You need to talk to the other side and those who are the perpetrators of violence and injustice."[40] At another conference an African-American participant expressed similar reservations, noting that the training models do not address the four hundred years of black slavery in the United States. He asked whether peace-building methods are able to produce an outcome that addresses the sense of injustice among African Americans.[41]

Training workshops have demonstrated that there are programs that can deal with micro and (some) macro obstacles to peace-building initiatives in Muslim communities. Successful application of those programs requires both careful design and implementation to address the kinds of skeptical attitudes summarized above. Utilizing the local and indigenous resources available in each community is an essential component of any intervention plan. The employment of those resources insures integration into the initiative of the important values and principles of the community.

For example, conflict resolution programs can involve teachers, selected groups of student leaders, women's organizations, and public health experts. Empowering such groups in the community can provide a solid basis for long-term changes in the community. Such groups often constitute the core leadership of the social or political movements that emerge to bring change to their communities.

Such peace-building programs must be developed by members of the community rather than being imposed by an outside agent. Outside agents can be good catalysts for change, but sustainable and authentic change can result only from the initiative of indigenous activists, who can impart to the voiceless a lasting sense of the possibilities of local action.

Some elements of peace-building training models have been applied in the Middle East by organizations such as Search for Common Ground and the Institute for Multi-Track Diplomacy (IMTD) in projects in Egypt, Palestine, Cyprus, Turkey, and Jordan. In these cases, the American organization that has the funding conducts an intensive training workshop for a selected group of community members, hoping to create a team of professional trainers and community activists who are committed to these principles of peace building. Then a center or an administrative infrastructure is created as a base of operations for the group. The trained team continues to design and implement training workshops and new projects. Gradually the influence and authority of the American organization is reduced to fund-raising activities and consultation (Abu-Nimer 1998).

The challenges facing such projects include (1) the inability of the American organization to select the appropriate set of participants; sometimes the selected groups of participants are unqualified and incapable of disseminating the ideas; participants may lack the initial commitment or may not have any legitimacy or authority in their communities; (2) the opposition of local authorities to the project, and the penetration, by security forces, of the workshop or the project staff, causing mistrust, discord, and splintering of the project group; (3) the unwillingness of the outside organization to allow the local team to operate their project and to take control of the initiative; a power struggle thus erupts over decision making, funding, the nature of the programs, and so on.

The local participants in peace-building initiatives often depend professionally and economically on the outside organizations, a dependence that often weakens them, hindering the emergence of local peace-building institutions. The sooner the outside organization can break this dependence, the more successful the local staff is likely to be in building and mobilizing their resources. However, to accomplish this objective, members of the outside organization have to help form a well-qualified and committed local group (for example, by providing financial compensation for local team members). Often, after one or two years of intensive training, these members are qualified to conduct training and initiate new projects. Their efforts become the crux of the fund-raising activities of the external sponsoring organization. However, the outside organization often does not pay these local trainers or pays them far less than they pay the foreign staff. This inequality prevents local empowerment, healthy relationships, and further growth and development of projects.

Local members often take enormous risks by engaging in such peace-building activities. When local members of peace-building initiative were arrested in Gaza and Jordan, there was a need for the outside organization to provide support and protection. Such intervention means contacting the local political authority and using the governmental ties that the organization has forged. The lack of such support from the outside organization could be an obstacle in building trust and in enhancing the commitment to peace-building initiatives.

Minimizing the role and responsibility of outside trainers in peace-building projects in Muslim communities will contribute to the empowerment of the local staff. Outside trainers can provide the concepts and even some basic tools. However, the actual application of the new tools to local realities must be the work of the community members themselves, even if the interveners are specialists in these strategies, motivated by a desire to promote global peace. When local members adopt these strategies, they earn more credibility and can be more effective in including all segments of the community. Knowing the cultural patterns of the community, the local interveners will be better able to transmit peace-building values to their peers.

5

Peace Building and Nonviolent Political Movements in Arab-Muslim Communities

A Case Study of the Palestinian Intifada

Mohammed Abu-Nimer and Joe Groves

In February 1989, in the West Bank city of Hebron, an Israeli patrol was chasing a group of *shabab* (Palestinian youth, ten to twenty years old, who were in the forefront of the street protests) after a stone-throwing incident. In the course of the chase, a young protester was shot and killed. As the chase continued, an Israeli soldier was cut off from the patrol and found himself surrounded by a group of angry shabab. Fearing for his life, he ran to the door of the nearest house and began beating on it with his rifle. A woman came and opened the door and, seeing the danger, admitted him to the house and refused to let the shabab enter and attack him. With the shabab milling around outside, she served the soldier coffee and waited for the mob to disperse so he could leave safely. The woman was the mother of the boy whom the patrol had just killed.

About a month later, in the course of a conversation in Hebron about nonviolence in the Intifada, the researcher asked a group of Palestinians what role religion played in their struggle. Ahmad, the host, replied, "Religion and custom enable us to preserve our humanity." When asked to elaborate, he told the above story and added, "This is why nonviolence is important to us. We will never become like the Israelis and hate our enemy; we will offer him hospitality. That soldier could come back again, and the woman would offer him coffee again." The family and friends sitting in the room nodded their assent to the story and the discussion.

This story illustrates several issues. First, it is a microcosm of the complex intertwining of violence and nonviolence that characterizes the Intifada and calls into question simple distinctions between the two. The shabab provoked the action by throwing stones, prompting the soldiers' fatal gunfire. One soldier's fearful response to potential violence resulted in nonviolent protection by the woman. By sorting out the complexities of these types of action and their interaction in the Intifada, perhaps we can further our understanding of how nonviolent resistance functions in movements of social protest. Second, the story hints at ways that Islam functions in relation to nonviolence. When asked about religion, Ahmad linked it with custom and proceeded to tell a story rather than turning to theory, theology, or narrowly defined religion. Therefore, exploring religion in its social context may help us understand the subtle interaction of religion and nonviolence in the Intifada.

Third, the story illustrates a particular way of talking about nonviolence. It does not recall a grand action of heroism or focus on a charismatic leader or deal in theological or ideological abstractions. It neither offers a database for sociological analysis nor develops systemic theories. But the anecdotal evidence it offers of the way that Palestinians were thinking and acting in a very real, very nasty struggle compels us to take it seriously. The model it presents of one family's attitudes and actions in the Intifada gives the story a moral and theoretical dimension and introduces potentially different avenues of approach to analyzing movements of social protest and the role of nonviolence in such movements.

The complexities that this story presents indicate some of the difficulties in identifying and describing nonviolent resistance in the context of Muslim societies. The goal of this chapter is to help the reader understand the ways in which nonviolence manifests itself in Muslim societies and to help identify the cultural and religious values and principles in the Arab-Muslim world that facilitate nonviolent and peace-building campaigns in their communities.

There are many illustrations of peace building and nonviolence in the political movements, campaigns, and actions initiated in Muslim communities (see chapters 1 and 2). There has been much discussion of these nonviolent movements, but few of the studies or research analyzes or examines the cultural and religious factors that influenced and supported them. Instead, researchers based their theoretical frameworks or analytical tools on internal and external political, economic, or social factors. One exception is Johansen's article (1997) on the Peshawar Pathan movement led by Abdul Ghaffar Khan. The peace studies analytical framework employed by Johansen helped identify the cultural and religious factors and conditions that made Ghaffar Khan's movement creative and effective. This kind of research is needed when approaching all cases of nonviolence in Muslim communities. Johansen's type of analysis may uncover more effective strategies and designs for mobilizing masses or small communities to seek improvement in the lives of their members.

Although there are a number of movements that we could examine, concentrating on one—the Palestinian Intifada—will enable us to go into greater depth and detail. This chapter will approach the Intifada by focusing on the cultural and religious values and principles that influenced the movement and made its technique of nonviolence possible in the Palestinian community. It will investigate those values and principles and their role in the emergence, dynamics, and outcome of the Intifada's campaign. This cannot be done without first examining the nature of the Intifada's strategies and addressing the debate that surrounds the labeling of the Intifada as either a violent or a nonviolent movement. Examining the Intifada from this cultural perspective does not negate or contradict the nature, objectives, and impact of the Intifada as an extension of the Palestinian national movement. The fact that secular nationalists, both Muslim and Christian, led and participated in the Intifada does not contradict the idea that certain values and principles inherent in the Muslim Arab culture and religion influenced the design and application of nonviolence in the Intifada movement.[1]

The Intifada: Background and Main Features

Researchers have identified many of the conditions that led to the Palestinian uprising in 1987. These conditions resulted from many regional, international, and internal political events and developments, including (1) the emergence of the Palestine Liberation Organization (PLO) as a major influence in all Palestinian actions; (2) Arab indifference to the Palestinian situation; (3) the undermining of the PLO that occurred when the United States channeled development money through Jordan and Israel; (4) the undermining of the PLO by Jordan through material advantages and external patronage; (5) deteriorating economic conditions; (6) high unemployment among the Palestinian intelligentsia; (7) the rise of Islamic movements; (8) the indifference toward the Palestinian issue exhibited by Reagan and Gorbachev at the Soviet-American summits; and (9) the refusal of the Palestinians to live under the authority of the Jewish state (McDowall 1994, 96–98; Melman and Raviv 1989, 205).

We will discuss only those causes and conditions we consider central to the Intifada's nonviolent actions. Following the invasion of Lebanon in

1982, both Palestinians and Israelis realized that the military option to end their conflict was not feasible (even the destruction of the PLO power bases in Lebanon had not resolved the Palestinian issue), and the Arafat–King Hussein accord in 1985 failed to engender any new hope of ending the Israeli occupation of the West Bank and Gaza. In fact, at the Arab summit meeting in November 1987, the Iran-Iraq war replaced the Palestinian question at the top of the Arab agenda. Arafat was not even invited to Amman for the summit by Jordan's King Hussein. Thus by 1987, Palestinians realized that they had to rely on themselves and their internal resources if they wanted to bring about political change. That realization sparked the Intifada as a way of emerging from a political cul-de-sac (Migdal and Kimmerling 1993, 266).

In 1986, Israeli policy in the occupied territories had two aims: to break the resistance of the nationalist groups and to promote the Jordanian option. Aid to those Palestinians who supported King Hussein and the appointment of Palestinian mayors who would promote the Jordanian option were the tools used to support these aims. To counter an increasingly difficult situation in the occupied territories, the deeply divided factions among the Palestinian diaspora reconciled at the eighteenth Palestinian National Council in Algiers in 1987. This reconciliation allowed for the formation of a unified leadership during the Intifada.[2]

However, the roots of the Palestinian popular resistance in the West Bank and Gaza go back further, to the 1970s. A strong popular movement began in the 1970s with the involvement of all the Palestinian political factions and with the creation of many institutions and organizations devoted to health, women, and agriculture and other professions. All these organizations were geared toward institution building in the occupied territories. Their experience in the 1970s and 1980s was valuable for its role in the sudden growth and later systematic organization of the Intifada. The most notable attempts to create a national coordination committee in the occupied territories after 1967 were the Patriotic Front in 1973–75 and the National Volunteering Committee in 1974, the Palestinian National Front (a coalition of professionals, trade unionists, and women's organizations), and the National Guidance Committee in 1981, which was dissolved by Israeli authorities in 1987 (McDowall 1994).

Perhaps the most important nonviolent groundwork for the Intifada was the development of alternative structures: charitable societies, professional associations, and mass organizations.[3] This organizational activity began in the first decade of the occupation with the growth of traditional charitable organizations (hospitals, relief aid societies, traditional women's organizations) and professional and cultural associations (art, theater, literary, journalistic, legal, and medical associations). The focus began to shift to mass organizations in the second decade with the growth of labor unions, voluntary work organizations, student organizations, and popular women's organizations. While the role and development of the different types of mass organizations differ, they all demonstrate the broad growth of nonviolent resistance in the occupied territories.

These organizations mobilized whole sectors of Palestinian society and cultivated the values of solidarity, service, and resistance. For example, the goals of the first voluntary work organization were "to combat selfishness and inculcate a collective consciousness; to promote women's rights; and to help the community" (Taraki 1989b, 452). Even in the early stages of their development, these organizations represented a conscious attempt to lay the structural groundwork for a future Palestinian state (436). Although mass organizations and more traditional associations are not revolutionary in nature, they constituted a significant level of resistance under the occupation. Without the groundwork laid by the mass organizations in the 1980s, Palestinian society would have lacked the organizational skills, the sense of self-sacrifice, the necessary solidarity, and the relationships that crossed traditional social and class affiliations and helped to sustain the Intifada. The degree to which the "constructive work" of building these alternative institutions permeated Palestinian society indicates the deep roots that nonviolent resistance laid down.

Women played a central role in the Intifada itself, but their prior organization was also an important factor that helped many activists in mobilizing new members. Women's working committees were formed by all the Palestinian political factions in the 1970s and were the most active segments in mobilizing women in political and national activities. Souad Dajani credited women in the Intifada with "radically challenging and transforming social relations and behaviors within Palestinian society" (1994, 67). The Union of Palestinian Medical Relief Committees (UPMRC) also contributed to this transformation by bringing the rural peasantry into closer touch with urban professionals. The UPMRC served fifty thousand patients, primarily in rural areas, and included seven hundred professionals by 1988 (McDowall 1994, 99).

A deliberate campaign of nonviolent resistance was launched four years before the Intifada. Although on a small scale, some successful initiatives were carried out by the Center for the Study of Nonviolence in Jerusalem and the Committee against the Iron Fist Policy, led by both

Palestinian and Israeli activists.[4] The center translated the wor'
Sharp, Mahatma Gandhi, and Martin Luther King Jr. into Arab.
promoted their dissemination and discussion. Members of the center in
tiated many activities in the West Bank and Jerusalem. Their pioneering
campaign can be credited with familiarizing Palestinians with nonviolent
methods of resistance before the Intifada. Even if their activities were limited in scope and only partially successful, the local political and ideological debates that they managed to create were highly important in educat-
ing many Palestinians about nonviolent resistance. In particular, the
Center identified several techniques that Palestinians had been using to
protest the occupation since 1967 as central to Gene Sharp's strategies for
nonviolent resistance. These techniques included demonstrations, obstruction of the Israeli policy of settlement, refusal to cooperate, constant
irritation of the Israelis, boycotts, strikes, internal solidarity and support,
the development of alternative institutions, and civil disobedience. All
these techniques were employed throughout the Intifada to various degrees and in different areas of the West Bank and Gaza. The impact of the
center's efforts is best illustrated by the increased awareness and familiar-
ity of the Palestinians with the nonviolent actions later adopted by the
Intifada's leadership (Awad 1984).

This brief background review leaves no doubt that there was a set of
systematic political, organizational, and economic conditions that led to
the Palestinian uprising. This contradicts the assumption made by some
journalists and policymakers that the Intifada was a sudden spontaneous,
unexpected development in the history of Palestinian national movements. In fact, as Phyllis Bennis argues, if that were true, then "it—the
Intifada—would have collapsed in just a few weeks. The ferocity of Israel's
counterattack left little hope for an ad-libbed resistance movement. But,
after one month, our [Palestinian grassroots political activists] earlier organizing efforts took root and gained control of the political motion of the
Intifada. That is what allowed the uprising to continue" (a popular committee member from Qabatiya; quoted in Bennis 1990, 22).

The Intifada surprised Israel's people and policymakers, its military, the
world—and not a few Palestinians as well. Part of the reason for that
surprise is the lack of understanding of how the quiet work of nonviolent
resistance goes on in a nonrevolutionary setting. If the Palestinian resistance is perceived only as an armed struggle, then the mass participation in
the Intifada and the shift to predominantly nonviolent tactics will be a
surprise and will be regarded as a tactical shift. But if the Intifada is seen

as a movement that grew out of historical experience and represents a stage of social maturation, then its nonviolence assumes a more significant role.

The triggering events for the Intifada have been identified as the truck accident in Gaza that killed several Palestinian workers on December 9, 1987, and the shooting of Palestinian demonstrators in the Balata refugee camp in the West Bank. These events triggered mass protests, demonstrations, and stone throwing in both the Gaza Strip and the West Bank. The Israeli response was massive and sweeping, utilizing extreme repressive measures approved by Yitzhak Rabin, the defense minister. They included allowing armed settlers a "free defense policy," instituting a policy of breaking the arms and legs of demonstrators, and allowing the free use of plastic bullets against demonstrators.[5]

Within two or three weeks, a massive coordinated effort by Palestinians resulted in an organized underground movement that lasted for at least two years and steered the entire community through nonviolent actions by way of weekly or biweekly fliers or communiqués. The coordinating group for the Intifada, the Unified National Leadership of the Uprising (UNLU),[6] regularly distributed flyers and communiqués to guide popular committees and to coordinate national strike days and other activities. The UNLU published its first leaflet in January 1988, announcing the Palestinian nonviolent struggle. At the same time, the Islamic Jihad Brigade renounced the use of weapons as a sign of solidarity and agreement with the unified leadership. Although Hamas did not join the UNLU, it cooperated with it on many occasions, particularly on issues of health and education (Salameh 1994, 23).

The high degree of coordination was certainly the chief characteristic of the first two years of the Intifada, not only at the national level of the UNLU but also at the grassroots level. For example, the UPMRC established a system for blood donations to help the injured and soon attracted fifty thousand names, an act that involved all segments of society and increased a sense of solidarity among the population. Also, each community created twelve different popular committees to address the various local and national needs and objectives, reflecting an enormous level of both national and local organization and coordination.

The Impact of the Intifada

The massive cost of the Intifada to the Palestinian population by 1991 was staggering. More than a thousand Palestinians were killed by gunfire and about a hundred by beating, tear gas, and other means. Another hundred thousand suffered injuries; fifteen thousand were held in administrative detention, without charge or trial, for at least six months; three hundred dwellings were demolished, leaving two thousand people homeless. Israel closed virtually every Palestinian educational institution, even kindergartens. In the context of Gaza and the West Bank, with a total estimated population of 1.6 million people and scarce resources, such numbers are thoroughly devastating to the entire community (McDowall 1994).

By 1990 massive Israeli repression and the stress it produced began to undercut the nonviolent tone of the Palestinian uprising. Both Islamic Jihad and Hamas advocated a limited return to violence and carried out a number of attacks on Israelis, both in the occupied territories and in Jerusalem, thus undercutting the influence of more traditional political factions. Attempts by these factions to reassert their control over the community resulted in considerable conflict and disillusionment among Palestinians, who were empowered by the Intifada's emphasis on local control. The lack of effective international response (beyond an influx of media figures and concerned activists) increased frustration and anger. The eruption of the Gulf War, exacerbated by the PLO's perceived support for Saddam Hussein, spelled the end of the Intifada.

But the uprising had a significant lasting impact on both Palestinians and Israelis. In terms of actual achievement, the Intifada's impact was more political than economic. The Palestinians managed to mobilize more international support and sympathy by nonviolence, which portrayed Israel as the aggressor. At the same time, they managed to make Israelis uncomfortable by raising their awareness of the consequences of the occupation. This resulted in mobilizing a minority of the Israeli left wing—both political activists and peace activists—to demonstrate and march in support of ending the occupation. These groups visited refugee camps and other Palestinian centers to express their sympathy (Bar-On 1996, 220). Therefore, despite the change in direction in the Intifada after the first two years, from an emphasis on nonviolent resistance to a partial use of arms, and despite the ability of the Israeli military to crack down on its various activities, the Intifada still managed both to move the issue of the occupation to the center of Israeli politics and to refocus the attention of the Arab and the international communities on the Israeli-Palestinian conflict.

Developing economic, social, and political organizations and institutions became a national priority to resist the Israeli policy in the occupied territories. In addition, voluntary and charitable organizations were instrumental in providing social services that had not been available previously, especially in the rural areas. The Family Enrichment Committee, the Committee for Health Care, Women's Work Committees, and numerous other organizations all worked in both urban and rural areas and helped unify the resistance. They helped develop literacy programs, train women for work, provide child care and education, create scholarships for students, care for political prisoners' families, and expand technical training. In health care alone, several local and mobile health centers provided much-needed services to the local population (Dajani 1993). These activities created connections between the urban and rural populations and among professionals, peasants, and the working class that did not exist before the Intifada. Many of the voluntary and charitable organizations worked across the boundaries set by the traditional political factions and created the possibility of new political alliances.

Dajani describes the impact of these actions as brief because of a lack of coordination with the PLO, Israel's harsh and systematic response, and, most important, the lack of a Palestinian strategy that connected means to ends and tactics to strategy. It is true that the UNLU, its coordinated resistance, and local governance through neighborhood committees all faded fairly rapidly. However, the sectoral and voluntary committees, the urban-rural and cross-factional connections, the deeper politicization, and the greater sense of possibility all remained. In addition, the nonviolent resistance during the Intifada targeted Israeli vulnerability and sensitized many Israelis to unnerving parallels between Israeli and Palestinian claims to victimization (Dajani 1993, 41). Palestinian nonviolent actions caused many Israelis to question the excessive use of force by the military. The military limited the impact of this questioning by rotating its soldiers, legitimizing the violence, and maintaining total separation between Israeli and Palestinian communities. Also the inability of the Palestinians to fully appreciate the value and impact that their nonviolent actions carried also limited the effect on the Israelis (42).

However, if these strategies limited the political impact of the Intifada, the uprising was nevertheless a source of enormous pride, a sense of empowerment, and unity for the Palestinian community. Regardless of the limitations of Palestinian nonviolent actions, scholars and observers agree that the Intifada proved the vulnerability of the Israeli occupation to nonviolent actions.

The Intifada was also influential in internationalizing the Palestinian problem, bringing it to the forefront of the international news and agenda. Images of Palestinian women and children facing up to Israeli soldiers had an impact on both Arab countries and Western governments. Both increased their support for Palestinian political organizations and NGOs.

Several factors contributed to the continued success of the Intifada. The diverse composition of the unified underground leadership allowed it to continue even when many of its top members had been arrested and imprisoned. And its birth within the occupied territories and its grassroots work within the communities gave it a sensitivity to the conditions of repression and the possibilities of resistance that previous external leadership had lacked. The PLO's underground political organization in the occupied territories provided trained cadres, continuity, and stability to the newly formed resistance movement. Constant contact and close cooperation (at least in the first two years) between the PLO in exile and local leadership broadened the reach of the Intifada and provided it with resources not available inside the occupied territories. The increasing organization of Palestinian communities when the Intifada erupted enabled new institutions to merge and strengthen when the Israeli grip on power weakened (Bennis 1990, 24).

Constructing a Nonviolent Analysis of the Intifada

The Intifada is one of the most thoroughly studied examples of political resistance in history. It would take a book-length bibliography to list all the analytical works on the Intifada, but few of these works deal with the role of nonviolence in the Palestinian resistance. The media phrase that dominated coverage of the uprising was "the violence of the Intifada." *Violence* as a word to describe the Intifada is not inaccurate—violence was abundant—but the phrase (and the media coverage) obscured the disproportionate nature of the violence, which was largely that of Israelis against Palestinians. Nor does it accurately reflect the predominantly nonviolent resistance of the Palestinians. Thus, the very presence and visibility of violence obscured the nonviolence. Second, Palestinians themselves were ambivalent at best about the use of the term *nonviolence*. Most of them rejected the term and felt that violence could play a role in their movement. The fluid and ever-changing nature of the Intifada, with much of the action evolving on the streets, meant that Palestinian leadership could not always clearly define or control the tactics that were employed. The need to maintain the unity of the uprising meant that they could not rule out violence because groups that played key roles in the Intifada—Islamic Jihad, the Popular Front for the Liberation of Palestine (PFLP) and the

Democratic Front for the Liberation of Palestine (DFLP)—felt the need for armed struggle. And both international law and the Universal Declaration of Human Rights affirm the legitimacy of violence to resist an occupying army. An analysis of the Intifada (or any other liberation movement) that focuses on nonviolence needs to begin with the recognition that international law affirms a right to violence. For Palestinians to totally disavow violence would be to surrender a recognized right. These factors all made it difficult for Palestinians to embrace nonviolence as an exclusive means of struggle or as a description of the Intifada.[7]

But nonviolence is treated as legitimate resistance while violent resistance is considered illegitimate by many peace analysts and activists. Frequently, governments will label liberation movements violent or terrorist in order to delegitimize them. Analysis that tries to highlight nonviolent resistance and understand its role needs to avoid these traps. When Palestinians practice nonviolent resistance, it should be regarded by the world community as a voluntary relinquishing of an international right.[8]

But nonviolence is far from irrelevant to the Intifada. Palestinians debated the nature and efficacy of nonviolent resistance. "We all believe in the tactics of nonviolence—if they work," was a frequent and typical statement in these debates. While questioning or rejecting the term *nonviolence,* most Palestinians readily embraced *civil disobedience* as an accurate description of the primary thrust of the Intifada. Indeed, in 1988 the goal of the leadership of the Intifada was to escalate the uprising to the level of "total civil disobedience."[9] To some, particularly the PFLP, civil disobedience is a stage in revolutionary development, succeeding the popular revolt that characterized the beginning of the Intifada and to be followed by mass armed struggle.[10] Others hoped or believed that civil disobedience would be sufficient to achieve the goals of the Intifada.[11]

Factors external to the Intifada also obscured the role of nonviolence. The U.S. and Israeli governments and many Middle East analysts have long associated the PLO with terrorist activity, thus creating an image of Palestinians that was difficult to overcome. Television emphasized rock throwing by the shabab and brutality by the Israeli military; newspapers catalogued deaths and injuries on both sides; talk of the "violence of the Intifada" was a constant. The violence was there—to a greater extent than the outside world recognized. Most coverage did not accurately reflect either the scope or thrust of the Intifada. Nor did it provide much space for Palestinians themselves to explain the nature of the uprising. Media coverage, with its thirty–second sound bites, its search for the dramatic, and its self-imposed limits on the amount and type of analysis, obscured the nonviolent dimension of the Intifada.

But the reasons go much deeper than media coverage. Many analysts, scholarly and popular, fail to recognize nonviolent resistance when it does anything but sit, stand, or march right in front of them. Violence is so much easier to recognize, categorize, and analyze weapons, physical attacks, injuries, and death compel attention. Nonviolent resistance is much more subtle, out of design or necessity. To a certain extent, nonviolent resistance must be defined in relation to the repression that it works against. Actions that are commonplace in one society constitute resistance in another. For Palestinians to gather the wild herb z'atar, a key ingredient for their cooking, was an act of resistance. The Israelis prohibited gathering the herb because the presence of Palestinians in the hills posed a security risk. Consequently, z'atar became a symbol of resistance. Since the Israeli military closed schools in the occupied territories for most of the Intifada, holding and attending class became a pivotal act of resistance. Neither the gathering of herbs nor the holding of classes are dramatic acts, but they are forms of nonviolent resistance central to the Intifada. But serving or asking about food, clothing, and daily activities escape most analysts who are cataloguing and categorizing the activities of a resistance movement.

But the problem reaches beyond that of the subtlety and contextuality of nonviolent resistance. Many analysts expect a nonviolent movement to be dedicated to principled and pure nonviolence, modeled on the civil rights movement and Gandhi's independence movement. This is a problem not only for researchers working from traditional social science models, but also for many researchers and activists working from a peace perspective. As we examine the Intifada, we see that it diverges from "pure" nonviolence in a number of ways. Rather than discarding the possibility that it is a movement of nonviolence, we need to ask whether the Gandhi-King model is the only valid form for nonviolent resistance.

This analysis will focus on the role of nonviolence in the Intifada. But we also need a wider-angle lens. We can understand the nature of nonviolence in the uprising only if we adjust for cultural specificity and stages of historical development, free ourselves from the prejudgment of Palestinian actions that permeates most discourse in the United States, and avoid imposing expectations of what a nonviolent revolution should be.

Two complementary analytical perspectives provide a basis for such an endeavor. Sharp's *The Politics of Nonviolent Action* (1973) analyzes the principles, methods, and dynamics of nonviolent resistance. His classification of 198 different methods of nonviolent action provide the broad sweep of tactics that will help us understand the multifaceted nature of resistance in the Intifada (Sharp 1973).[12] But Sharp, although aware of the historical developments and the sporadic, frequently spontaneous nature of much nonviolent resistance, chooses to concentrate on theory.

The Intifada began not with a theory but with nonviolent resistance making itself felt in the streets in an unarticulated, mixed, and uncontrolled form—and then having shape and direction applied to it. James Scott (1985) and Don Nonini (1988) offer perspectives on everyday, nonrevolutionary resistance among peasants and workers, thus providing a complementary approach to the dynamic aspects of the Intifada. Although neither author excludes violent acts from the analysis, their work demonstrates the centrality of nonviolence to everyday resistance. Their analysis (Scott's in particular) undergirds this study in two ways. First, they understand that seemingly spontaneous resistance movements have their origins and staying power in indigenous, unarticulated, practical, everyday forms of resistance (Scott 1985, 28–37).

Second, Scott's definition of resistance will enable us to assess more fully and freely what constitutes resistance in the Palestinian context. All too frequently, theorists consider only planned, coordinated, directly confrontational movements as true resistance. The surprise of the Iranian revolution and the Intifada, where sustained resistance seemed to emerge from nothing, demonstrates the weakness of this concept. Scott defines resistance as "any act(s) by member(s) of a subordinate class that is or are intended either to mitigate or deny claims (for example, rents, taxes, prestige) made on that class by superordinate classes (for example, landlords, large farmers, the state) or to advance its own claims (for example, work, land, charity, respect) vis-à-vis those superordinate classes" (290). Although he focuses on class-based resistance within a society, his definition can easily be applied to the resistance of a society under occupation. A society under occupation is more conscious of being oppressed and more active in its resistance even when that resistance is sporadic and uncoordinated. The definition is of particular value because it removes the condition of direct confrontation, of mass coordinated action, and turns attention to the intention of the participant, not the success of the action.

The Presence and Ambiguity of Violence in the Intifada

It is impossible to discuss the nonviolent aspects of the Intifada without first addressing the question of whether the activities carried out by Palestinians in the first two years of the uprising could be termed nonviolent. The mere presence of nonviolent actions and attitudes in a resistance movement does not mean that the movement itself is nonviolent. The Algerian revolution, which no one would classify as nonviolent, incorporated many tactics associated with nonviolent resistance. To understand the role of nonviolence in the early stages of the Intifada and to see what possibly distinguishes it from a violent revolution, one must examine tactics that are questionable or clearly violent.

The Question of Stones

A primary activity of the Intifada was stone throwing, something that was both a tactic and a symbol. The primary use of stone throwing was in demonstrations. Crowds of shabab (the primary street activists) confronted Israeli soldiers clad in riot gear and armed with tear gas, rubber bullets, plastic bullets, and live ammunition. The shabab directed barrages of stones at the soldiers to occupy their attention, provoke them into retaliation, and keep them at a distance. Stones were frequently used outside demonstrations as well. They were thrown at Israeli installations such as police stations, military encampments, and administrative buildings, and at Israeli vehicles.

Stone throwing appears to be a violent tactic and is regarded as such by many Palestinians as well as by the Israelis.[13] But not all Palestinians agree. When the interviewer asked one Palestinian, Ahmad, about stone throwing, he said, "The stones are just to tell the soldiers what we want. You cannot talk to machine guns. Stones are not violence."[14] Stone throwing was portrayed as an exercise in deliberate restraint in the use of force. Stones injured some soldiers and settlers in confrontations and in attacks on institutions and vehicles, but in most cases their use by Palestinian protesters was not as lethal weapons. Palestinians claimed that they could have used lethal force if they wanted to. "We are not afraid to die, and we could take many Israelis with us if we wished. We have knives, we have heavy stones, we have our hands—and we have guns. We have surrounded soldiers in our neighborhoods many times, but we choose not to kill them." This quote synthesizes the attitude expressed in many conversations in the West Bank. Yasser Arafat claimed that there were ten thousand weapons in the occupied territories but that the PLO ordered that they not be used. While Arafat's claim may be questionable, and the attitudes above may reflect exaggeration and bravado, restraint in the use of force was deeply ingrained in the thinking of the Intifada. It appeared in both UNLU and PLO statements, and was embedded in numerous stories conveying standards of behavior.

Why this restraint? The reason most frequently cited, that Israeli military power would make the use of weapons by Palestinians counterproductive, misses the complexity of the tactic. The Intifada placed constraints on the actions of both sides. Israel was constrained by its claim to high moral ideals, the rule of law for its own citizens, and international pressure. These led Israel to publish "rules of engagement" for combating the Intifada. These rules included soldiers shooting only from specified distances, shooting at the ground or at the legs, and relying on "nonlethal" ammunition such as rubber and plastic-coated bullets unless their lives were in danger. In the fall of 1989 these rules changed significantly. Soldiers were allowed to shoot at any masked or fleeing demonstrator who failed to heed a warning to stop. This both indicated Israel's acknowledgment of the effectiveness of stones and posed a challenge to that effectiveness. Would stone throwing continue to be an effective tactic if the soldiers began to retaliate more violently? The stones were effective under the old rules: Demonstrators could maintain their distance and stand behind walls to protect their legs. One purpose of the stone throwing was to get soldiers to break the rules and inflict severe casualties. This use of stones embodied an important principle of nonviolent resistance: Turn an opponent's superior force to your own advantage. This "political jujitsu" is a primary dynamic of nonviolent resistance in its effect on both the opponent and the resister (Sharp 1973, 3:657–97). Stones against automatic weapons is an unfair fight, and the massive Israeli retaliation against stone-throwing shabab upset the status quo by damaging morale in the Israeli army and increasing public sympathy for the Palestinians.

More important is the effect that the successful reliance on stone throwing had on the Palestinians' self-image. They no longer feared Israel's superior weapons because they had discovered the power of numbers, solidarity, and nonlethal weapons. Thus, the success of stone throwing was a step along the road to understanding the effectiveness of nonviolence and creating a situation of courage, confidence in spite of weakness, and personal empowerment that are key elements to a fully nonviolent strategy.

Some Palestinians summarized their restraint in the use of force by saying, "We do not hate the Israelis; we do not wish to kill them. If we resort to the use of force in the way that they do, we will become like them, violent and full of hate, and we refuse to do that." The stones were a way for people to stand apart from the cycle of fatal violence that has characterized the Israeli-Palestinian conflict and from being absorbed by the hatred for and dehumanization of the enemy that may accompany killing. Thus, even though stone throwing is a violent act, the attitude behind the stone throwing for many Palestinians is central to nonviolent resistance. These Palestinians saw the enemy as human beings whose lives were important and who should not be killed. They acknowledged the dehumanizing effect of violence on themselves and wished to minimize it. They recognized restraint in the use of force as necessary for breaking the cycle of violence.

But the use of stones also undercut nonviolence. Because stones can inflict injury and project an image of violence, they were less effective in placing the Palestinians on "higher moral ground" than absolute nonviolence. When Israel argued that the "violence of the Intifada" had to be countered with violence, Palestinians could not argue that violence came only from Israel. They could only argue that the violence was disproportionate.

Was stone throwing really necessary? Could not the same objectives have been achieved with absolute nonviolence? As one Palestinian said, "I wish that my people would use no violence. Let all of us sit down in the street; let the Israelis arrest all of us. We will choke their jails and the world will be appalled."[15] His statement reflected the views of many North American activists as well. But this assessment, based on comparisons with the Civil Rights Movement and Gandhi's struggle for independence, may not take sufficient account of the different context of the Intifada.[16] The demands that Gandhi's movement made and the threat that it posed bear some resemblance to the Palestinian situation, but Gandhi had advantages that Palestinians lacked. Gandhi was a Western-educated (and, at the beginning of his work, Westernized) Indian who was able and willing to speak the language of Christianity, appeal to the ideals of English civilization, and thus command international recognition and moral stature. More important, Gandhi had distance, numbers, and space. Britain was a long way away, and the British occupying force was small in comparison to the vast indigenous population. They could not control that population when significant numbers decided to resist. They were quite willing to fill the jails and keep them full, but the numbers were so vast that they were able to imprison only a small portion of the resisters. And, when resistance flagged or the British were successful in muting it, Gandhi had the option of retreating to the vast countryside to sustain the struggle.

And, finally, India was not home or holy for the British in the way that Israel is for many Jews.

Given the ineffectiveness of international law, there was no superior government to limit Israeli tactics of repression. Palestinians were not protected by Israeli law but, instead, subject to a complex and arbitrarily applied web of non-Israeli laws that severely restricted their rights and their opportunities for legal redress.[17] The occupied territories were governed according to a mixture of Jordanian law (in the West Bank), Egyptian law (in Gaza), Ottoman regulations, British military conventions, and Israeli military orders. The occupation was far more complete than was British control of India: the occupied territories are small; their borders are contiguous with Israel; and Israelis outnumber the Palestinians living in the territories. Consequently, Israel is a pervasive presence and exercises tight control over the population, which has no place to retreat, no room for safety. Israel has proven its willingness to imprison large numbers of Palestinians for long periods of time without charging them, deporting those they regard as troublemakers, using lethal force, and disregarding international law.[18]

Given Israel's ability and willingness to crush dissent, stone throwing was probably a natural response to the conditions of the occupation. As important as the symbolic value of the stones was, their practical purposes were more crucial. The stones created a breathing space for the Palestinians that permitted the growth of political and economic infrastructure. The stones seriously contested Israeli control of towns, villages, and refugee camps. In some cases, they created "liberated zones" that lasted a few hours, days, or even weeks or months.

Stone throwing is a complex tactic. It is not nonviolent. It can inflict injuries that are potentially, if rarely, fatal. It can be a reflection of hatred and enmity. But it is not strictly violent either. For many Palestinians, it represented nonviolence, while creating space for the creative work of nonviolent institution building. So, given the choice between calling stone throwing violent or nonviolent, Ahmed made a defensible choice of nonviolence. His statement reflects a problem in analyzing stone throwing that goes beyond a mere distinction between terms: the binary opposition between violence and nonviolence that is embedded in much of our thinking. If this dichotomy reflected neutral observational language for the purpose of "objective" analysis, it might be an adequate and useful categorization for certain situations. But the use of the dichotomy is highly value laden. Many times governments, particularly those of the United States and Israel, will label actions violent and call for nonviolence as a means of discrediting and squelching resistance to oppression. Many times nonviolent theorists and activists maintain the dichotomy to insist on the "purity" of nonviolent resistance.

But perhaps there are alternatives to the dichotomy of violence and nonviolence that would make it more useful to move beyond the binary classification. Gandhi, for example, did not see violence and nonviolence as opposite ends of a scale. In an oppressive situation, he felt the opposite of nonviolence was cowardice and inaction. Violent resistance in a just cause is preferable to passively accepting oppression and injustice (Merton 1965, 33, 37, 39). Furthermore, Merton saw little difference between "the nonviolence of the weak" and violent resistance (39). By questioning the relevance of a scale of violence and nonviolence, Gandhi also indicated that they were not necessarily absolute values. Looking at the presence of violence and nonviolence needs to be coupled with other values, such as the justice of a cause. Using nonviolence to further oppression does not make that oppression just. Nor does the justice of a cause necessarily make the use of violence good.

Stone throwing defies simple categorization. To speak of it as nonviolent, as some Palestinians do, is to dilute and distort the term *nonviolent* in such a way as to rob it of meaning. To refer to stone throwing as limited or restrained violence links it clearly with violence, which does an injustice to its intention and effect and some of the attitudes that accompany it. Perhaps we should refer to it as using nonlethal force or as unarmed resistance.[19]

Violence in the Intifada

If stone throwing was ambiguous, other actions of the Intifada—the use of Molotov cocktails, the killing of Palestinian collaborators, and the use of lethal force against Israeli soldiers and civilians—were indisputably violent. Among the more violent actions were knife attacks on civilians in East Jerusalem; a Palestinian grabbing control of a bus and driving it off the side of a mountain, killing seventeen people; the killing of several soldiers by dropping large stones from a roof. We need to take this violence seriously.[20] But we also need to examine it in relation to other tactics of the Intifada rather than using it to dismiss the role of nonviolence. Yes, some Palestinians employed serious and lethal violence against Israelis during the Intifada. However, what was remarkable about the uprising was not the presence but the infrequency of these incidents and the degree to which they stood outside the strategy and structure of the resistance as a whole.

There were exceptions to the restraint generally employed in the sanctioning of violence by the UNLU. Two leadership statements (nos. 37 and 40) sanctioned lethal force. Call 37, issued March 3, 1989, stated, "Let knives, axes, and Molotovs be increased. Let us increase the dropping of large stones from buildings."[21] The reference to large stones came in the context of the death of an Israeli soldier in Nablus, thus condoning lethal violence. However, this Call was ignored in practice: Neither the lethal use of stones nor the use of knives or Molotov cocktails increased. Call 40 asked for the death of one soldier or settler for each Palestinian killed by Israeli death squads (Nusseibeh 1989, 9). The Call did not encourage retaliation for all Palestinian deaths or for any deaths inflicted in demonstrations; it called only for retaliation in cases that violated Israeli law. Although there were Israeli deaths after this Call was issued, the UNLU did not claim that the deaths occurred in response to the Call. Thus, neither leadership statement that sanctioned lethal force had a practical effect in the Intifada.[22] But the willingness of Palestinian organizations to claim responsibility gave some sanction to lethal force, and the UNLU's silence on the issue created ambiguity. The incidents themselves did not set the Intifada apart from the Civil Rights Movement or Gandhi's independence movement; both of the latter were marked by violence outside the control of the leadership. But the UNLU's reluctance to condemn killings and the occasions when leadership sanctioned or claimed responsibility for lethal force did differentiate the Intifada from nonviolent resistance movements. Both King and Gandhi were quick to condemn such violence and even called off resistance efforts when violence occurred or an urge toward violence developed. The UNLU, as a collective and partial leadership, lacked the single or collective authority to effectively condemn such actions even if it wished to.

However, two indisputably violent actions, the use of Molotov cocktails and the punishment of collaborators, were explicitly sanctioned and encouraged by both the UNLU and the local popular committees, making them official acts of the Intifada. Molotov cocktails were directed primarily against property and vehicles. But civil administration buildings were attacked while employees were at work, putting people at risk of serious injury or death. Molotovs thrown at buses and automobiles injured a number of Israelis, both soldiers and civilians. The firebombing of vehicles protested the presence and restricted the freedom of movement of Israelis in the West Bank. These are violent tactics and indicate that the UNLU and the popular committees did not have an unequivocal commitment to nonviolence. However, even though the use of firebombs and Molotov cocktails increased during the course of the Intifada, it was still a limited and nonlethal use of force.

The punishment of collaborators was the one use of lethal force sanctioned by Palestinian leadership and regularly carried out by local committees and, consequently, was part of the structure of the Intifada. These acts of violence were directed against other Palestinians, not against Israelis. Not all treatment of collaborators was violent. Nonviolent forms of pressure (social ostracism, economic boycotts, taunting, harassment) were more common. Violent treatment was usually employed only when nonviolent pressure failed. Dealing with collaborators was crucial to the success of the Intifada. As in most situations of occupation, Israel's control of the occupied territories was strengthened by assistance from the occupied people. Before the Intifada, the Israelis had built a network of overt and covert collaborators. The overt collaborators (policemen, civil administration employees, and officials appointed by Israel) enabled Israel to control the territories through Palestinians who could work from within the social structure through their network of family and friends.[23]

As social and economic pressure and some use of violence by Palestinians undercut these networks of collaborators, Israeli intelligence services, according to Palestinian sources, recruited as collaborators "problem" Palestinians (criminals and drug addicts) over whom they had power.[24] Consequently, Palestinians came to see collaborators as a double problem: informers for Israel, thus a threat to the Intifada, and a criminal element in Palestinian society, thus a threat to ordinary safety and stability. When, after the resignation of Palestinian police, the popular committees assumed policing functions in towns and villages, the issue of collaborators intersected with the problem of law and order. As a result, the punishment of collaborators was both part of the struggle with Israeli occupation and part of the creation of an alternative system of justice.

In this context, the physical punishment of collaborators ranged from beatings to death. After a collaborator had been beaten, knifed, strangled, or hung, the body was sometimes left in a public place, sometimes tied to a telephone poll, for the Israelis to remove. These public displays were intended to shock and thus deter collaboration. Although the purpose of the violence was to create and preserve safe space in the Palestinian community in order to allow the nonviolent work of the Intifada to continue and grow, the graphic display of violence to intimidate and control goes against fundamental principles and attitudes of nonviolence. While such action might have been warranted in the Intifada and could possibly be understood as contributing to larger nonviolent goals, it stands in stark contrast to the principles of nonviolent resistance.

Accordingly, the Intifada involved violent resistance as well as nonviolent. The UNLU and the popular committees were willing to sanction and encourage some uses of violence; other actions lay outside their control. Arson, Molotov cocktails, and the killing of collaborators make it apparent that the Intifada was not completely guided and controlled by nonviolent principles. But, to get a full perspective on the Intifada, we must understand the balance between nonviolent resistance, nonlethal resistance, and the resort to violence. Even in its violence, the uprising exercised restraint. Sanctioned violence against Israelis consisted largely of attacks on property, not people. Lethal violence was directed internally against collaborators and as part of police functions. While the number of violent incidents may seem large, when spread out over more than two years and weighed against the total activity of the Intifada, they were minimal. Sari Nusseibeh's assessment of the shape of the Intifada seems to reflect the balance: "The voice of violence on the Palestinian side is still peripheral" (1989, 9).

The Intifada's Nonviolent Patterns

The term *intifadah* in Arabic means shaking off or arising, as in getting up in the morning and shaking off sleep (and any bugs that joined you in the night). The use of this term implies that the Palestinians wanted to shake off the Israeli occupation, remove external controls, and take their destiny into their own hands. To this end, one of the first (and lasting) acts of the UNLU was to call a shop owners' strike. Businesses opened and closed on their own schedules rather than at times dictated by the Israelis. The Intifada established a situation, unprecedented in the occupied territories, where people could "enjoy their families and normal interaction of life when they choose to, and tenaciously refuse to permit the occupation to establish their mood" (Strum 1992, 18; cited in Salameh 1994).

The UNLU declared that the primary objectives of the Intifada were to end the occupation and its devastating impact on local communities, live in a Palestinian state alongside Israel, survive without a connection to Israel, and expose the Israeli military policy of dehumanization and oppression. In analyzing the Intifada's nonviolent potential, Dajani (1993, 49) argues that those objectives could have been achieved by operating on three levels of nonviolent strategy: strengthening Palestinian resistance, undermining and polarizing Israel from within, and creating rifts between Israel and the international community.

Motivated by their need for self-determination and improved living conditions, Palestinians initiated a wide range of nonviolent strategies and actions designed to send a clear message to the Israeli, Arab, and international communities (see Calls 18 and 20). For the first two years, these actions dominated the daily lives of most Palestinians. Every day, Palestinians, mostly youths, marched in the streets, burned tires, raised their illegal flag, and chanted slogans decrying the occupation, supporting Palestinian self-determination, and declaring the PLO as their political representative. Pictures of children of all ages chased by Israeli soldiers firing tear gas bombs and rubber bullets were transmitted by the Israeli and international media. These images had a dual impact: They revealed the horrors of the occupation to Israeli society and the international community and, at the same time, they increased solidarity and communal mobilization among the Palestinian community and the Arab world.

This analysis focuses on nonviolent resistance in the Intifada and gives an indication of its extensive, even dominant, presence. Sharp's categorization of nonviolent actions is a useful tool for understanding the scope (although not the force and depth) of nonviolent resistance. Of his 198 categories of nonviolent resistance, 168 are applicable to the Intifada's resistance to occupation (Sharp 1973, vol. 2).[25] Of those, at least 87 strategies were employed in the Intifada,[26] ranging across all of Sharp's major categories.

The Calls issued by the UNLU provide a quick glimpse of the range of nonviolent actions employed. They constituted an official call to action agreed upon by the factions in the UNLU. The leaflets were distributed widely in the occupied territories and constituted the UNLU's primary tool of communication with the Palestinian masses because the underground leadership lacked any access to the public media. The leaflets provide us with the most accessible overview of the direction that the UNLU wished the Intifada to take.

An analysis of leaflets 18 through 39 reveal three major categories of nonviolent actions. Almost 20 percent of them recommended some sort of strike. The next largest percentage asked Palestinians to help support the communities particularly vulnerable to Israeli reprisals by doing things such as visiting the graves and families of those who were killed by the Israeli settlers and troops, giving financial assistance to organizations and groups, visiting prisoners and hospitalized resisters, and helping work the land of those killed, injured, and imprisoned. The third greatest number of directives instructed the people to stage demonstrations and marches; praying and fasting were recommended almost as much (Kishtainy 1990). The UNLU leaflets called for a wide range of other nonviolent actions: replacing Israeli-controlled institutions with indigenous ones; withholding taxes; boycotting Israeli products; displaying the Palestinian flag; refusing to work for Israelis; resigning from offices that supported the occupation; defying Israeli school closures; refusing to cooperate with Israeli officials; holding symbolic funerals; ringing church bells; refusing to pay fines; breaking curfews; ostracizing collaborators; blocking roads into settlements; marching in religious processions; mounting graffiti campaigns; engaging in national mourning; organizing strikes and sit-ins; arranging delegations to meet with Israelis; exposing conditions of the occupation to international media and delegations; and, most important, creating an alternative economic, social, educational, and civic infrastructure to reduce dependence on the existing Israeli systems. These directives were often adopted and implemented in various degrees by the local popular committees that were formed in neighborhoods and local communities.[27] In the leaflets, the UNLU conveyed a message of humanity and justice through its willingness to negotiate with Israel and its assertion that Palestinians did not seek the destruction of Israel. This implicit, and later on explicit, recognition of Israel was a basic principle in the work of the UNLU and represented the view of the majority of the Palestinian community.

Nonviolent actions were not new to the Palestinian community. Many, perhaps most, of these tactics had been used since the beginning of the occupation. But they were used intermittently and only in local, limited protests. For example, Palestinian Muslims successfully applied nonviolent means to defend al-Aqsa Mosque and the Dome of the Rock from Jewish fundamentalist groups. The mosque's leadership employed a nonviolent guard unit, mass demonstrations, and a strategy to mobilize support for a strike to protect these holy sites. These strategies were employed on many occasions after the 1970s (Crow, Grant, and Ibrahim 1990, 54). As mentioned earlier, in the pre-Intifada period there were a series of attempts to move the Palestinian masses to nonviolent resistance. Most notable was the work of the Palestinian Center for the Study of Nonviolence in Jerusalem. Their activities were designed to challenge the actions and policy of the Israeli army and the settlers by replanting trees that had been uprooted, defying certain military rules (such as the division of Hebron into two parts), and supporting Palestinian businesses in Hebron.[28]

This brief analysis gives some idea of the scope of nonviolent actions in the Intifada. But to gain a sense of the pervasiveness and depth of these actions, we need to make a more detailed examination. In this examination, we need to include anecdotal evidence and specific examples in order to gain a better sense of the interrelation of actions and attitudes among the participants and to understand the historical, cultural, and religious roots of nonviolent resistance. The first part of the analysis is organized around Sharp's major categories for nonviolent resistance: economic noncooperation, social noncooperation, protest and persuasion, political noncooperation, symbolic expression of nonviolent resistance, development of alternative institutions, and changes in attitude.

Economic Noncooperation

In the first twenty years of the occupation, the West Bank and Gaza were an economic boom to Israel; they were the largest market for Israeli goods, and the occupation was financed by taxes and licenses paid by the occupied people. Consequently, a key goal of the Intifada was to reverse this situation and make the occupation unprofitable for Israel (Sharp 1973, 2:219–84).[29] One of the earliest testing grounds for the uprising was a general strike by Palestinian merchants.

After a brief but fairly successful total strike by merchants at the beginning of the Intifada, the UNLU decided that a limited strike by merchants would be an effective ongoing tactic. Their call for all merchants to open their shops only from 8 A.M. to noon allowed Palestinians to conduct necessary business while still challenging and protesting Israeli control of the economy. The authorities retaliated by demanding that shops be closed from 8 A.M. to noon and open the rest of the day. They tried to enforce this demand by forcibly opening the shops, frequently destroying merchandise and fixtures. But when the merchants refused to obey, the Israelis capitulated. The 8 A.M. to noon shopping hours became standard in the occupied territories. Shopping hours may seem a minor issue for a key confrontation, but both sides perceived it as a confrontation not about hours but about control. The success of this tactic meant that the Israelis had lost control over the merchants, who preferred to side with the UNLU and the shabab, even at the cost of retaliation by the Israelis and loss of income.

This example illustrates several key elements of nonviolent resistance: the intertwining of the symbolic and the practical; the limited effectiveness of superior force in countering a well-chosen nonviolent tactic; the willingness of nonviolent resisters to bear more suffering than they inflict. The success of the merchants' strike encouraged the UNLU to extend the call for economic noncooperation to a boycott of Israeli goods by both merchants and consumers (where a Palestinian alternative existed) and a policy of austerity. The boycott and the austerity measures had decided effects, although they were not completely successful.

The merchants' strike was an indirect blow to Israeli control over the economy of the occupied territories. A more direct attack was tax resistance. The UNLU called on all Palestinians to refuse to pay any tax or assessment to the Israeli government unless the UNLU granted a waiver (as in the case of licenses for taxi drivers and Palestinian factories). The major taxes avoided were automobile taxes (which the Israelis used as a major source of funding for the occupation), sales taxes, and the value-added tax (VAT). Refusal to register automobiles, to register shifts from private vehicles to public taxis, to renew driver's licenses, and to purchase plates was widespread. Tax resistance was particularly successful in Ramallah, Bethlehem, and Beit Sahur. The case of Beit Sahur is particularly well known and well documented.[30] People avoided sales taxes and the VAT by fostering a barter economy and exchanging goods for services.[31] While news reports focused on demonstrations, deaths, and injuries, Palestinians saw economic noncooperation as the most crucial aspect of the Intifada. At the heart of this effort to make the occupation unprofitable to Israel lay time-tested tactics of nonviolent resistance.

Palestinians exerted economic pressure against Israel by withholding payment of taxes, customs fees, and water bills as well as by interrupting tourism and refusing to provide cheap labor. Boycotting Israeli goods and other items exported to the occupied territories through Israeli companies also cut into any increase in the estimated $5.5 billion profit already realized by the Israeli economy from the occupation. The deployment of so many Israeli military personnel to counter the Intifada added to the cost of the occupation (Crow, Grant, and Ibrahim 1990). The monthly cost of the Intifada to Israel was estimated to be $120 million for security forces and $88 million in indirect economic costs (McDowall 1994, 101).

The strategy of exerting economic pressure on Israel subjected the local communities to tremendous difficulties (Melman and Raviv 1989). New institutions and initiatives had to be launched to address those difficulties. For example, small home-based health clinics and schools had to be created to meet the needs of the communities whose hospitals and schools had been shut down. Alternative labor markets had to be created to compensate for the Israeli closure of its borders and the Palestinian boycott of Israeli markets. These initiatives were a response to the UNLU call for "economic self-sufficiency" (Melman and Raviv 1989, 200).

Social Noncooperation

The Palestinians also practiced social noncooperation (Sharp 1973, 2:183–218), in the form of social boycott, suspension of social and sports events, boycott of social affairs, and stay-at-home actions. The merchants' partial strike grew out of the use of a general strike best described as a "stay-at-home" action (2:199). With the move to a daily merchants' strike, the UNLU did not abandon the general strike but limited their appeal for one to approximately once a week through its Calls. On general strike days, all activity ceased. Factories and shops closed all day, public transportation ceased, people avoided driving, no one dealt with the civil administration. Only doctors were granted immunity from the strike. Everyone else was expected to remain at home or to engage in marches and demonstrations. Just as the merchants' strike was a struggle over control of the economic sector, the general strike was a struggle for control over the social sphere. If Palestinians were willing to forego the needs and rhythms of everyday life once a week or more, then they were both denying Israel control over their activities and affirming their solidarity with the forces of resistance. The sacrifice was actually greater for Palestinians than for Israelis. Strike days significantly disrupted the pattern of their daily lives and cut into their productivity, especially with a labor-intensive economy relying heavily on income from migrant workers. Thus, the general strike emphasized the Palestinians' willingness to embrace economic hardship and social disruption in order to regain control over their lives.

The ill treatment of prisoners was often a major cause and mobilizing force for strikes during and before the Intifada. Hunger strikes were often used by the UNLU, especially by women, who protested at the Red Cross offices in Jerusalem, Bethlehem, and other cities. Prisoners also used hunger strikes in an attempt to improve conditions in the prisons. The hunger strike at Ansar 1, 2, and 3 (containing fifteen thousand Palestinian prisoners among the three Israeli prison camps) against the harsh desert conditions was one of the most influential events in the Intifada. It not only demonstrated solidarity among prisoners across factional lines under extreme duress but also mobilized sympathy protests throughout the occupied territories.

Protest and Persuasion

Marches and demonstrations were often held on strike days. They were methods not so much of social noncooperation as of protest (Sharp 1973, 2:152–68). The Intifada used many tactics of protest not included in any of Sharp's categories. The long list included public speeches; letters of opposition and support; declarations by organizations and institutions; slogans, caricatures, and symbols; banners, posters, and displayed communications; leaflets, pamphlets, and books; newspapers and journals; records, radio, and TV; deputations; fraternization; humorous skits and pranks; performance of plays and music; singing; processions; parades; demonstrative funerals; homage at burial places; assemblies of protest and support; protest meetings; camouflage meetings of protest; and teach-ins.

Of all the protest tactics, marches were the most popular. The marches had varying purposes. Sometimes they were directly confrontational and accompanied by stone throwing. But, although the marchers were always prepared for confrontation, many marches did not have confrontation as their goal. Frequently, marches simply commemorated special events: the death of a national hero, Palestinian Independence Day, the war of 1948, Land Day, or the martyrdom of a local person. These marches and demonstrations instilled and promoted Palestinian identity and signaled solidarity with the Intifada. They were times of celebration and even of liberation because when Palestinians held a two-hour march of six hundred people in one village,[32] they, rather than the Israelis, controlled the village for that period of time. Such periods of liberation could range from an hour to several weeks—and they were always tenuous—but they were still a powerful nonviolent assertion of identity, social solidarity, and control.

Demonstrations were also important tools for political mobilization and protest, and Palestinians had had a long and rich experience in demonstrations since the beginning of the 1967 occupation. However, during the Intifada, the UNLU took a direct role in organizing these protests. For example, Call 8, issued in February 1988, asked women and old men to organize a protest march to Red Cross headquarters and to prison detention camps in every city, village, and refugee camp at least once a week between Monday and Thursday (Lockman and Beinin 1989, 337). The same Call encouraged marches to start from mosques and churches on Fridays and Sundays too.

Political Noncooperation

Especially in the arena of political noncooperation, nonviolent actions predate the Intifada (Sharp 1973, 2:285–356).[33] The basic act of withholding acknowledgment of Israel's right to rule the West Bank and Gaza illustrates an evolving use of nonviolence. Originally, Palestinians and other Arabs refused to acknowledge Israel's right to exist and attempted to challenge Israel militarily through both the armed forces of other Arab countries and guerrilla activities. After 1974, Palestinian willingness to accept the existence of Israel gradually evolved with increasingly clear statements from the PLO. The Intifada created a situation in which the PLO and the Palestinians in the West Bank and Gaza acknowledged Israel's right to exist (in exchange for a Palestinian state in the occupied territories), minimized the use of armed struggle, and emphasized political noncooperation.[34] The shift is marked by a move from formal, external, and violent resistance to Israel to actual, internal, and nonviolent noncooperation in the West Bank and Gaza.

During the early years of the occupation, many Palestinians accepted Israel's de facto rule over the territories by cooperating with the civil administration. Many Palestinians accepted employment in the bureaucracy administering the occupation. The Israeli search for cooperation culminated in their controlled election of mayors in the towns and villages of the occupied territories in 1976. However, the election produced political noncooperation instead of greater Israeli control. PLO-supported candidates won most of the seats and pushed a political agenda of resistance and local control. The Israelis responded by deporting or dismissing the mayors, replacing them with their own appointees and creating the Village Leagues (town councils that offered pro-Israel leadership in place of pro-PLO officials). The decade of 1978–88 was marked by increasing reluctance among Palestinians to cooperate with the civil administration. Then, during the Intifada, the UNLU demanded that all Palestinians withdraw from the Village Leagues and resign their posts in the civil administration, especially in the tax and housing departments. This severance of Palestinians from the occupiers was largely accomplished with the help of social pressure, nonviolent activities directed at the Village Leagues, and the use of threats and intimidation. Political noncooperation included a wide range of acts of civil disobedience in which Palestinians refused to acknowledge the validity of the laws and directives by which Israel governed the territories. People did not just refuse to pay taxes on their cars; they continued to drive them in defiance of the law. They did not just close down their shops; they opened them in defiance of military orders. They did not accept Israel's closure of schools; they tried to carry on education apart from the schools. While they sometimes accepted Israeli-imposed curfews, they usually broke them covertly and sometimes challenged them overtly. This movement from violence to nonviolence in the political sphere, rather than lessening resistance to Israeli control, heightened it and made it more effective.

The Symbolic Expression of Nonviolent Resistance

Economic, social, and political noncooperation are classic examples of nonviolent resistance. Their centrality to the Intifada indicates that non-violence played a crucial role. But to understand the full scope of nonviolence, we need to consider less widely recognized methods as well. The symbolic element may be more important in a resistance movement that relies on nonviolence than it is in a violent revolution (Sharp 1973, 2:135–45). Although Sharp relegates symbolic action to a subcategory of protest and persuasion, it played such a central role in the Intifada that it warrants separate consideration.

Forms of symbolic protest in the Intifada included the display of flags and symbolic colors, the wearing of symbols, prayer and worship, delivering symbolic objects, the destruction of one's own property, the display of portraits, paint as protest, signs and names, symbolic sounds, and rude gestures. And the Intifada was replete with symbols: olive trees, flags, colors, portraits, posters, graffiti, and names. The symbols were omnipresent. A primary activity for the shabab was painting graffiti (Palestinian flags, stenciled pictures, slogans) on every available wall. Israeli soldiers regularly pulled Palestinians out of their houses and ordered them to paint over the graffiti—only to have them reappear the next day. Graffiti was another form of communication, dialogue, and debate for the various factions and organizations involved in the Intifada. They also functioned as a form of direct communication with the UNLU when urgent action was called for, particularly if the newspapers had been closed by the army.

Flying the Palestinian flag or wearing Palestinian colors were offenses punishable by imprisonment, yet every protest march was replete with flags, villages were festooned whenever possible, and women's groups engaged in making enough flags for every occasion. The use of Palestinian colors as protest, however, was more subtle. Since wearing red, black, white, and green was a punishable offense, people wore close substitutes. In Hebron, clothes were decorated with large red, blue, yellow, and green diamonds. The design was particularly popular on young men's sweaters and toddlers' pajamas. In Jerusalem, because this open display of colors could lead to harassment or arrest, young men wore bracelets of the colors under their shirtsleeves. This use of color was quiet, indirect, and individualistic, a type of action frequently not regarded as significant resistance, but for the wearers it was an act of defiance signaling their dedication to the cause and placing them in considerable danger from the authorities.

The nonuse of firearms was another symbol of nonviolent resistance. Early in the Intifada, the national leader of the Israeli-sponsored Village

Leagues was forced to resign by his fellow villagers. When he surrendered the Israeli-supplied guns that he had used to maintain control, the villagers disabled them and left them for the Israelis to pick up. In the village of Beita, when an Israeli settler began to shoot at a crowd of Palestinians (and succeeded in hitting an Israeli hiker he was supposedly protecting), villagers wrested the gun from him and disabled it rather than use it (Collins 1988; J. Kuttab 1988b).[35] While these incidents were limited and there were many cases when a weapon taken from a soldier was kept and used, one impulse with strong nonviolent symbolism in even the most stressful situations in the Intifada was to disable weapons.

The Development of Alternative Institutions through Popular Committees

Of all the forms of nonviolent resistance used in the Intifada, the most important was the development of alternative institutions. While Sharp recognizes this type of activity, he treats it only as a subcategory of nonviolent intervention (Sharp 1973, 2:357–445).[36] But Scott's definition of resistance (1985, 290) again reveals the significance of these tactics. They did not involve direct confrontation with the authorities, but concentrated on increasing the control that Palestinians had over their own lives. They were the very center of the Intifada. They combined elements of economic, social, political, and symbolic resistance and created a positive framework for all resistance activity. The Intifada was not just opposition to Israeli control or the denial of Israel's right to control. It was the creation of an alternative to that control. The UNLU had an all-encompassing vision of alternative systems. They envisioned the decision-making apparatus of each locality being invested in popular committees that were subdivided to cover the daily needs of the people: medical relief, food distribution, strike forces, agriculture, merchants, public safety, education, information, and solidarity with the families of martyrs and prisoners. When these popular committees were combined with sectoral committees (women, students, labor, teachers) and were represented by different factions in the PLO, Palestinian society had an alternative decision-making apparatus that was broadly based and provided a voice for a spectrum of constituencies. Consequently, the Intifada developed a structure that allowed Palestinians to bypass Israeli authorities and its own traditional hierarchy (much of which the Israelis had co-opted). Local popular committees were a key reflection of coordination and solidarity among factions in the Palestinian community. They operated on all levels and were particularly targeted by the Israeli authorities for their efficiency and strength in organizing the community. Their work was a major reflection of nonviolent efforts to sustain the constant mobilization of local communities.

But the creation of a decision-making network was only a beginning. That network was responsible for developing and administering attempts to create alternative health, education, economic, judicial, and agricultural institutions. For example, when Israel closed the schools in the West Bank, education committees attempted to carry on popular education through the Palestinian Council for Higher Education, an organization established in 1990 that had close ties to both the UNLU and the PLO. In leaflet 6, published in February 1988, the UNLU called on teachers to organize for home schooling to compensate for the closure of the schools. The UNLU "called for an educational operation on a national basis" (Lockman and Beinin 1989, 333). A Palestinian student testified to spending "three years taking classes in students' houses, where every session was held in a different house in order to avoid the military arrest" (Salameh 1994, 27). While this attempt was initially successful on all levels of schooling, an Israeli crackdown on alternative schools made popular education at the primary and secondary levels sporadic and university education difficult. But by that time, the Intifada had managed to shift the focus in government schools away from highly censored Jordanian material to a more relevant, popular, and action-oriented education.[37]

Because of Israeli control over government hospitals,[38] Palestinians were reluctant to use them and had begun creating their own multilevel medical system even before the Intifada. The first level consisted of traditional hospitals built and run by charitable institutions. While several of these hospitals, such as al-Muqassed in Jerusalem, had been operating for many years, Palestinians saw a need to build a more complete alternative hospital system. A second level was accordingly created: village clinics that provided basic emergency aid and preventive health care. A third level consisted of popular medical committees that provided mobile health clinics to villages that could not afford their own and engaged in basic health education and training. When the Intifada began, the work of the popular committees expanded to provide emergency assistance to wounded Palestinians. The role of the committees was encouraged and strengthened by the UNLU in a leaflet that stated, "To the sectors of doctors and health services; we call upon you to always be ready and to immediately join the medical committees which organize campaigns of medical aid to camps and besieged areas" (Lockman and Beinin 1989, 332). The Intifada necessitated yet a fourth level: neighborhood medical committees that would work with the hospitals and popular medical committees to train local people to give emergency aid to those wounded in the fighting. Thus, Palestinian society moved not only toward the creation of a separate hospital system but also to an alternative model of broadly based and popularly controlled medical care that incorporated and empowered nonprofessionals.

Probably the most difficult task that faced the Intifada was the creation of an alternative economy. In fact, because of the lack of economic development and Israeli control over imports and exports and the licensing of new industries, the task was impossible. So Palestinians decided to increase their economic self-sufficiency by patronizing their own products, developing an indigenous agriculture and industry, and practicing austerity. The UNLU's tactics illustrated the flexibility and pragmatism of the Intifada. Since an absolute boycott of Israeli goods was impossible, they called for people to purchase Palestinian goods where possible, under the guidance of the local committees. For example, the UNLU called for the purchase of Palestinian cigarettes instead of the more favored American and Israeli brands. Since Palestinian cigarettes were taxed by Israel, even their purchase was a compromise that contradicted tax resistance. But the jobs and money that the cigarette industry provided the economy, the acknowledgment that Palestinians would smoke in any event, and the decision therefore to take small, achievable steps outweighed any idealistic tendencies toward total boycott.

Agricultural self-sufficiency was a more fully developed goal. After Israel occupied the West Bank and Gaza in 1967, young men began to seek wage work in Israel. Palestinian agriculture therefore started into a sharp decline. With the Intifada, that decline was reversed, at least temporarily. Agricultural committees were encouraged and praised in leaflet 6 (April 14, 1988), which stated: "We appreciate the role of our people, our agriculture and popular committees and area committees, for their response to the call of participating in planting at home and plots through agricultural cooperatives. We call all of our committees and people to expand and enrich agriculture and cooperatives until they encompass all areas in our beloved land" (Lockman and Beinin 1989, 348).

These cooperatives, which were particularly successful in villages around Nablus and Bethlehem, allowed for better distribution and sale of locally produced food. In the villages, families planted more vegetables, olive and almond trees, and raised more livestock. In towns and cities, the committees taught Palestinians various techniques for gardening and raising chickens on small urban lots.

This attempt to create agricultural self-sufficiency could have potentially far-reaching effects on Palestinian society. It demands that Palestinians change, not just their diets but also their attitudes toward food; it necessitates a change in work patterns in order to combine "normal" work (professional and wage labor, etc.) with labor-intensive food production; and it tends to strengthen ties with the land, the family, and the community.[39] Israeli peace activists who visited Palestinian villages to express their solidarity with them were given tours of the agricultural accomplishment in each site. The development of alternative agriculture also challenged traditional hierarchical values associated with land ownership and production in Palestinian society by creating a new decision-making apparatus, the agricultural popular committee, stressing cooperative agriculture and sharing of resources. The Israelis acknowledged the seriousness of the agricultural challenge by outlawing the agricultural committees and arresting and imprisoning leaders.

The creation of an alternative system of justice began in the pre-Intifada period, but it accelerated when the Intifada began. Palestinian lawyers had periodically boycotted Israeli civil and military courts because of the futility of defending Palestinians against charges and the legitimacy that participation in the judicial process bestowed on the occupation. Although Israeli civil rights lawyers continued to handle complaints for Palestinians, many Palestinians refused to have a lawyer or to appeal convictions handed down by the court. But until the beginning of the Intifada, Israel successfully managed law enforcement in the occupied territories through Palestinian police. However, in the early months of the Intifada, the UNLU called for the resignation of all Palestinian police. Numerous immediate resignations, followed by social pressure that forced more, eliminated them as an effective force. This absence resulted in nearly total noncooperation with the Israeli system of justice. In many areas, popular committees took over both civil and criminal court functions. The UNLU called for disputes to be settled within families if at all possible. If families could not resolve a dispute, then a local committee arbitrated it. Criminals, when discovered, were confronted with their crime and given the opportunity to repent and make restoration. If they refused or continued their criminal activity, then they were punished by local committees.[40] Sometimes the punishment was nonviolent, such as social ostracism; other times it involved beatings or even death.[41]

The creation of alternative social and economic structures is rarely recognized as nonviolent resistance. Yet they are crucial to a nonviolent strategy seeking revolutionary change, such as Gandhi's independence movement or the Intifada.[42] To some observers and activists, the Palestinians' ability to continue the uprising depended on the successful creation of these alternative structures as support systems for confrontational activity (Nusseibeh 1988; Sayigh 1989; Abu-Amr 1989; Khalidi 1988, 513). Furthermore, these structures indicated the depth and scope of the nonviolent alternative in Palestinian resistance. Because they were a focus for positive and creative expressions of energy, they provided an outlet for the rage and frustration caused by the ever-increasing casualty figures and the continued lack of movement toward settling the Israeli-Palestinian conflict. Consequently, they not only sustained the Intifada in practical ways but provided psychological support for the continuance and enlargement of its nonviolent aspects.

Changes in Attitude

But nonviolent tactics do not necessarily make a movement nonviolent. When a movement is a mix of violence and nonviolence, the balance and interaction between the two is crucial, as are the attitudes conducive toward or indicative of nonviolence. If these attitudes are present, they indicate a basis for nonviolent resistance that extends beyond mere tactical necessity. While the Intifada reflected massive anger and resentment toward Israelis and others who cooperated in the occupation, it also demonstrated attitudes that are consonant with, even central to, nonviolence.

The willingness to bear more suffering than your opponent without retaliating in kind was a central feature of the Intifada. While that has frequently been treated as a tactic necessitated by the imbalance of power, it entailed much more. People who have engaged in nonviolent resistance know that it takes more than mere willpower to refrain from retaliation; restraint is sustained by certain attitudes toward opponents and toward the resister's own cause. To maintain restraint over the lengthy period of the Intifada points to the presence of more than necessity and willpower. One crucial feature is the attitude that resisters take toward their enemy. Although it is based on limited interviews, the frequent expression of their lack of hatred for Israelis was striking.[43] The rejection of hatred was expressed in many ways: "We do not hate the Israelis; we simply want our land"; or "We refuse to hate them; it robs us of our humanity; we will not become like them"; or "At the funeral of my nephew [killed by soldiers], there was one soldier weeping; that is why we do not hate them." These brief statements alone reveal a variety of reasons for this attitude: political practicality, self-interest, moral principle, recognition of compassion in the enemy. Rejection of hatred carries over into more positive attitudes as well: Palestinians consistently spoke of Israelis as opponents worthy of respect rather than as dehumanized others.[44] These attitudes are necessary but not sufficient components of nonviolent resistance. They set resisters on the road to nonviolence by restraining violence, encouraging positive action toward the oppressor, and enhancing the prospects for negotiation and compromise. If the oppressor recognizes these attitudes in the oppressed, the sense of threat is reduced and the willingness to resolve the conflict is increased.

The Intifada also helped Palestinians break out of a zero-sum mentality in which they considered any gain for the opponent to be a loss. They came to recognize that both sides can gain from a recognition of Israel's right to exist in exchange for independence. In the Gandhian ideal of *satyagraha* (the force, born of truth and love or nonviolence, employed to bring social and political change), one side recognizes that both parties to a conflict hold partial truths. The struggle involves clinging to one's own truth, discarding error, accepting the truth in the opponent's stance, and reaching a mutually beneficial solution. Few Palestinians embraced this ideal process. They did not find "truth" in Israel's existence, but they recognized its reality and the need to adjust to that reality. While such compromise did not achieve the triumph over resentment that the Gandhian search for truth seeks (Juergensmeyer 1986, 3–66), Palestinians achieved a measure of peace with themselves and a willingness to be at peace with their opponents in accepting what they regarded as a less than just solution. This was no small concession. It recognized the need to concede over half the land that they regarded as their own to their opponent, to see that solution as beneficial to both sides, and to accept their opponent's gain at their expense. This willingness to see a solution to a conflict as a win-win situation is a second essential attitude for nonviolence (Fisher and Ury 1981). It reduces the need to resort to violence by diminishing the threat to the opponent and offering a basis for nonviolent resolution of the conflict.

The willingness of Palestinians to cooperate with and accept the help of Israeli peace groups grew out of these attitudes and took them a step further. The cooperation and respect that Palestinians exhibited for Israeli peace activists was a concrete indication that they did not view them as monolithic opponents. Cooperation indicated that Palestinians recognized a mutuality of interests between the two sides, a mutuality that could transcend the barriers of resentment and alienation created by the occupation.[45]

While not all attitudes in the Intifada were consonant with nonviolence, key ingredients were present: acceptance of suffering, lack of hatred, respect for the enemy's integrity, avoidance of dehumanization, rejection of the zero-sum game, and acceptance of contact and cooperation with the opponent. While some of these ingredients, such as transcending the zero-sum game, were attitudes that defined the Intifada, others were held less universally. Nevertheless, these attitudes underlay the actions and goals of the Intifada and made its nonviolent tactics more than mere tactics. They were in part expressions of how Palestinians regarded the nature of their struggle.

Culture and Religion in the Intifada

The Palestinian Intifada was primarily a struggle for national identity. Its leadership included both Muslims and Christians, both observant and nonobservant. The leaders were motivated by a desire to end the Israeli occupation. The UNLU deliberately avoided religious affiliation and terminology and used a national narrative to unify the entire community under its leadership. Thus, the Intifada was a nationally motivated movement in which religious affiliations were subordinated, even pushed aside, by its secular leaders.

Nevertheless, it is impossible to argue that these leaders and their followers could escape or isolate the impact of Arab and Muslim culture in their language, values, and actions. There are at least two avenues in which cultural and religious values assisted or lent themselves to the nonviolent campaign. First, certain cultural norms, values, and symbols were prevalent in the UNLU Calls and in the call for implementing those nonviolent initiatives. Political justification is not sufficient for local communities to engage in such activities. Cultural, social, and religious explanations had to be found.

In fact, Mubarak Awad, a Palestinian leader of nonviolent campaigns carried out before and during the Intifada, said that during his work in Palestine, his center (the Center for the Study of Nonviolence) in Jerusalem translated into Arabic a book on the life of Abdul Ghaffar Khan (the Muslim leader from Pashtun who led an Islamic nonviolence movement during the 1930s against British colonialism). "We used to distribute the book free in the Palestinian villages to mobilize people and illustrate that the concept of nonviolence is not strange to Islam."[46] This statement illustrates an attempt by Palestinian activists to directly link Islamic religious values and the Intifada's various nonviolent actions. Second, the popular masses who carried out the nonviolent actions utilized their values, norms, and beliefs in explaining and applying such tactics.

Nonetheless, this discussion is not an attempt to prove that the Intifada was an intentional and direct Islamic nonviolent movement, nor that its nonviolent strategies were designed around Islamic values. Such characterization cannot be true due to the nationalist and cross-sectarian structure of the leadership of the Intifada. Rather, the limited objective of this discussion is to identify the features in Palestinian society that allowed the emergence and application of the nonviolence movement, and to discuss the linkage of such features to Arab and Muslim values, norms, and beliefs.

A consideration of the role of religion in the Intifada can be explored through the impact of Islamic organizations, the role of Islam among the broader population, and the response of the leadership. This can proceed with a traditional sense of defining religion as a set of beliefs, symbols, rituals, and attitudes toward a divine reality and its effects on human reality. But the final inquiry moves beyond that realm and addresses the function of religion as a creator and sustainer of social structures and modes of human interaction. Since Islam regards itself as a religion that encompasses all areas of human existence and seeks to establish a social context and complex of human relationships, this broader definition will guide the inquiry. To be more specific, the Intifada occurred in an "Islamicate" society; that is, a society "in which the Muslims and their faith are recognized as prevalent and socially dominant" and in which "non-Muslims have always formed an integral, if subordinate, element" (Hodgson 1974, 57–60). The complex of social relations and the shape of the culture in an Islamicate society is deeply imprinted by Islam, whether the specifically religious dimension of Islam has a direct impact or not. Thus, even the 15 to 20 percent of Palestinians who are not Muslims are part of this Islamicate society and embedded in its social and cultural nexus. We will need to consider what effect this has on violence and nonviolence in the Intifada.

Hamas and Islamic Jihad

As a result of the Iranian revolution and the rise of Hizbullah and other militant Islamic groups in Lebanon, scholars and the media, when addressing the impact of Islam on political situations, have concentrated on movements they describe as fundamentalist, revivalist, or Islamist. Consequently, when the role of Islam in the Intifada is discussed, whether in a brief reference or an extended treatment, the focus is on the two leading militant groups: *al-jihad al-islamiyah,* or Islamic Jihad; and Hamas, the Arabic acronym for *harakat al-muqawamah al- islamiyah,* or Islamic Resistance Movement (see esp. al-Ghazali 1987; Shadid 1988; Taraki 1989; Wright 1988). While the attention is fully warranted (and more is needed), limiting discussion to these movements obscures the larger role that Islam played in the Intifada. This narrow focus particularly affects how we view the relation of Islam to violent and nonviolent aspects of the resistance. While a full treatment of this topic is outside the scope of this study, sketching out some of the ways in which Islam functioned in the uprising may further the discussion of nonviolence and raise issues for future consideration.

Since Hamas and Islamic Jihad are the two Islamic organizations that were directly involved in the Intifada, we will begin by examining their role in relation to violence and nonviolence. But since the committed followers of these groups were estimated at fewer than 10 percent of the Palestinian population, focusing on them alone will miss the functioning of Islam in the life of most Palestinians. Mohammed Shadid's study of Palestinian religious attitudes concludes that 49 percent of Palestinians are "strongly religious," and another 20 percent are "moderately religious" (1988, 662–64, 681–82).[47] While Shadid concludes that this 70 percent of Palestinian Muslims are susceptible to the message of the Islamic movements, we also need to turn the question around. If so many religious Palestinians were *not* involved in Hamas or Islamic Jihad, then what role did Islam play for them as they worked in the Intifada? How and to what degree did the leadership of the Intifada respond to the religious dimensions of Palestinian society in its language and actions? The broader societal effects of Islam also need to be considered. Palestinian culture is embedded in and grows out of an Islamic milieu. How did that affect violence and nonviolence in the uprising? What religious and cultural values were expressed in the Intifada's nonviolent strategies and actions?

If we are to judge the contribution of Islam to the Intifada solely by the role played by Hamas and Islamic Jihad, then we must conclude that Islam contributed to heightening the violence. Islamic Jihad was regarded as central to the beginning of the Intifada. Several actions by that group in the Gaza Strip—actions that resulted in the deaths of several Israelis and Palestinians between October and December 1987—spurred Israeli violence, Palestinian counterdemonstrations, and the subsequent escalation of repression by the military (Taraki 1989a, 32; Wright 1988, 25). Islamic Jihad also claimed credit for forcing an Israeli bus off the road on July 6, 1989, resulting in the deaths of seventeen Israelis. Although Islamic Jihad worked in conjunction with the UNLU, it consistently advocated more violence and less compromise with Israel than other groups represented in the leadership. Hamas stood further apart from the unified Palestinian position on the Intifada; it called separate strike days and enforced them with violence and threats of violence; it advocated more violence against Israelis than did the UNLU; it rejected any compromise with Israel and continued to call for its destruction. The ethos of Hamas is both triumphalist and exclusivist: God will give victory over Israel when Palestinian Muslims return to true Islam; Islam is the only true way for the salvation of humanity. Although there was talk of closer cooperation between Hamas and the UNLU, Hamas frequently contributed to internal discord among Palestinians, since "Godless communism" among Palestinians is considered a greater threat than Israel.[48] Consequently, both Hamas and the Islamic Jihad, in both their attitudes and their actions, reinforced the presence of violence in the Intifada; and, although they planned and participated in many nonviolent actions, they tended to undercut the nonviolent tone of the uprising. Before the rise to prominence of the Islamic Jihad in the 1980s and the formation of Hamas early in the Intifada, the Muslim Brotherhood (of which Hamas is an offshoot) opposed *any* resistance to the occupation. They argued that religious purity was necessary in order to overcome oppression and must precede any action against the oppressors. The brotherhood opposed resistance so strongly that they violently attacked members of the resistance movements.

But we should also note that both these Islamic groups (Jihad and Hamas) used many of the uprising's nonviolent techniques to recruit and mobilize their supporters. As indicated earlier, the Islamic Jihad was represented in the UNLU during its first year.[49] However, both groups expanded their political resistance to include attacking Israeli military and civilian targets and even using suicide bombs. For these and other reasons, a political rift developed between the UNLU and those two groups after 1989. In short, the overall impact of the organized Islamic groups was to undercut nonviolent resistance either by opposing all resistance, by fostering dissension among Palestinians, by accenting violence, or by resisting any compromise with Israel.

Islam and Nonviolence in the Intifada

The structures, rituals, customs, and attitudes associated with Islam, however, affected the Intifada in other ways. Most obviously, mosques provided actual and symbolic focal points for the uprising. Although some mosques were linked to Hamas and Islamic Jihad, the role of the mosque extended far beyond these organizations. As the only natural community gathering places in most Muslim villages and towns, many mosques became organizing and teaching centers. Although preachers had to be circumspect about their language in Friday sermons, many of them overtly or covertly exhorted worshipers to participate in the resistance. Frequently, marches and demonstrations began at mosques, especially on Fridays after the noontime communal prayers. As the most visible and important structure in a town or village, the mosque was also a center for graffiti. The shabab linked the mosque to national aspirations by covering walls and minarets with Palestinian flags and slogans of the uprising. The mosque was also a communication link during demonstrations. Sometimes leaders used mosque loudspeakers to direct demonstrators or to exhort and encourage them in their efforts. The use of mosque loudspeakers could also be a point of contention among Palestinians. After one demonstration in Tequa (March 1989) in which the loudspeakers were used to call out religious exhortations, a lively argument ensued over whether that was proper. While most of those present felt that it was, others felt that the mosque should be used only to announce the death of a martyr in the demonstration. The Israelis helped focus attention on the mosques—and radicalize religious Palestinians—by surrounding them with soldiers during prayers and frequently attacking worshipers with tear gas and bullets. As one older Palestinian lamented, "We are forced to pray with guns to our heads."[50] The degree to which the mosque contributed to violence or nonviolence in the Intifada is moot. That it contributed to the presence of Islam in the uprising is unquestionable.

The mosque was also used as a symbol of religious unity. The UNLU leaflets referred regularly to "mosque and church" to indicate their desire for this unity, and it was enacted on numerous occasions. One striking example was the Rishon Lezion massacre in 1990, in which an off-duty Israeli soldier lined up a group of Palestinians waiting for day work in Israel and shot them with his automatic weapon, killing seventeen. The UNLU called for fasts in response. In Beit Sahur there was a day-long fast in the mosque called by both the mosque's imam and the priest of the Greek Orthodox church in the village. All day long, the imam sat on the left side of the *mihrab* (prayer niche) and the priest sat on the right, with a circle of Orthodox seminarians and Muslim religious students in front of them. The group spent the day in prayer, silence, and quiet discussion of the Intifada, with a large group of villagers, media, and other observers standing quietly behind them. At the end of the day, the imam, the priest, and the students rose and marched to the Orthodox church to break the fast. The religious tone of the day and the concluding march were decidedly different from the secular rallies and marches that occurred more frequently in the Intifada.

This broader influence of Islam on the Intifada, centering on the role of the mosque, the effect of ritual practices, and the promotion of traditional values and modes of interaction, is not directly linked to nonviolent resistance, but it created an atmosphere in which Palestinians could see and react to more than occupation, repression, violence, and anger. It therefore helped preserve a sense of perspective, kept them from responding to provocations with violence, and helped the Intifada create the psychological and spiritual balance it needed to sustain nonviolent resistance.

Islam influenced the Intifada in less visible forms than the mosque. Many Palestinian Muslims stated that their faith and practice gave them the strength to face the rigors of the uprising and a foundation for their attitudes of reconciliation toward Israel (also see Bjorkman 1988). As one woman said, "Anyone who had circumstances like ours and did not have faith would go crazy or become a communist." She was a supporter of Hamas, but her emphasis on her faith reflects that of other, more traditional Muslims. This sustaining faith might simply steel people for the struggle and make no clear contribution to nonviolence. But for some Palestinians, the two were linked. Several people spoke of the ability of ritual actions such as prayer and reciting the names of God to calm them and center them on a higher reality than the Intifada. The centering, the inner peace, and the relativizing perspective on the struggle were all enabling attitudes for the preservation and promotion of nonviolence.[51]

Other Palestinians regarded the fast of Ramadan as important in building and sustaining the ethos of sacrifice and sharing resources that characterized the Intifada. During the month of Ramadan, Muslims fast from sunrise to sunset, and the rich are expected to share their good fortune with the poor. Some Palestinians viewed the sacrifices required in the Intifada as an extension of Ramadan. That attitude allowed them to link the uprising to an obligatory religious ritual. Consequently, the values of sacrifice and sharing acquired a logic and authenticity rooted in the community, rather than being innovations for a revolutionary situation.

The story of the soldier in Hebron who was protected by the Arab family also indicates ways in which Islam, as a bearer of social customs and values, provided an anchor for nonviolence for some Palestinians: "Religion and custom enable us to preserve our humanity." The story, and the explanation that framed it, indicate that values such as hospitality, generosity, and protection were operative in the Intifada and that they worked to preserve humanity in the face of oppression. The story's narrator, Ahmad, added in explanation, "If you come to my house, I will open the door for you and invite you in and offer you what our house has to offer—regardless of who you are. When we drink tea together, we become brothers. I cannot hurt you then or later. I cannot even think about hurting you. I must protect you, and I will." These attitudes called on Palestinians to regard the enemy as fellow human beings, or at least encouraged them to treat enemies as worthy of such regard. This attitude goes beyond merely refraining from violence; it calls on them to protect an enemy who has requested hospitality from violence from others. The demand is not conditioned by an enemy's actions or attitudes. It is a self-imposed obligation rooted in communal values. This particular discussion occurred only within a single family circle, but the Intifada produced other examples of Palestinians protecting Israelis from violence. In the village of Beita, when young Israeli hikers were attacked by demonstrators, Palestinian women protected the hikers, pulling some of them inside their homes. The values of hospitality and generosity also underlay some of the frustration and anger of the Palestinians. Soldiers forcing their way into homes and breaking, destroying, soiling, and robbing (a common occurrence) would be deeply upsetting and offensive to anyone. But many Palestinians said that they were angry not just at the violation of their homes but also at the violation of their values of hospitality and generosity. "If they had only asked, I would have let them have my furniture," was a frequent refrain. That attitude carried over into the larger issue of coexistence on the land. More than one person said, "We are a generous people. If the Israelis would only acknowledge that they do not have the right to take our land, then we can be generous." Thus, Islam and the customs that have grown within its orbit provide operative values that reinforce nonviolence toward enemies.

Ahmad pointed to the emphasis on family, a characteristic of Islamic societies, as a source for sustaining their humanity. "Our families are our neighbors. We visit each other every day. Even the Intifada does not stop that. We never forget that we care for each other and that we are required to behave well toward each other. Other people might forget all but anger and killing and shooting. But the visiting keeps us from doing that; we think about our family, we share stories, we play with our nephews and nieces." These everyday rites acted as a counterpoint and balance to the violence and anger of the uprising. The round of evening visits, with their mixture of discussing the day's events, politics, religion, and family affairs in a warm, enthusiastic, frequently jocular setting, provided a striking contrast to the tension and violence of the day.

The UNLU, although largely a secular nationalist leadership, linked the Intifada to Islam in its leaflets. These leaflets frequently used Islamic symbols, such as "the people of al-Qassim." This reference to Shaykh Izz-ad-Din al-Qassim, who organized an armed rebellion in Palestine in 1935 that led to the uprising of 1936–39, called forth an image of Islam engaged in revolution.[52] But the language of the Calls was not narrowly sectarian. They sought symbols that were balanced, such as references to both mosque and church, or multivalent, such as shahid.

In the Intifada, the shahid (witness or martyr) became a central symbol that was deeply rooted in Islam but open to a variety of understandings. Most Palestinians, religious and nonreligious, applied the term *shahid* (pl., *shuhad'a*) to those killed in the uprising. The UNLU leaflets referred to them repeatedly; their pictures were prominently displayed and their names chanted in parades; rituals of visitation to and remembrance for their homes and graves became a regular activity. Their families displayed pictures of them in their sitting rooms and frequently gave photographs or posters of them to visitors. The UNLU designated special days for visiting the families and graves; foreign visitors were taken to the homes of the shahid; and, if necessary, their families received financial support from the community.

But the use of this central religious symbol in the Intifada was complex, with Palestinians holding quite distinct attitudes about the religious significance of the shahid. Some, particularly those inclined to support the Islamic organizations, held the traditional view of martyrdom:[53] The shahid died in the cause of religion and now is in heaven; the family should be sustained by this knowledge. In this view, only true Muslims can be *shahid*, reinforcing the exclusivity of their ideology. But other religiously inclined Palestinians were less sure about the nature of the martyrdom. For Ahmad, his family, and friends, a shahid was a martyr and witness to the Palestinian struggle; whether the shahid went to heaven was "a matter for God to decide." Leaving the decision to God is also a time-honored Muslim attitude. There are questions that lie beyond human ability to answer, and we should not presume to know the answers. This attitude has the very practical effect of religious tolerance and political flexibility. It does not presume to judge the credentials of secular and Christian Palestinians who died in the struggle. It allows religious Muslims to honor them equally and provides a religious sanction for Palestinian unity in the uprising. Palestinians with a more secular orientation also used the term *shahid,* but, while recognizing the religious roots and religious power of the term, they rejected any religious connotations. For them, the shahid was a human witness whose reward was to die for the people and, in death, to continue to inspire their struggle.[54] The use of the shahid as a symbol in the Intifada signaled a turn from violence to nonviolence. Before the Intifada, a primary symbol in the occupation was the armed guerrilla. Now, in place of this symbol of heroic armed aggression stood a symbol of innocent suffering.[55] Thus the symbol of the shahid demonstrates how a religious symbol can play an important unifying role in an uprising. Most people agree on the importance of the symbol and accept some differences in the interpretation of its religious significance.

In this way, the UNLU related Islam to the need for religious cooperation. The language of the leaflets was carefully balanced, referring to mosques and churches, Muslim and Christian holy places, and Muslim and Christian religious festivals. This attitude, which differentiated the UNLU and the majority of the participants in the Intifada from the Islamic organizations, stemmed from a tradition of religious cooperation. Not only did Muslims and Christians work together in the resistance, but most Muslims accepted their Christian brethren as equal participants in the struggle and in the community. While some Palestinian Muslims were willing to talk and argue at great length about the superiority of Islam to Christianity, they would also state that their religious differences created no barriers between them and Christian Palestinians and took the Qura'nic verse "There is no compulsion in religion" (2:256) as their guide in interreligious relations. For them, Palestinian nationalism neither excluded non-Muslims nor suppressed religious differences, but embraced religious as well as political pluralism. They extended this openness to Jews as well by expressing their respect for Judaism as a religion and way of life and their willingness to share holy places sacred to both religions.[56] Their attitude of openness was backed by actions such as cooperating with Israeli peace groups and welcoming sympathetic American Jews into their homes. Islam was a force for tolerance, pluralism, and reconciliation in the Intifada as well as a force for division and enmity. Both the UNLU and many Palestinian Muslims looked to Islam to enhance cooperation and openness in the Intifada and thus support nonviolent aspects of the resistance.

The structure of Islamicate society also affected the Intifada by guiding both the nature of its leadership and the development of alternative structures. The collective leadership was one of the most striking and successful features of the Intifada. Not only did the different organizations within the PLO collaborate in the UNLU, but leadership responsibilities were also shared with popular committees at the local level. Even at the local level, the popular committees depended on various sectoral committees both for carrying out the basic functions of the uprising and for assessing the needs and desires of their constituency in order to develop a community consensus. The ability of the UNLU to reconstitute itself after arrests and detentions without missing the publication of a single leaflet and their ability to distribute these leaflets throughout the occupied territories despite the security net demonstrated its depth, flexibility, and inventiveness. But most important for a resistance that relies largely upon nonviolence, it maintained discipline and restraint in the absence of a visible charismatic leader. While in some ways analysis of the civil rights and Indian independence movements has generally overvalued the role of King and Gandhi, these two leaders were certainly instrumental in controlling the drift toward violence and sustaining the creative nonviolence of their respective movements. But the Intifada, restricted by circumstance to an underground leadership and involving a far larger percentage of the population than either of those two movements, maintained its discipline and limited the degree of violence under even harsher conditions of repression.

The ability of the Intifada to function successfully with this leadership is tied up with its Islamicate context. Although both historical and contemporary societies in the Islamic world have been characterized by autocratic political leadership and economic hierarchy, they have also been characterized by processes of consensus in local and family leadership and in dispute settlement. Islam even has a (largely theoretical) consensus process for choosing leaders and exercising leadership—Shurah, or consultative assembly (see discussion in chapter 2). Sunni Islam, of which Palestinian Muslims are a part, is, in theory (and sometimes in practice), egalitarian. Its religious leaders, the 'Ulama, are not accorded any significant degree of authority. Even the authoritarian political leadership, which is the norm in the Muslim world, is usually accepted because of its power, not because people regard it as legitimate. Their submission to political hierarchy does not mean that they grant it religious legitimacy. Instead, Muslims look for guidance to those family members and local figures who are worthy and devout. The leadership of the Intifada can be seen as an extension and development of this popular tendency in Islamic societies to work through consensus. Such processes were evident in many of the gatherings that we observed in the occupied territories. In many discussions, statements about the Intifada were not frequently made as an individual opinion, but a speaker would look to the group for modification, disagreement, assent, and finally affirmation. The process was easy and comfortable, based on common experience. It was not an overnight innovation.[57] The consensus process that characterized the leadership and the daily operation of the uprising required the trust, give and take, flexibility, and sharing of responsibility associated with nonviolent resistance. Palestinian society, through its family and communal structures developed in the context of Islam, had modified leadership modes inherent in these structures to provide a flexible, deep, and creative leadership for the Intifada that was a key to its discipline and restraint. Under severe duress, Palestinian leadership turned not to charisma, but to communality rooted in their social structure.

The Intifada's attempt to develop self-sufficiency produced a complex interaction with the traditional values and structures of Palestinian society, some of which are specifically religious, all of which were involved in its Islamicate context. One trend that illustrates this interaction was the return to cultivating the land. On a visit to Tequa, a village outside Bethlehem, Dawud, a young college-educated professional, took visitors on a tour of the newly planted gardens and groves that dotted the landscape, told them of the new pastureland that his father had purchased for him as a wedding gift, and showed off the chickens, sheep, and goats that his family were raising. With these new developments in the Intifada, he was expected both to continue his white-collar job in Bethlehem and to participate in the care and tending of the livestock and the garden. While he was acutely aware of the strains that his life in two worlds entailed, he regarded the reincorporation of traditional life as positive: "It strengthens our society and returns us to our roots." The emphasis on the cultivation of the land was accompanied by a renewal of interest in Islam in Tequa. However, religious revival in the village did not mean turning to Hamas or the Islamic Jihad, but renewing the more traditional Islam of Dawud's parents, accompanied by a greater politicization and the strengthening of family and community ties needed for cooperative endeavors. While Dawud was not a practicing Muslim, he applauded Islam's role in the uprising because of the greater family and village solidarity that it fostered.[58]

But the structures and relations that pertained in the Intifada were not strictly the old traditional ones. They involved the transformation of traditional forms or the interaction of the traditional and the new. In particular, Palestinians did not return to the old models of authority in which large landowners and the wealthy few dominated all decision making.

Their dominance had already been undercut by the rapid proletarianization of Palestinian society under the occupation. Rather than a return to the older hierarchical models, the Intifada saw the development of cooperative models of authority, with the popular and sectoral committees dominating decision making in food production and distribution, dispute settlement, security, support for the needy, price regulation, education, and most other areas of community concern. But the committees worked from the structures of family and neighborhood, building upon traditional forms and relationships at the same time that they altered them.

Self-reliance and its necessary counterpart, austerity, affected some religious rituals directly. The fast of the month of Ramadan and the feasts of the Muslim religious calendar are usually times of family and community festivity as much as they are times of religious observance. In the Intifada, the UNLU and the local committees called on Palestinians to observe religious holidays as times of austerity, not lavish celebrations, and to be particularly aware of the dedication and austerity that the Intifada required. Thus, while the UNLU did not directly appeal to religion in relation to the observances, its call for austerity created an atmosphere of simplicity, remembrance, and rededication that revived a deeper, purer, politicized religious sense for the rituals. Thus, while the call for more self-reliance drew upon traditional values and relationships already present in Islamic society, it also altered them by drawing upon the Sunni tendencies toward egalitarian attitudes toward authority and austerity in living. The resulting interaction, if successful, would have not only created structures of self-reliance but enhanced and developed ways of being Muslim in Palestinian society as well.

Religious and Cultural Values That Strengthen Nonviolent Resistance

Having examined the nonviolent nature of the Intifada and its direct and indirect relationships to Islam culture and religion, we can now discuss those relationships and values that helped to initiate, promote, and sustain nonviolence in the Intifada. Identifying these values should help us construct a nonviolent framework from an Islamic perspective. The values we will discuss are unity, solidarity, justice and empowerment, commitment and discipline, forgiveness, and *sumud* (steadfastness).

Unity. Preserving and calling for national unity was a main code of conduct in the early stages of the Intifada. The national, cultural, and historical unity among all Palestinians and the notion of one destiny for all was emphasized again and again in the leaflets distributed by the UNLU.

This sense of unity is one of the main cultural mores that Arabs and Muslims desire to achieve and preserve. Both Qur'anic verses and Islamic tradition praise the notion of unity and support it as a central value for Muslims. Palestinians realized the power of unity and collective endeavor during the first few weeks of the Intifada, and Palestinian Arab and Muslim culture and religion provided an easy and fertile ground to nurture such values.

There are many examples from the Intifada that illustrate the sense of unity. Ze'ev Schiff and Ehud Ya'ari (1989, 214) see this unity reflected in the friendships formed in Israeli prisons between erstwhile rivals and in the connections made between rival factions in the universities. The full participation of both rural and urban Palestinians in the Intifada indicated that a sense of unity transcended "the period in which urban merchants, traders, labor contractors and professionals among whom national activism was common, and a rural population which was still to a great extent preoccupied with more immediate matters" (McDowall 1994, 96).

Solidarity. Expressing sympathy and solidarity among the various segments of the Palestinian community was an essential principle in the Intifada. Such solidarity allowed the entire community to be involved in the popular movement and committees, particularly in the early stages of the uprising. Solidarity meant providing economic, social, and moral assistance to neighbors (the family next door or in the next village or city). It meant blood donations (fifty thousand donors were on the UPMRC list) and membership and involvement in the various local popular committees. In fact, Hamas's organizational infrastructure and policy strongly mirrored such values of solidarity, taking care of the needy and fostering a strong collective identity (Schiff and Ya'ari 1989). Those values were also identified as major factors in the success of the Pashtun nonviolent movement against British rule in India-Pakistan (Johansen 1997).

Palestinian solidarity was woven around two dimensions of identity: the secular national Palestinian identity promoted by the UNLU, and a Muslim-Arab identity highlighted by the Islamic groups Jihad and Hamas. This solidarity was different from the solidarity fostered by the Pathan leader Abdul Ghaffar Khan, which focused mainly on the religious identity of a homogeneous religious and tribal community. Due to the diverse religious affiliations of members of the Palestinian community and the nature of the national Palestinian movement itself, an exclusive focus on Islamic religious values would have worked against a successful national mobilization.

Justice and Empowerment. A belief in justice and in fighting injustice was a central objective and a unifying force for Palestinians in the Intifada. Fighting injustice is a cultural as well as a religious value for both Arabs and Muslims. The chapter on the values of peace building in an Islamic society provides evidence to support the duty of Muslims to pursue justice in their daily lives. In conveying the sense that all community members were being subjected to an injustice from the Israeli occupation, the UNLU created a powerful tool for mobilizing all segments of Palestinian society.

The Intifada had a major psychological impact on Palestinians. Their collective national identity was boosted by a sense of empowerment and strength. It was as if the pursuit of justice through nonviolence provided a sense of pride and dignity to many. The stories of the Prophet opposing and defeating powerful enemies during his early period were constantly repeated among people and by preachers in mosques. A belief in the justice of their cause was a strong empowering force that motivated people to take part in the resistance movement.

The self-reliance encouraged by the Intifada's leadership also fostered a sense of pride, dignity, and empowerment in many of the people who were involved in grassroots activities. UNLU leaflets 3 and 4 (January 1988) stated: "Our people of all sectors and classes: let us begin today boycotting the Israeli goods for which an alternative is produced in our national products and factories, especially such products as chocolate, dairy items, and cigarettes. . . . Honorable nationalists . . . we call upon you to join us in the following: concentrating all energy on cultivating the land, achieving maximal self-sufficiency aimed at boycotting the enemy's goods" (Bennis 1990, 108–10). This new sense of empowerment, pride, and dignity was also one of the factors that allowed Palestinians to make political concessions, such as accepting a two-state solution, recognizing Israel, and negotiating with the Israeli government.

Commitment and Discipline. The success of the nonviolent resistance in the Intifada was due in large part to the high level of commitment and discipline among local and national leaders. The commitment and discipline were demonstrated in the local popular committee work and in the sacrifices made by all segments of the society (particularly youth and women) in the early stages. Those values are praised in the Arab Islamic tradition. Islam as a culture and religion instructs people to express their commitment and to be disciplined in their pursuit of just causes.

To carry out the Calls of the UNLU, community members needed to exercise much discipline, commitment, and dedication to the cause, values that are inherent in the culture and religion of the people who took part in the actions. Social norms had to be altered. For example, parties, loud music, and lavish celebrations were prohibited. The new norm was to sympathize with each other and live modestly. Enforcing such arrangements required a great deal of commitment and discipline from both the people and their leaders. The strong discipline is also reflected in the fact that during the Intifada there was a lawless period. The Israeli military administration lost its control over the population. Thus the police system did not function. In spite of that, the crime rate—drug and other public violations—went down during that period. The Islamic culture of discipline allowed the various communities to exercise control over their own deviant members.[59]

Forgiveness. Forgiveness is highly valued in Islamic and Arab culture. In fact, it is one of the major values that provide honor, pride, and dignity to Arabs in traditional dispute settlement. Thus the use of forgiveness cannot be viewed as totally secular or coincidental but needs to be analyzed within the cultural and religious context of the Palestinian community. The UNLU recognized the importance of such a value and used it in their nonviolent political campaign. A day of forgiveness was declared by the Palestinian leadership in order to allow collaborators and informants to surrender their weapons and rejoin their community in its struggle against the occupation. Many responded positively and came to the different mosques. The act was aimed at achieving a higher level of unity in the various local communities and reducing the damage that these collaborators could have caused to the movement.

Sumud. Steadfastness as a concept was introduced by Palestinian national activists to the political ideology of the Arab world. By steadfastness, they were referring to the ability of Palestinians to face the various oppressive Israeli policies after 1967 without giving up. *Sumud* is associated with patience as well as resistance and perseverance. The PLO leadership used the term to refer to the political activities and resistance of Palestinians in the West Bank and Gaza. Use of the term was intensified during the Intifada by both internal and external leadership. Steadfastness requires patience, endurance, and the ability to sacrifice. These qualities are often associated with the call for *sumud*. In fact, the PLO had special funding to compensate Palestinians who lived in those territories for the sacrifices that their steadfastness entailed. Local communities were aware that they had to pay a heavy price for their *sumud* and also that their sacrifice and endurance were needed for the success of the Intifada. Thus actions of sacrifice became the norm during the Intifada.

There is no doubt that *sumud* and its associated values are derived from the Muslim cultural and religious context, such as patience and the endurance of difficulties for the sake of one's religious principles. Often the life of the Prophet and his early followers is alluded to as an example of *sumud*. Patience (*sabr*) is one of the main virtues of Islam. Suffering for one's faith and rights is a quality that Muslims are brought up to respect and accept.

The actions of Palestinians imprisoned during the Intifada are a good example of the quality and importance of *sumud*. Prisoners were expected to maintain total silence or to give up only minor details, even during long debilitating sessions with practiced interrogators. Members of the Islamic organizations were especially known for their endurance and resilience facing Israeli interrogators (Schiff and Ya'ari 1989, 230). Often Palestinians who were arrested during the Intifada described with pride and dignity their steadfastness against interrogators and despised those who were "broken" under interrogation and torture. Palestinian political prisoners have developed an entire narrative and a social and political system that relate to such experiences.

Rituals and Religious Symbols. As mentioned earlier, mosques were often used as refuges by those who sought protection from assault. The use of the local mosques for the purpose of forgiving the collaborators and informants indicates the extent of direct use of Arab and Islamic cultural values and principles by the Intifada's leadership. The mosques were also used for mass mobilization during the Intifada. The weekly Friday prayer functioned as a meeting place for many activists, not necessarily just those affiliated with Hamas or Islamic Jihad, as mistakenly believed. There are Palestinian Muslims who belonged to other political factions, supported the UNLU, and still observed Islam. It is an Islamic custom for Muslims to congregate in the mosque, not only for prayers but also to discuss religious affairs (Kishtainy 1990, 23; also see Satha-Anand 1998). Considering this practice, it is not strange that the UNLU intentionally used the mosques as the point of mobilization and recruitment for their nonviolent political acts.

Conclusion

Islam played various roles in the Intifada. On the one hand, it reinforced the element of violence that is frequently present and always looming in Palestinian responses to Israeli repression. But it also contributed to and was a source for nonviolence. The importance of this aspect of the Intifada is difficult, perhaps impossible, to assess. In Palestine, as in most Muslim countries, Islam has not developed an explicit ideology of nonviolence; and Muslims have done little preaching or teaching about nonviolence as a way of life.[60] Thus, as indicated by Saad Eddin Ibrahim (1990), nonviolent political struggle is still a very long way from being a dominant sociopolitical philosophy and practice in the Middle East. But the roots, the tradition, and the need are all in place, creating fertile ground for the dissemination of important ideas.

The pluralistic nature of Palestinian society (which includes secularists, Muslims, Christians, and Druze), combined with the need to reach an accord with Israeli Jews, served to minimize the religious basis for theory and action. When organizations such as Hamas and Islamic Jihad put forth political programs based in Islam, the programs tended to be divisive and frequently contributed to violence. While a countertactic might have been to face them with an ideology that worked from a tolerant, nonviolent understanding of Islam, that was not a realistic option for the Palestinian nationalists who led the Intifada. Instead, they concentrated on one of Islam's strengths: its focus on the practical and the everyday. That is how Palestinians expressed their comprehension of nonviolence: in the actions and restraints of the Intifada, not in formulations of principles. Support for the Intifada's nonviolent, nonlethal resistance was strongest among traditional Muslims and moderate nationalists of all classes. Militant Muslim groups sometimes pushed the Intifada toward violence and intolerance. The Popular Front for the Liberation of Palestine and the Democratic Front for the Liberation of Palestine, while they were in the forefront of organizing civil disobedience, saw it as a stage that would be followed by armed struggle. Their continued rejection of Israel's right to exist contributed to rigidity and hostility between the two sides. Nonviolent resistance was most firmly grounded in the traditional, frequently religious, middle ground of Palestinian society. It was centered not among a small elite but among the common people. The new leadership of the Intifada sensed this and was able to use it to empower the broader Palestinian population and organize it in a way that enabled a new form of resistance to emerge—one based largely on nonviolence.

The Intifada was not a religious uprising, but one in which religion played a multifaceted role. The foundation of the uprising was a pluralistic nationalism that allowed space for the religious elements in society —both Muslim and Christian—as well as for a variety of secular perspectives. The revolt sprang from a society firmly embedded, both historically and currently, in the milieu of Islam. The Intifada's nonviolent campaign, qualified by some as nonlethal/violent resistance, was as Muslim as the Civil Rights Movement was Christian and Gandhi's movement was Hindu.[61]

This analysis supports Johansen's explanation when examining the case of nonviolence among Pashtun Muslims. "More widespread knowledge of this case—Pashtun—and others could enable people elsewhere to recognize that the highest values of Islam may be compatible with militant nonviolence that has power to liberate and to resolve previously intractable conflicts" (1997, 66). Many other features of the Intifada as a political and social popular movement could be explored. However, the objective of this study is simply to show that at least in the early stages of the Intifada, the intensive application of nonviolent action was based directly or indirectly on cultural and religious values drawn from Arab and Muslim tradition.

The Intifada as a social and political movement was perceived as threatening, not only to the Israeli military administration, but also to the Arab political regimes and elites. Thus it was alarming to all authoritative political elites. Leaders of the Intifada have long claimed that they did not get the active support of Arab political leaders because they were perceived as a threat to their regimes.[62] The Intifada is an excellent example of a political movement in which the masses of people were able to take control of their destiny and bring political change into their environment by organizing themselves to fight oppression using nonviolent tactics.

6

Conclusion

This study provides abundant evidence that there is a need to move the discussion of the relationship between Islam and peace beyond the question of whether Islamic religion and tradition are inherently inimical to nonviolence or pacifism. It suggests that future discussions proceed from the assumption that Islamic traditions, religion, and culture are potentially fertile sources of nonviolence and peacemaking. For whatever reasons—colonialism, imperialism, or internal political and social structures—systematic discussion of this premise has been missing from scholarship on peace, conflict resolution, and Islam. Syed Sikandar Mehdi writes, "Islam and the Muslim world still remain, to a considerable extent, rather neglected areas of peace studies and peace research. Being very largely a colonized world engaged for years, for decades, in the bloody liberation struggle against (a) colonial yoke, the Muslim world remained busy for quite sometime waging peace and striving to create a decolonized, just and peaceful society rather than producing sufficient peace literature explaining Islam's position on the issues concerned" (1994, 117).

There are numerous studies on war and the use of force in Islamic religion and tradition, but very few on peace building and conflict resolution in an Islamic context. Such research needs to be undertaken by scholars and practitioners. Shifting the emphasis from war to peace in the study of Islamic religion and culture can contribute to furthering the understanding among Westerners and Easterners, Muslims and non-Muslims, believers and nonbelievers.

Islam does not need to be understood and interpreted as an "absolute pacifist" religion for Muslims to justify nonviolent resistance campaigns and activities. There are abundant clues, symbols, values, and rituals in Islamic religion and culture that can provide policymakers and other people with the opportunity to pursue nonviolent options in responding to conflicts. The fact that certain groups and policymakers have chosen another path does not abrogate the possibilities for nonviolent practice among Muslims.

Single and multicase studies are appropriate and effective ways to begin addressing specific questions and generating hypotheses for research and practice. Some questions that ought to be included are: What are the contextual conditions that facilitate the application of Islamic values of peacemaking and nonviolent resistance in social and political conflicts? Are conflict resolution and nonviolent principles and values reflected differently in the various Islamic religious texts, such as the Hadith, Shari'ah, and the Qur'an itself? How are Muslim responses compatible with nonviolence and peace-building methods? How do nonviolent and peacebuilding values differ when the conflict is between various Muslim factions or between Muslims and other groups? How do Islamic texts relate to other values that support the application and belief in nonviolent frameworks? Is the term *nonviolence* appropriate when investigating these values, or is *quietism* more apt? What are the obstacles that inhibit the wider application of such strategies, particularly on the political level?

The case of the Pashtun movement (Johansen 1997) and the study of the Intifada lead us to conclude that vastly different traditional cultures can draw upon Islamic resources to provide a basis for launching nonviolent campaigns for justice and peace. This was particularly evident in the Palestinian case and in the context of traditional dispute resolution in Arab-Muslim culture. The relevant guiding principles to be utilized in policy, research, or theory building are: (1) Islamic religious identity provides an effective basis for recruiting people to join a nonviolent campaign by nurturing strong identity and discipline; (2) Islamic religious values provide a strong basis for nonviolent activists' goals of serving others and implementing broad social, economic, and political reforms; (3) Reinterpretation of religious values can mitigate violent tendencies in a conflict, encourage activists to avoid intolerance toward other people, and enable them to overcome their time-honored inclination to use violence against adversaries, both in interpersonal and intergroup conflicts; (4) Nonviolent actions enable many Muslims to be politically more effective than they were when using violent tactics; (5) Muslim religious teachings and discourse can provide a basis for enabling people to question the meaning of their own tradition; and (6) Muslim religious commitments have sustained the determination and courage of their nonviolent leadership.

Extracting such principles and conditions from case study–oriented research can help develop a comprehensive nonviolent framework in Islam. The analysis of new case studies of nonviolent strategies implemented by Muslims or non-Muslims in an Islamic context is essential to developing and promoting peaceful political and social change among Muslims around the world. The use of nonviolent strategies in Kosovo by Muslim leaders in 1996 was dismissed or neglected by politicians and scholars, yet it is precisely such cases that will help inform our understanding of the conditions for the successful applications of peaceful political strategies in Islamic contexts.

In addition to research, conferences and informal frameworks for dialogue among Muslims can also be of value. Some new initiatives have been emerging in this direction, such as the Islamic Peace Chair at American University and Nonviolence International in Washington, D.C., both of which have sponsored conferences on Islam and Peace that have dealt with some of the aforementioned issues.[1] In the past, very few conferences have focused on such subjects as nonviolence and Islam. At a pioneering 1968 conference on the world religions and world peace, G. K. Sayidain identified a contribution that Islam could make in this field: "The best contribution that Islam can make to the world is to assist in the process of the emergence of the new man who will be able to define his priorities more intelligently and compassionately and live by these priorities, who will be more concerned with giving than with taking, and who will strive for peace with resource of his being" (quoted in Homer 1968, 56).

Every religion can foster either violence or nonviolence. It is the responsibility of those who follow a particular faith to cull these resources for nonviolence from their religious scriptures. Altaf Gauhar has pointed out, "In Islam power flows out from the framework of the Qur'an and from no other source. It is for Muslim scholars to initiate universal *Ijtihad* at all levels. The faith is fresh, it is the Muslim mind which is befogged. The principles of Islam are dynamic, it is our approach which has become static. Let there be fundamental rethinking to open avenues of exploration, innovation, and creativity" (1978, 48).

Arab-Muslim culture is also a rich source of nonviolent and peacebuilding practices. The research in this book clearly illustrates the enormous potential of various peacemaking practices that are used on a daily basis among Arab Muslims and non-Muslims in the Middle East. Such traditional mechanisms of peacemaking have been essential in maintaining peace and social and political order among fighting or competing groups for many centuries. They have also saved many lives and promoted harmony in many communities, as exemplified in the strong respect for and impact of codes of honor and public image in social and cultural peacemaking, virtues that have been underestimated in the political arena.

The Middle Eastern traditional dispute resolution methods of gaining entry and credibility, if considered systematically, can enhance the policy-makers' ability to work effectively and constructively with many internal conflicts. Another potential tool of traditional dispute resolution is the use of a community's venerable rituals and symbolic interactions, which can be easily applied in postconflict peace-building processes. Many of the rituals applied in traditional dispute resolution can be transmitted into the political arena as well. For example, the notion of restoring the dignity and honor of the victims in public as an act of restorative justice can allow the parties to negotiate and settle their differences. Exploring the possible adoption of such traditional practices in Islamic communities would be an extremely important contribution to the larger study of nonviolence and peace.

Cultural and religious values are powerful means of mobilizing people in social and political movements. Islamic nonviolent and peace-building cultural and religious values are no exception to this rule. The Palestinian Intifada illustrates how religious symbols, rituals, and beliefs can play a role in promoting the strategies of nonviolence in a secular, national-liberation context. Neither the leaders nor the people involved in the Intifada could have succeeded in applying nonviolent strategies without the fertile Islamic cultural and religious context of the Intifada. The Pashtun nonviolent movement illustrates how an Islamic religious movement can adopt a strict nonviolent strategy; the Intifada provides strong evidence of the contribution of Islamic religious and cultural values in promoting a nonviolent political movement led by a secular and national leadership.

The case of the Intifada clearly shows the connection between the Islamic values expounded in this book and the type of religious values and norms utilized, consciously or unconsciously, by the movement's leadership to promote nonviolence in the Palestinian context. Values such as patience (sabr), solidarity, sacrifice, and universal human dignity were core elements in the Intifada's political message and mobilization process.

On a theoretical level, the role of culture and religion has been strongly confirmed as an essential factor in understanding the causes, dynamics, and solutions of conflicts. The cultural worldviews of the parties involved in any conflict constitute an important element not only in the escalation of the conflicts, but also in the process of change. Thus scholars and activists in the field of conflict resolution and peace studies should explore the dynamics and effects of shifts in the religious and cultural identities of conflicting parties.

Guidelines for Intervention

Beyond the contribution to a new research agenda, the use of nonviolent peace-building strategies and activities in Muslim communities has potentially far-reaching consequences in terms of political and religious leadership, nongovernmental organizations, and third-party interveners. The following guidelines illustrate potential outcomes if agents of change (peace-building and development workers) were to integrate or take into consideration cultural and religious frameworks in their initiatives. There are at least six such guidelines, which can be applied whether the initiatives are carried out by an indigenous or foreign organization.

First, Islamic religion and culture encompass values and norms that promote peace building as well as the use of force and violence. Hence it is pointless and misleading to stereotype Muslims as more receptive to violence than any other community. This image hinders the credibility of an intervener and local peace builders in any Muslim community.

Second, there is an abundance of cultural and religious indigenous practices and values in Muslim communities that can be drawn upon in designing models of intervention to promote social and political change and development; there is no need to mechanically import Western-based models. Western models may at best produce a short-term outcome, but in the long term cannot be expected to take root in the life of the community.

Third, in most effective peace-building projects community members who actively participate eventually run up against certain problematic core values in the sociocultural structures of many Muslim communities (especially in the Muslim Arab context), such as hierarchy, authoritarianism, patriarchy, and so on. These structures are threatened by the democratic participatory elements of community peace building. This is an inevitable confrontation that ought to be anticipated by both interveners and community members. Utilizing the community's local forces for change in such projects is an important step in overcoming some of these structural challenges.

Fourth, to increase the efficacy of peace-building initiatives in Muslim communities, development projects ought to be designed and implemented in accordance with values and principles derived from their specific context. Emphasizing justice, empowerment of the weak, social solidarity, and public support is essential for any initiative to become effective.

Fifth, for interveners it is nearly impossible to function in a Muslim community without knowing its members' cultural and religious worldviews. This is something an outside intervener may have enormous difficulty acquiring in two weeks or "even" a month. Official and nonofficial (NGOs) teams who initiate projects in those communities therefore must include local people in their planning and implementation. This does not mean a token representation of locals in such projects—on the contrary, it requires full incorporation and local ownership of such projects, and a clear and unconditional long-term commitment by the outside intervener to the overall interest of the specific community.

Sixth, long-term conflict resolution and socioeconomic development projects are inseparable. Many organizations who fund and implement development and peace-building initiatives in Muslim areas (particularly those areas affected by conflicts and violence) are often run by professionals (locals and foreigners) who have lost or never had contact with grassroots or day-to-day concerns of the community. Therefore, they neglect local resources who are well versed in the religious and cultural context. The success of socioeconomic development and peace-building projects depends on local leaders feeling free to use their skills in responding to their communities' genuine needs in the face of tension, conflict, and change. Local residents must be able to sustain the resolution of their conflicts and the development of their community beyond the period of outside involvement and support. In short, building independent and local capacities for peace should be the ultimate objective of intervention in any community.

Notes

Introduction

1. Several practitioners have been implementing such strategies; for example, John Paul Lederach (1995, 1997) has assisted local communities in Latin America (Guatemala) to develop their own local initiatives for peace-building and nonviolence approaches. See also Abu-Nimer 1996a on conflict resolution training workshops in Gaza.

2. Training workshops in peace building have been conducted by organizations such as Search for Common Ground, the Eastern Mennonite University Summer Program, American University's International Peace and Conflict Resolution Program, the Institute for Multi-Track Diplomacy (IMTD), and Catholic Relief Services.

3. The term *Islam* is used in this study not as an essentialist notion but in reference to a set of religious and spiritual beliefs and practices, as a multicultural civilization that has existed for centuries, and as a historical narrative that provides Muslims with cultural, political, and religious identity. For more details on civilizational or nonessentialist approaches to Islam, see Khadduri 1984 and Sachedina 2000.

4. A discussion of such relationships between the West and Arabs took place in summer 1998 at a conference held at Oxford focusing on the Arab image in the West. The conference was sponsored by the Royal Institute for Inter-Faith Studies; the Jordan Middle East Center; St. Antony's College; and the Center for Lebanese Studies.

5. It is important to point out that the author uses the term *Islam* mainly in reference to the Middle Eastern Muslim community, particularly when the discussion is focused on cultural and traditional norms and values. The author by no means intends to say that Muslims around the world have only one generic culture. On the contrary, Islam has valued the diversity of local cultures in coexistence with Islamic principles, which remains a distinctive theme in conceptualizing the Muslim community, or the Ummah. In addition, the major bulk of data for this research, particularly for chapters on the Palestinian Intifada and the sociocultural obstacles for peace building and dispute resolution, are derived from a Middle Eastern Arab-Muslim context. Being an Arab Muslim living in the Middle East provides the individual certain cultural attributes that cannot be found or shared

with other Muslim countries or societies. Thus the main reference in the analysis and discussion relates to Middle Eastern Arab-Muslim communities (see chapter 1 for further discussion on this point).

Part I: Peace Building and Nonviolence in Islamic Religion and Culture: A Theoretical Framework

1. Edward Hall is mostly known in the field of culture and communication. His study (1976) of generic patterns and attributions of high- and low-context societies is a classic example of an etic approach to culture.

Chapter I. The Study of Islam, Nonviolence, and Peace

1. These features are suggested in part by Reinhold Niebuhr (1960, 244–54, based on King 1957, 165–67). However, Gandhi and Martin Luther King Jr., who articulated (1957) the above five features of the nonviolent approach, are the classical sources for defining the meaning of nonviolence.

2. This list of assumptions is based on a wider and more in-depth discussion of the various developments in the field of conflict resolution and its theoretical models that appeared in Abu-Nimer 1999.

3. Fasting is one of the main values and practices that Gandhi associated with Islam, particularly during his early imprisonment (McDonough 1994, 122).

4. A number of Islamic scholars have emphasized the legitimacy and importance of the different interpretations of Islamic texts. See Esack 1999; al-Hibri 1992.

5. Muslims and non-Muslims share other characteristics, including communities that are based on tribalism, ethnicity, and religion and that maintain strong social and territorial boundaries (Zubaida 1992a; Barakat 1993).

6. In fact, many of the discussions and writings on Islam and peace or nonviolence have emerged from non-Arab-Muslim regions, particularly South Asia. However, among Middle Eastern Muslim communities (Arab and non-Arab), there are significant cultural differences, for instance the cultural differences among Sudanese Arab Muslims and the Persian or Afghani Muslims. Even among Arab Muslims themselves there are subcultures and differences that would be difficult to capture in one generic term. For example, the attitude toward Europeans is different among Arab Muslims in the Gulf area than those in North Africa.

7. This process has been described by scholars researching democracy and other ideologies. Ibrahim Abu-Rabi' best summarizes this notion: "Most secularist Arab thinkers hold tenaciously to the proposition that the universalization of modernity and its acceptance by Arab society and the Arab mind in the nineteenth century was inevitable, and that an appeal to traditionalism in the form of authenticity is just an escape from the new conditions created by modernity" (1996, 249).

8. The scope of violence in Western societies (on individual and group levels) is dangerously high and has been described by scholars of peace studies and other policymakers as a social disease or even war (Turpin and Kurtz 1997).

9. Contemporary political leaders have attempted to define new secular identities for their nation-states. They affirm the broader compatibility between the Western and the Islamic worldviews using harmonization, accommodation, and reformulation as the primary principles in the process of adaptability. They keep Islam as the religion of the state, but through the free and liberal interpretation of Islamic laws and values, they seek to introduce Western concepts into the social and political life of Muslims. Opposing them are the traditionalists, who reject the harmonization thesis and call for an "Islamic solution." They perceive Western concepts such as democracy, the nation-state, and secularization as contrary to Islamic religious thought because those concepts rely on human rather than on divine authority (Abed 1995, 120).

10. Dan Quayle, Patrick Buchanan, Daniel Pipes, and others best represent such policymakers and politicians, who often have compared Islam with communism and Nazism (Esposito 1992, 168).

11. The review of such research and publications in this study is brief and limited due to (1) the nature of these studies (which avoid or neglect peace building and nonviolence); (2) the fact that they represent the majority of studies in the literature; (3) the specific purpose of this study (focusing on peace building in Islam); (4) the fact that reviewing war and jihad have been the typical way of covering Islam as a religion or society by both the defenders and the attackers of Islam; and (5) there have been several studies in English and many in Arabic that have reviewed these studies and uncovered their cultural biases and limitations. See Esposito 1992; Esposito and Voll 1996.

12. There are numerous studies on Islamic fundamentalism; the scope of this research does not allow a full listing of them. However, in addition to the present list, see Martin E. Marty and R. Scott Appleby's three edited volumes in the series on fundamentalism (Fundamentalism Project, University of Chicago Press, 1993).

13. For Qur'anic verses, I have relied on the translation by Abdullah Yusuf Ali (1991) except where the quoted scholars have used other editions.

14. Based on excerpts from Moulavi Cheragh Ali 1977. In my note on the Companion of the Prophet, I relied on Tabarsi 1958, commentary on sura 2, 212.

15. When studying Islam in general and political Islam in particular, there is an emphasis and even domination of such stereotypes and generalizations among scholars and writers described in the above quote. Andrea Luego (1995, 11) supports the notion that although many people are able to see and treat Christianity as culture rather than religion, Islam when viewed by people in the West cannot be associated with culture but with religion only. The negative characterization of Arabs and Muslims has significant political implications. Two prime examples come from leading politicians and scholars of Islam. Former U.S. ambassador to the United Nations Jean Kirkpatrick questioned the ability of Arabs to reach a rational decision: "The Arab World is the only part of the world where I have been shaken in my conviction that if you let the people decide, they will make fundamentally rational decisions" (quoted in Luego 1995, 16). Bassam Tibi gives the

impression that Middle Eastern people are addicted to oppression: "The Arab masses follow their dictators and despots till they are bitterly disappointed; they must first undergo painful periods of self-deception before they finally do realize that they have been deceived. However, they do not learn their lesson; though they let their heroes fall, they again pledge allegiance to the next dictator. This is a characteristic of the political culture of the Middle East" (quoted in Luego 1995, 16).

16. In support of this notion of limited violence and war, the Prophet's son-in-law—the first of the imams, Caliph Ali—laid down rules and conditions in great detail for the ethical guidance of his army. "The conditions prohibit attacking first, looting, humiliating women, killing children or fleeing people or injured fighters, stripping a dead soldier, molesting or outraging the modesty of a woman, hurting old or enfeeble persons, etc." (Saiyidain 1994, 174).

17. In support of this notion, scholars point to a historical event: "In one battle, the Muslims, left with little to eat, looted a herd of goats they saw. When the Prophet heard about it he came and overturned all the cooking utensils in which the goats were cooked, saying, 'Eating looted things is like eating a dead carcass.'" *Kitab al-Sunan: Sunan Abu Dawud (Kitab al-Jihad)* (1998, 2:13).

18. Algeria, Egypt, Palestine, Lebanon, and Afghanistan are only some examples in which military and political conflicts exist as a result of the disagreement over the conditions of appropriate leadership of the country. The Islamic groups in these countries have declared war against the existing leadership, arguing that these leaders are not worthy of the Muslim communities' obedience, so that fighting them is, according to Islam, a righteous cause to pursue.

19. These include the legacy of Martin Luther King, Gandhi, and others too obvious to be ignored.

20. The two priorities of inclusivity and creativity are the purpose of applying the principles of *shurah* and *ijtihad*. These are core values in conflict resolution and approaches to nonviolence (see the discussion of assumptions in chapter 2).

21. Muslim writers and preachers who aim to convert people to Islam or speak out only on the basis of faith statements were excluded from this category.

22. Satha-Anand (1993a) discusses the destruction that might result from nuclear warfare and concludes that such warfare is prohibited by Islamic teachings and principles. A similar conclusion was reached by K. G. Saiyidain as early as 1968 in a conference presentation on Islam and peace. He suggested that any type of total war cannot be carried out within the conditions proscribed by Islam. See Homer 1968.

23. Peace scholars and practitioners have been promoting such a paradigm shift since the late 1980s. For more information on such arguments, see Burton 1990.

24. Jawdat Sai'd is a Syrian religious scholar who was jailed for many years by the Syrian government for his reformist views of Islam.

25. Although the authenticity of this Hadith is not provided by Jawdat Sai'd or

others who have cited it, the saying is nevertheless well known and often cited in social gatherings.

26. It should be noted that although Ahmadiyya is being identified by Ferguson (1978, 136) as a pacifist movement or sect, nevertheless he recognizes their teaching of the "necessity to use armed defense against aggression." Such a statement disqualifies this group from "absolute pacifism."

27. Obviously, this presentation of *al-da'wah* has a missionary objective and motivation. In addition, Wahiduddin Khan does not clarify how *al-da'wah* can be applied in a conflict situation. Even if all people became Muslims, how would that help in reducing violence and how would conflicts be resolved among them?

Chapter 2. Islamic Principles of Nonviolence and Peace Building: A Framework

1. Several Qur'anic verses (e.g., 90:17) emphasize the value of compassion among people. The same value is stressed in: "He who does not show compassion to his fellow men is undeserving of God's compassion" (M. al-Bukhari 1959, book 34, ch. 53, 47–48).

2. Howeidy cites al-Zamakshari: "and in this—pursuing justice with enemies—there is a great warning that justice is a duty to be applied when dealing with the infidels (*Kuffar*), who are the enemy of God. If it had such a powerful characteristic with enemies, then what duty and impact will it have among the believers, who are God's supportive favorites!" (1993, 121).

3. Based on Barazangi, Zaman, and Afzal 1996. The prophetic tradition supports such a notion of moderation and fairness: "You should act in moderation." Sahih al-Bukhari, vol. 7, book 70, no. 577; vol. 8, book 76, no. 470. (Except where indicated, all Sahih al-Bukhari Hadith citations in this study are based on the translations in Khan 1983. These were verified with the Arabic edition of Sahih al-Bukhari, 1998).

4. "He who believes in God and the last day must honor his guest for one day and one night as well as granting him hospitality for three days. More than this is considered *Sadaqah*. A guest, then, should not stay longer in order that he might embarrass his host." Sahih al-Bukhari, vol. 8, book 73, no. 156.

5. In peace studies there is an emphasis on all aspects of justice (distributive, procedural, and restorative components).

6. In addition to articulating what God has forbidden to Muslims, the Qur'an makes it clear that God also expects Muslims to cultivate that which is good. Being a Muslim involves not only repulsing what is bad but actively enjoining the good. The Qur'an articulates in concrete terms what it means to enjoin the good to thus achieve a balanced and just life in a social, community context.

7. Zakah is also encouraged and described in detail, along with its rewards, in verses 2:262–72.

8. The Prophet liberated the slave Bilal, who was among the first believers in

Islam, and instructed Muslims to do the same with their slaves. In fact, Bilal occupied a leading role among the companions.

9. In support of such an interpretation see verses such as 41:34, 7:56, 7:199, and 28:54, in which Muslims are expected to exercise self-restraint and to control their anger and their reaction to evildoing.

10. The complete saying of the Prophet is translated by Mohammad Muhsin Khan: "A Muslim is the one who avoids harming Muslims with his tongue and hands. And a *Muhajir* (emigrant) is the one who gives up (abandons) all that Allah has forbidden" (1972).

11. There are Muslim groups (e.g., Sufism, Ahmadiyyah) that emphasize the spiritual rather than the physical jihad. The Sufi teachings explain that "The warrior (*mujahid*) is one who battles with his own self (*nafs*) and is thus on the path of God" (Nurbakhsh 1983, 2:76). Other groups suggest that *da'wah* (the call to spread Islam through preaching and persuasion) is the major form of jihad for Muslims.

12. For full details of these events in the life of the Prophet, see Ibn Hisham 1992, 288.

13. See Khadduri's discussion (1984) of philosophical justice and its roots in Islamic tradition by analyzing the work of the great Islamic philosophers al-Farabi, al-Kindi, Ibn Rushd, and Ibn Sina.

14. In his discussion of the debate between traditionalist *naql* (transmitted knowledge) or *'aql* (reason), George Hourani (1985, 227–73) identifies four major approaches to interpretation of the Islamic sources on ethics: (1) revelation and independent reason, which includes revelation supplemented by independent reason (itjihad), and independent reason supplemented by revelation (Mu'atazilite); (2) revelation supplemented by dependent reason, which called for the return to tradition; (3) revelation alone; and (4) revelation extended by imams. That reason preceded revelation was mainly supported by Muslim philosophers such as al-Farabi (870–950), Ibn Sina (980–1037), and Ibn Rushd (1126–1198), who was more forthcoming on the role of religion and faith in the individual's life. Al-Ghazali (1058–1111) attacked all the previous philosophers for their perceived departure from religion and revelation.

15. Saiyidain went even further in encouraging scholars to engage in interpretation: "Even if my competence to undertake an authentic interpretation of the message of Islam would be in doubt, I strongly affirm the right of any serious, honest and intelligent person to do so. Such reinterpretation becomes necessary in every age for a variety of reasons" (1994, 3).

16. Shari'ah is the divine will for human behavior interpreted by Muslim scholars and is presented through specific legal codes (*fiqh*), the science of Islamic law. For more on the much debated "closing of the doors of itjihad" and the present need for reform and dynamism, see Iqbal 1930; also see Sonn 1996.

17. Another saying supports such a forgiving attitude when the Prophet entered Mecca: "There is no censure from me today on you (for what has happened is done

with), may God, who is the greatest amongst forgivers, forgive you" (Ibn Sa'd 1957, 2:142).

18. Ibn Is'haq 1978, 184; *Life of Mohammed* (English trans. of Sirat Ibn Is'haq) 1955, 193.

19. Sachedina (2000, 105) identifies two social goals as underlined in the holy book: to place moral and legal restrictions on the process of retribution, and to offer an alternative way to restore relations through forgiveness, blood money, and other compensation.

20. Interview with Sheik Arimiyawo Shaibu, an Islamic scholar in Pakistan, March 1998. See Catholic Relief Services 1999.

21. See other verses emphasizing the same principle of individual choice and responsibility: 5:8, 9:6, 16:125, and 42:48.

22. The ethical axioms in Islam are: (1) unity (*tawhid*); (2) equilibrium (*al-'adl wa al-ihsan*): the desirability of an equitable distribution of income and wealth, the need for helping the poor and the needy, the necessity for making adjustment in the entire spectrum of consumption, production and distribution relations, and others. This is all to prevent or correct *zulm;* (3) free will (*ikhtiyar*): man is capable of choosing the right choice if he follows the correct path of God. But man is also capable of making the wrong choice. Man is free to make the choice, but his freedom is not absolute; and (4) responsibility (*fard*): responsibility toward himself, God, and others. By doing good things and observing his faith, man can insure his correct path. The person is thus an integral participant of society. Man will not be responsible for what others have done and will not be questioned about others' deeds. Naqvi 1994.

23. Based on the Abdullah Yusuf Ali interpretations (1991, 28, comm. 61) of sabr in the Qur'an.

24. Some of those verses are: 10:109; 11:115; 16:126–27; 20:130–32; 40:55, 77; 46:35; 50:39; 70:5; 73:10–11.

25. Islam attempted to abolish the dependence on tribal solidarity by emphasizing a higher order of unity among individuals; however, it remains a strong norm among many Arab and non-Arab Muslims.

26. Farid Esack (1998) has completed a pioneer study on the Islamic theology of liberation based on the experience of Muslims in South Africa in fighting apartheid. He describes the use of Islamic beliefs and values in mobilizing Muslims to resist the South African system, particularly by building community coalitions with non-Muslims. Such experience affirms the great potential to construct coalitions across religious boundaries and identities in resisting war, violence, and injustice.

27. Akbar Ahmed (1988) supports this notion of the Ummah being a diverse religious and individual community, particularly in the Medinan period, in which the Qur'an mentions the concept of community forty-seven times, as compared to only nine times in the Meccan period.

28. Aziza Al-Hibri (1992: 12) establishes the principle for Islamic systems of governing—the will of the people shall be the basis of the authority of the govern-

ment. She identifies *bay'ah* as "the act of accepting and declaring allegiance to a potential ruler." This process of contracting with the people is recognized as a participatory and democratic principle in Islam.

29. A good example of such consultation is the Battle of Uhud, in which the Prophet, contrary to what he thought, agreed to meet with Quraysh's army outside of Medina. See Ibn Hisham 1978; cited in al-Hibri, 1992.

30. See, for example, Qur'anic verses 88:21–22. Another Hadith in support of this principle is: "If all Muslims agree on a matter then it cannot be wrong." Muhammad ibn Yazid Majah, 2 Sunan 3951 at 1303 (n.d.), cited in al-Hibri 1999, 506.

31. Freedom and choice are supported in the Qur'an (2:256, 18:29, 17:107, 10:99).

32. In addition, the Qur'an stresses the legitimacy of differences in verses such as 11:118–19 and 30:22.

33. The authenticity of this Hadith is in doubt; nevertheless it is widely used among Muslims.

34. Ibn Kathir (Tafsir, 2:588).

35. This notion of a gap between reality and the ideals of Islam has been discussed by Islamic scholars (see Nasr 2000).

Part 2. Social, Political, and Cultural Applications of Nonviolent Strategies in Muslim Communities

1. The data in this section are based on my professional experience in peace building and nonviolence training between 1992 and 2001.

2. Based on evaluation reports (1993–2001) from these projects and my professional experience as a trainer in this field.

3. In several workshops conducted in Europe and the United States, in which most of the participants were non-Muslims and had little knowledge about Islamic tradition and culture, some participants expressed doubts about the applicability of nonviolent, peace-building concepts by Muslims based on their stereotypes of the Islamic religion and Muslim societies. However, their statements have often lacked a solid argument or any accurate knowledge of the context. Some of those statements were expressed by members of other religions in a discussion of the religious approaches to peace. In such discussions, those participants would typically argue that "Christianity, Judaism, or Buddhism are more peaceful religions than Islam: look at the jihad."

4. Community Conflict Resolution Workshop, Gaza 1996.

5. Andrea Luego supports the existence of this notion of stereotyping and its implications for the process of dialogue: "The stereotype of a supposed irrationality in Islamic countries sharpens the polarization between West and East. The modern West is sensible, the backward East more or less crazy. As a result, it is necessarily impossible for the East to be an equal and valid interlocutor. Madmen

are unpredictable and dangerous, one cannot have an equal relationship with them, it is better to keep oneself—or them—at a distance" (1995, 17). As a result, she suggests creating channels of meaningful and symmetric dialogue between West and East or between Western culture and Islam.

6. For full information on this case, see Easwaran 1984.

Chapter 3. Peace Building and Nonviolence in a Sociocultural Context: Traditional Arab-Muslim Mechanisms for Dispute Resolution

In addition to a review of the existing literature, data in this chapter is based on interviews I conducted from 1995 to 2001 with traditional mediators in the Galilee (northern Israel) and Gaza (Palestine) and among the Awlad Ali, a Bedouin tribe in northwestern Egypt.

1. There has been much discussion and research on the extent to which different tribal traditions have been influenced by Islamic religion and culture. However, researchers agree that there are many tribes who currently live in the Muslim Arab world whose traditions have been preserved and that Shari'ah codes are not fully absorbed by these communities or their leaders. Instead, they abide by tribal 'urf (tradition) (Zinati 1992). Also see Cole 1975; Fadl 1982; Isma'il 1986; S. Musa 1984; Pasha 1983; Owadi 1982.

2. Interview with tribal leader (arbitrator) of the Awlad Ali, Marsa Matruh, Egypt, 1995.

3. In 1996, I witnessed a reconciliation based on tribal customs in a northern Egypt tribal community. A similar process was used to settle an interpersonal conflict between two clans, where the mediators-arbitrators used their tribal constitution and rules to reconcile the two parties. Each statement was supported by a verse from the Qur'an and a saying from the Hadith.

4. Gradually some techniques used in the customary laws are disappearing; for instance, the technique used to determine a person's innocence or guilt (basha'ah) is not implemented any more. In this procedure a person would place his tongue on a hot tool (knife, spoon, etc). If the act left a mark on his tongue, he was considered guilty; he was deemed innocent if no marks were left (Zinati 1992, 411).

5. Islamic scholars identified, according to the Shari'ah, five necessities or basics of life: preserving religion, life, reason, honor, wealth (Hanafi 1992).

6. According to Islamic law, honor is considered one of the bases to determine the nature of criminal offenses. The remaining concerns in criminal offenses are often categorized as relating to person, property, state, religion, public peace and tranquility, and decency and morals (Abu-Hassan 1995, 26). Thus, the code of honor occupies a central role in the making of the Muslim person and community.

7. This does not necessarily take place in every sulhah.

8. For more details on the procedures and some examples of these dispute mechanisms in practice, see Elias Jabbour's monograph (1996) on sulh.

9. The Prophet's tradition is often invoked in this context through the descrip-

tion of his reaction to the people of Quraish, who were fighting against him at that time in the reentry of Mecca. The Prophet forgave the Meccan leaders and warriors: "Peace be with you. I can only tell you what Joseph had said to his brothers. Today, there is no blame on you. Go! You are free." This is a well-known event in Islamic history (Kishtainy 1990, 15).

10. In fact, Mubarak Awad, a Palestinian political activist who was the first to systematically introduce nonviolent actions into the Palestinian occupied territories, has attempted the use of the term *sabr* to describe the nature of the nonviolent campaign in Palestine between 1984 and 1986 (see Crow, Grant, and Ibrahim 1990).

11. Interview with local arbitrator in El Buraij refugee camp, Gaza, summer 1998. His statements were translated from Arabic.

12. Ibid.

13. For the full story, see Ibn Hisham 1998.

14. Sometimes the person's oath is not enough, as supported by the Arabic saying: "They asked the person who does not know God to take the oath; he said: it is easy."

15. Several of those Hadith not documented in the main sources of Hadith are from al-Bukhari or Sahih Muslim; nevertheless they are being cited by the religious leaders.

16. El Buraij, Gaza, summer 1998.

17. There are many anthropological studies supporting such a hypothesis (e.g., Witty 1980; Antoun 1997).

18. Interview with Deputy Mayor Marsa Matruh, Egypt, summer 1996.

19. Interview with participant in a dispute resolution process in El Buraij, Gaza, summer 1998.

20. Interview with local mediator El Buraij, Gaza, summer 1998.

21. Interview with Gazan participant in a case arbitrated according to Shari'ah procedures, Gaza, summer 1998.

22. Based on interviews with Awlad Ali tribal elders, Marsa Matruh, Egypt, summer 1996.

Chapter 4. Nonviolent Peace Building Initiatives in Arab-Muslim Communities: Myths and Obstacles in a Training Framework

1. Due to a narrow analysis or fear of their communities' and government's responses to such an internal critique, scholars and writers often blame or focus their analysis on such external factors (colonialism, imperialism, or Zionism) without considering their society's internal factors as well.

2. It is difficult and complex to capture the historical relationship between Islam as a religion and Arab culture; however, it is agreed upon or assumed that Arab culture had a central role in Islamic religion, and that Islam has been a dominant factor in shaping Arab culture. Such culture or society has been termed an Islamicated context. A similar interaction took place between Islam and other

cultures that adopted it as a religion (Persian, Central Asian, African, etc.) See Mursi 1989, 18–19.

3. By the same token Salem (1994, 146) describes a reality that in all political parties and national movements, except the Islamist, there was a cross-sectarian representation of Christians and non-Muslims. In fact, in several political parties, such as the Communist and Ba'th Parties, Christians and non-Muslims were over-represented.

With the exception of the Gulf area, there are Christian minorities in all other Muslim countries. Such communities have suffered in many cases from persecution and discrimination, as a result of governmental policies and popular attitudes. See sources on Christian minorities in Egypt, Jordan, Iraq, Syria, etc.: A. Hourani 1947; Hudson 1977; McLaurin 1979; Nisan 1991; Schulze, Stokes, and Campbell 1996.

4. Barakat (1993, 42) argues that culture in the Arab case contains several cultural foci and that it is a dynamic and changing culture. Although it has many subcultures (religious, class, regional, etc.), nevertheless Arab culture has its own dominant features, constructed from what is most common and diffused among Arabs. In addition, cultural and traditional Islam has adapted different elements from various cultures and civilizations to its own requirements and blended them within its civilization. Islam, then, came up with unique discoveries through the course of its own development (Peretz 1994, 39; Hudson 1977, 42).

5. The discussion of these challenges is based on workshops in conflict resolution and other nonviolent methods conducted in Egypt, Jordan, the West Bank, Gaza, Turkey, Israel, Philippines, Sri Lanka, and the United States. It is also based on interviews with other trainers of nonviolence who operated in these areas and others.

6. *Associated Press,* August 30, 1997. Deborah Seward estimated the number of people killed at seventy-five thousand. Seward, "West Eyes Opening to Algeria Massacres Mount in the Seventh Year of Struggle," *Rocky Mountain News,* January 12, 1998,

7. "A Revolution to End the Revolution," *Economist* 345 (October 25, 1997).

8. In May 1998 a wave of massive protests took place in several cities in Jordan. Forces were deployed and curfews imposed to restore control. *Reuters,* July 22, 1998.

9. *Los Angeles Times,* May 23, 1998; *Christian Science Monitor,* June 9, 1998.

10. On the various stratification systems that exist in Arab society, see Barakat 1993.

11. Daryush Shayegan (1992) describes a set of values and behaviors related to technocratic culture and mentality in Iran that contributes to the cultural and social stagnation of the society. These technocrats either have no ideological loyalty or they adapt to the new regime for their own interests.

12. In every training workshop in the Middle East, participants engage in informal and formal discussions attempting to analyze the factors preventing the re-

vival and awaking of the Arab and Muslim political and cultural influence. Thus, most participants see in such meetings a forum for exchanging ideas on social and political change. When participants are asked about their primary motivation for taking part in these meetings, they share the following: frustration about current reality, the desire to gain more liberties, the achievement of social and political equality, and the righting of socioeconomic and political injustices. An Egyptian participant best summarized these feelings: "The technocratic system has prevented the advancement of any new leadership in the various ministerial offices, and people wonder why change has not arrived in our governments." Conflict Resolution Workshop, Cairo, March 1997.

13. Jurists and theologians from Islamic al-Azhar University declared that the Camp David treaty with Israel was not contrary to Islamic law (J. Jansen 1986), a decree that contradicted the 1968 decision by another group of jurists and theologians at the same institution (Tessler and Grobschmidt 1995). Islamic religious leaders who control official institutions have been subject to pressure and co-optation by the political ruling regimes, particularly in the Arab world. The case of al-Azhar in Egypt illustrates the point. In 1961 the Nasser regime formally changed the function and leadership role of al-Azhar to coincide with Egyptian policy at that time. Every president has carried out the same "nationalization of the religious institutes" (Haddad 1980, 117).

14. Many researchers have supported the link between political repression and the growing strength of Islamic political movements: "As long as the Arab governments resist political participation and refuse to tolerate different political opinions, the strength of Islam as an alternative political ideology will continue to grow" (al-Suwaidi 1995, 92). Wright (1991) and Garnham and Tessler (1995) also support the conclusion that the power of radical Islamic groups did not originate in a vacuum, but as a result of the combination of economic hardship, political failure, and social turmoil. There are many studies explaining the impact of globalization on Muslim communities too. For instance, Ronald Inglehart (1997, 184, 243) supports the argument that "fundamentalist" movements in the Islamic societies are only a temporary reaction to the changes brought by modernization and globalization. Thus, these movements will eventually disappear or lose their appeal once the Islamic countries and societies are fully modernized.

15. Many observations have been made in regard to the tension and rising internal conflicts in the Arab-Muslim countries as a result of modernization. "On the social level, uneven modernization has accentuated the differences between classes: the gap between the literate and the illiterate, the rural and the urban, the commercial, landed upper middle classes and the new salaried technocrats, the old and the young, even women and men. On the political level, modernization has set in motion a bare-knuckled conflict of ideology, which contributes to the persisting instability in the region" (Hudson 1977, 129). Dessouki (1998) stresses that religion became a source of rebellion in a context characterized by the weakening of traditional bonds.

16. The Taliban regime in Afghanistan, for example, issued a decree in 1998 to destroy all television and satellite equipment in Afghanistan, accusing such technologies of destroying the country's culture and fomenting social and cultural problems. *New York Times,* July 6, 1998. Muslim leadership in Palestine, Egypt, and Algeria has urged abandoning the Internet because of its negative impact on the young.

17. Mernissi (1992, 44) in explaining the reasons for the underdevelopment of Arab-Muslim countries, cites that Middle Eastern states bought more than 40 percent of all arms sold throughout the world in the 1980s, wasting on hardware the wealth that could have financed full employment.

18. Fuad Khuri (1997, 131) states that in Arab-Muslim society, the whole theory of social and religious differentiation rotates around the "power syndrome." To mention only a few ethnographic details: "the weak tribes are client tribes, the strong are patrons (*usul*)." He argues that the Arab-Muslim culture lacks the participatory tradition, or even the notion of public, which makes it difficult to establish true democratic cultures or regimes. "The social fabric of the Arab society, which rotates around the concept of endogamy (*al-usuliya*), inhibits the rise of a civic public, and this fact weakens the democratic process." He also identifies the social individual solidarity (*'asabiyah*) as another value that decreases the possibility of democratic processes.

19. Barakat (1993, 80) best summarizes the Muslim economic reality of the 1990s: (1) dependence on the world capitalist system, in which Arab countries lost control over their own resources; (2) widening disparities in terms of development, which resulted in widening the gap between rich and poor in all Arab countries; (3) disparities between rich and poor Arab countries; and (4) lack of balanced development due to poor distribution of resources and poor development strategies.

20. See the political and economic conditions in countries such as Jordan, Egypt, Palestine, Lebanon, Syria, and Algeria, where poverty is shaped by either a war economy or a powerful economic elite. These countries have an average annual growth rate (1985–95) of –0.03, while low- and middle-income countries had a rate of 0.4 and high-income countries 1.9. Based on Korany, Brynen, and Noble 1998.

21. Dependent modernization "is a distorted form of modernization that is neither modern nor traditional, but it manages to prevent and limit participation of powerless members of society because of the continuing control and dominance of single leadership." Sharabi 1988.

22. Many feminist scholars and writers have supported such statements. Two of the classic writers on this theme are Fatima Mernissi (1975) and Nawal El-Saadawi (1982).

23. Based on the Gender Development Index (GDI), a measure of typical living conditions (on a scale of 0 to 1). This measure is based on three criteria, each given equal weight: life expectancy, educational attainment (including literacy and primary and secondary enrollment, at 2/3 ratio, and tertiary enrollment, at 1/3 ratio),

and per capita gross national product (GNP). The index for Arab-Muslim countries is 0.537, compared to 0.856 for industrial countries and 0.374 for sub-Saharan Africa. Women are severely underrepresented in the governments of Arab-Muslim countries: 2 percent, in comparison to 12.5 percent in industrial countries (5.5 percent in all developed countries) and 6.6 percent in sub-Saharan Africa. In addition, all Arab-Muslim states discriminate against women and have recorded substantial violations of women's rights, based on statistics gathered by Korany, Brynen, and Noble (1998). Valentine Moghadam argues that Islam as a religion is not the main factor that determines the status of women in the Middle East, but that women's roles and status are "structurally determined by the state ideology (regime orientation and judicial system), level and type of economic development (extent of industrialization, urbanization, proletarianization, and position in the world system), and class location. A sex/gender system informed by Islam may be identified, but to ascribe principal explanatory power to religion and culture is methodologically deficient, as it exaggerates their influence and renders them timeless and unchanging" (1993, 14). She also argues that a patriarchal system is not static but ever changing, even in the Middle Eastern and Islamic countries. Modernity and economic and sociocultural changes are taking place in which women are able to overcome the limits of the traditional patriarchal system. She provides examples from Iran, Afghanistan, Algeria, Egypt, and Yemen. Thus the patriarchal system exists, but both emerging middle-class and working women fight such a system on a daily basis. The creation of a feminist movement in countries like Algeria has been an indicator of such change and of the ability to address new challenges, particularly facing the various Islamist movements (50).

24. Many researchers have discussed the impact of tribal values on Muslim Arab political regimes and society. Philip Khoury and Joseph Kostiner (1990, 18) argue that several new Arab states, when formed, failed to create completely centralized bureaucracies and therefore did not have a monopoly on authority. They had to adapt to new arbitrary borders. While many Middle Eastern states today still contain tribal societies within them, tribal states do not exist in any meaningful sense of the term. Tibi (1990) puts it more bluntly, arguing that Middle Eastern tribes have not integrated into the national communities. Despite the effect of rapid and disruptive social change (what some theorists call modernization), there has been little national integration along the lines of a nation-building model. See Khoury and Kostiner 1990.

25. An Egyptian diplomat in conflict resolution training, Cairo, 1998.

26. Saad Eddin Ibrahim (1994a) argues that even after the Gulf war, most Arab-Muslim regimes remain in power. In response to the various Islamist movements that undermine these regimes' legitimacy, these regimes stretched their coercive measures of control to the point of diminishing returns. Thus, Arab regimes eventually will have to strike some kind of coalition or make concessions to the secular opposition.

27. Korany, Brynen, and Noble (1998, app. 5) identify gross and substantial

violations of civil and political rights in nineteen Arab-Muslim states. Violations include killings and disappearances, torture, lack of due process, lack of freedom of speech or freedom of association, violation of workers' rights, discrimination against women, and discrimination against minorities.

28. The process of liberalization reflected in *ta'addudiyah* (multiparty system) is far more advanced and developed in these countries than the process of democratization (*dimuqratiyah*) (Korany, Brynen, and Noble 1998, 7). Such a distinction is also emphasized by Garnham and Tessler when they pose the question: "Can democracy take root and flourish in societies which lack, or may lack, a prior commitment at popular levels of freedom of expression and dissent, to organized partisan competition, to political tolerance and respect for diversity, and other liberal political principles?" (1995, xii).

29. All Arab-Muslim regimes and the political rulers of other Muslim countries are subject to this generalization of authoritarian relationships. For instance, between 1993 and 2001 the Palestinian National Authority had at least nine different branches of security to control a small population of 2 million Palestinians (Robinson 1997).

30. On several occasion peace-building training workshops were canceled by political authorities in Kuwait, Jordan, and Palestine (1994–99) due to a suspicion that such training might undermine security.

31. A great deal of research has investigated the problems of the Muslim and Arab worlds. In fact, both secular and religious scholars have been arguing over the explanation of the decline in Arab and Muslim cultures and global influence. However, secular and religious scholars differ in their analysis and conclusions as to what can and must be done, as well as how. Discussing the relationship between Islam and peace from a religious or faith perspective, Hassan Hanafi (1987) has identified several problems in the Muslim world. He highlights the absence of Muslim ideals in the life of Muslims as the core problem. This, however, is a result of economic, political, and social injustices, which first must be removed in order for Muslims to be able to live in an internal and an external world of peace. Hanafi presents seven forms of injustice for which jihad is relevant: (1) the occupation of Muslim land; (2) internal oppression and dictatorial regimes (including Marxism, socialism, democracy); (3) the polarity between rich and poor; (4) the dismantlement of the Muslim world through artificial borders; (5) the underdevelopment or backwardness of the Muslim world; (6) the Westernization of Muslim identity, in response to which Islamic fundamentalism is growing; and (7) the lack of mass mobilization for a huge project of global renaissance, leaving the masses vulnerable to the expansion of underground groups. Hanafi raises valid points in terms of economic and political stagnation. He proposes, however, a set of Islamic revivalist rules without ruling out the use of violence in removing any of these obstacles—a proposition contrary to peace-building aims and methods.

32. The data reported in this area of application is based on my professional experience as practitioner of conflict resolution and peace building since the early

1980s. (I have led hundreds of Palestinian and Israeli Jewish dialogue groups in Israel and Palestine.) The data is also derived from interviews and exchanges with Muslims and non-Muslims in the Middle East (both individuals and groups from Palestine, Egypt, Jordan, Turkey) and outside the Arab and Muslim worlds as well. I have conducted thirty-two different workshops in peace building (conflict resolution, dialogue, nonviolent community building and organization) since 1992 (on average, one every three months). At least 550 Muslim participants took part in these training workshops. These participants were often community leaders, professionals, and politicians. The workshops often were sponsored by such international organizations as Search for Common Ground and the Institute for Multi-Track Diplomacy. Such workshops are designed and implemented by experts in conflict resolution and peace-building practices. The design usually includes a series of two or three workshops (four to five days each) that aim to train local trainers in conflict resolution and peace-building strategies and skills. A typical workshop design includes concepts such as the causes and dynamics of conflict, problem-solving techniques, mediation, group facilitation, effective negotiation strategies, nonviolent strategies of resistance and change, community problem-solving methods, and basic communication skills. The participants of such workshops are often recruited by a local sponsoring organization. The type of participant often depends on the interest, scope, and mission of the local organization network. For a full description of such training workshops, see Abu-Nimer 1998.

The data for this research was gathered through direct observations of participants in these workshops, unstructured and unscheduled interviews with a random number of participants, and structured interviews with selected group members who expressed interest in the theme of Islam and its relation to conflict resolution or nonviolence. Due to the sensitivity of the issues and themes discussed in this research and in the training workshops, names and specific locations of those individuals cannot be publicly shared. However the general location and date of the workshops is usually cited.

33. Such a critique is valid when considering the broad range of conflict resolution activities that can be included in any training workshop. For example, a training in the Alternative Dispute Resolution (ADR) system may very well emphasize the notion of a settlement without addressing issues of justice and deep-rooted causes of intractable conflicts. For examples of such short-term outputs of intervention, see Kriesberg 1998, 202.

34. Nonviolence International and the Mohamed Said Farsi Islamic Peace Chair at the American University (Washington, D.C.) sponsored two conferences (1997, 1998) on this theme. Some of the participants (or panelists) argued the above notion.

35. It is important to distinguish between several types of communities in Arab-Muslim societies. First, those who live in a traditional context of social structures, often secluded in small villages and towns away from the urban areas, and less influenced by technological changes. The second category is the transitional com-

munities, whose members often live in an urban setting and have on average a higher level of education; and their types of consumption and general lifestyle are different than those of the first group. Such communities are not fully urbanized in the sense of Western industrial and urban societies, but they have acquired a non-traditional set of norms and values as a result of their education and exposure to other lifestyles. This allows members of the transitional community to share more commonalities with individualistic, consumerist, and highly competitive cultures. In general, transitional societies share more values and norms with Western indus-trial societies than with traditional ones (Barakat 1993).

36. Conflict resolution workshop, Gaza city, fall 1994 (sponsored by Search for Common Ground and the Gaza mental health program).

37. It can be argued that part of such an attitude is related to the perception and actual status of academicians and researchers, as professionals who should not deal with the applied aspects of ideas. Certain scholars who participated in the conflict resolution workshops believe that the further you remove yourself as an academician from the applied aspects of conflict resolution and the practical role of the agents of social change, the more objective, and therefore better, your analy-sis becomes.

38. Certain scholars of Islamic studies have contributed to these widespread misperceptions too. John Voll (1994) defuses some misperceptions when he cites some of the changes and developments that have taken place in three cores of Islamic civilization (the Middle East, Central Asia and China, and the Indian Ocean), as identified by Janet Abu-Lughod (1989). The end of the unity of a single Islamic empire did not mean the end of the development of Islamic civilization.

39. "Conflict Resolution and Community Building," workshop for community organizers, Gaza, summer 1997.

40. Conflict resolution workshop for regional staff and directors of CARE International, Amman, May 1998.

41. Conflict resolution workshop, Conflict Resolution Skills Institute, Ameri-can University, Washington, D.C., September 1997.

Chapter 5. Peace Building and Nonviolent Political Movements in Arab-Muslim Communities: A Case Study of the Palestinian Intifada

This chapter is based on a paper by Joseph W. Groves (1991), professor of religious studies and director of peace and conflict studies at Guilford College, Greensboro, N.C. The paper grew from two three–week visits to the occupied territories, one in March 1989, sponsored by the American-Arab Anti-Discrimina-tion Committee, the other in June 1990, for Middle East Witness (an initiative launched by International Fellowship for Reconciliation to express solidarity with victims of Middle East conflict). The majority of both visits were spent in Hebron, the Bethlehem area, Jerusalem, and Gaza, with much of the time spent living with Palestinian families. The focal points of the visit were observing the conditions of the Intifada and conversing extensively with the families and their friends about experiences and attitudes. All names used in the paper are pseudonyms. The at chapter has been supplemented by material from my numerous visits to the occupied territories, a third month-long visit by Dr. Groves (sponsored by Grassroots International in September 1995), and additional revision and analysis by both of us. The material for the chapter is drawn primarily from the first two years of the Intifada, when the nonviolent tenor of the resistance was predominant.

1. Thus, this chapter offers an alternative perspective to the argument made by some who argue that the Intifada had nothing to do with Islam—that it was a purely nationalistic endeavor that repressed religious aspects. According to Mubarak Awad, a well-known and respected Palestinian leader of the nonviolent campaign before and during the Intifada, "At early stages of the Intifada there was no Christian or Islamic religious figure or clergy involved. In fact, we tried to bring them on board as early as possible but they gave us many excuses why they could not be involved." "Hamas and Jihad also were not on board at that point." Interviews with Mubarak Awad, American University, Washington, D.C., March 26, 2000, February 19, 1999.

2. The Palestinian factions were fighting internally after the PLO withdrew its armed soldiers from Beirut and departed to Tunisia in 1982. Opposition groups in the north of Lebanon engaged in a militant confrontation with forces loyal to Arafat. In fact, some have argued that the leadership and people of the West Bank and Gaza have provided the PLO with legitimacy and life by insisting on representation via PLO officials only. The PLO was in its weakest state after the 1982 war. The Intifada brought it to life again as a political and national liberation movement. Interview with Mubarak Awad, Nonviolence International, Washington, D.C., March 2000.

3. For a thorough study of the development and role of mass organizations, see Taraki 1989b and Hiltermann 1991.

4. The Center for the Study of Nonviolence was started by Mubarak Awad, a Palestinian American who returned to Palestine and intensively worked on applying nonviolent strategies and methods to the Palestinian reality.

5. It is hard to capture the human dimension and other factors that triggered and sustained the Intifada; however, the suffering of the community on all levels stretched the limits of tolerance for the Israeli military administration. One of the central factors was the combination of the following: constant economic pressure on businesses to pay high fines and taxes; permission for mobility and other daily necessities, which became hard to get without the approval of local collaborators (before, local mukhtars and other dignitaries could help people gain access to resources, but during the Intifada the Palestinians who collaborated with the Israeli administration became the gatekeepers); the arrest of professionals and respected members of the national elite (doctors, lawyers, and members of the Nusseibeh and Hussaini families), and the detention of youth from major cities, not only from refugee camps. These elements compounded the pressure on the

Palestinian elite as well as the refugee population. Interview with Mubarak Awad, Nonviolence International, March 2000.

The use of plastic bullets was introduced as a tool to reduce lethal injuries to protestors. However, the bullets caused thousands of disabilities among Palestinians.

6. The PLO was represented in the UNLU by four main factions: Fatah, the Popular Front for Liberation of Palestine (PFLP), the Democratic Front for the Liberation of Palestine (DFLP), and the Communist Party (CP). In addition, Islamic Jihad participated for a brief period. The PFLP, DFLP, and CP form the "progressive wing" of the PLO. The CP, mainly based in the West Bank and Gaza, has never advocated armed struggle for the liberation of Palestine.

7. As indicated by many Palestinian interviewees, it is important to distinguish, as does international law, between terrorism and legitimate armed resistance. Because the Palestinian resistance prior to the Intifada used both terrorism and armed struggle, Israel and the United States have managed to blur the distinction between the two. For the right to resistance, see Armanazi 1974.

8. Jerome Segal (1989, 67–72) has stated a persuasive case for this relinquishment.

9. This term was used many times by the UNLU, beginning at least as early as Call 18 (May 28, 1988).

10. Several interviewees associated with the PFLP in the West Bank and Gaza held this position. The PFLP's analysis of the nature and role of civil disobedience appears frequently in articles in the magazine *Democratic Palestine*. The following articles demonstrate their developing analysis of the Intifada: "Mass Resistance," 27 (1987): 25–27; "Palestinian Fists Challenge the Iron Fist," 27 (1987): 28–31; "From Stones to Civil Disobedience," 28 (1988): 9–13; "Civil Disobedience," 29 (1988): 12–14; "Armed Struggle and the Uprising: Interview with Comrade Abu Ahmad Fuad," 29 (1988): 18–19.

11. Most of the interviewees held such beliefs. And the Palestinian Center for the Study of Nonviolence advocated civil disobedience for many years. See Awad 1984, 1988a,b; Feffer 1988; Wilsnack 1986. Other writers have implied that reliance on civil disobedience alone is the necessary strategy: Hijab 1989; Khalidi 1988; B. Kuttab and J. Kuttab 1988; D. Kuttab 1988; Siniora 1988.

12. For a description and historical examples of methods, see vol. 2 of Sharp's *The Methods of Nonviolent Action*. Sharp also responds directly, if briefly, to the Intifada in a 1987 interview with Afif Safieh.

13. Based on interviews we conducted between 1988 and 1992, it is safe to say that both the supporters of unconditioned nonviolence and those who affirm the need for armed struggle to overcome Israeli repression would regard stone throwing as violent.

14. The quotes in this section arise from a number of discussions held in Hebron, Dhaisheh refugee camp, and a village near Bethlehem in 1988 and 1989.

The nature of these discussions, as well as the quotes, is significant: the discussions were a group process, with the members of the group agreeing on the main points while disagreeing on some specifics.

15. Interview with Nafez Asseley of the Palestinian Center for the Study of Nonviolence, Jerusalem, March 27, 1989.

16. The Civil Rights struggle did not take place in a situation of occupation by a separate nation. White southerners who opposed the movement were constrained by a federal government that wielded power over them (even though the government was reluctant to take action against them). The Civil Rights Movement held the high moral ground from the beginning: it was a church-based movement in a Christian country; the southern establishment was held in low esteem for various reasons; as fellow citizens of the United States, southern African-Americans could effectively appeal to shared ideals of freedom and equality. Consequently, Southern authorities could not openly resort to lethal violence. They could not jail Civil Rights leaders without raising an outcry in the North; and their ability to jail anyone for a long period or without charge was limited. Furthermore, the demands of the movement were modest: it was not asking for land or independence, but for equal treatment under law. Thus, the threat posed was less severe than the threat the Israelis perceive from Palestinians. As a result, nonviolent resistance was a practical option for the Civil Rights movement.

17. The reports of Raja Shehadeh (1982, 1985, 1988a,b) give a good sense of the application of law by Israel in the Occupied Territories.

18. One Israeli response to the Intifada was to open numerous new prisons to increase the period of administrative detention (a legal process that allowed Palestinians to be held in prison with no formal charge) from six months to one year. For a detailed study of Israel's tactics during the Intifada, see Law in the Service of Man 1988. Israel's willingness to act forcefully against nonviolent actions was indicated by its response to the Ship of Return in 1988. The PLO hired a ship to carry Palestinian exiles back to Israel for a symbolic return, accompanied by the international press, nonviolent activists, and several sympathetic Israeli citizens. The Israelis assassinated the three PLO officials who had purchased the ship and sank the ship in a Greek harbor with an explosive device. Particularly striking was the lack of any international concern over Israel's action, indicating that the Palestinians have yet to seize the moral high ground so important to nonviolent resistance. See McReynolds 1988; Hurwitz and Kennedy 1988.

19. In fact, several of the Israeli peace activists and scholars have used this latter term. For example, Reuven Kaminer states that the Intifada "was non-violent in the sense that an unarmed civilian population developed the capacity to confront an army of occupation and create, by virtue of internal cohesion and discipline, an alternative source of power." They exercise that power "in order to deny the occupier of his most cherished assets: stability and all the semblances of normality that go with it" (1996, 42).

20. From the beginning of the Intifada to September 1989, approximately fifty Israelis died in Intifada-related violence; some two thousand attacks with knives, bombs, and Molotov cocktails were reported; some eighty-five Palestinians were killed by other Palestinians as collaborators. The statistics vary considerably depending on the source, but these give an indication of the degree of Palestinian violence in the first twenty-two months of the Intifada. The PBS program "Intifada: The Palestinians and Israel," aired on September 6, 1989, quoted Israeli figures of under fifty Israeli deaths, a thousand incidents of arson, and approximately two thousand uses of Molotov cocktails since the beginning of the Intifada. A report on NPR's *All Things Considered* (September 4, 1989), in addition to quoting similar figures, stated that half the firebombs had been directed at Arab targets. U.S. newspapers (July 28, 1989) stated that eighty-five collaborators had been killed. In contrast, it was reported that 657 Palestinians were killed by Israelis. *Al-Fajr Weekly,* September 11, 1989.

21. Anonymous translation of Call 37, issued March 3, 1989. References to the Calls (*bayan*) are based on careful examination of the English translations of the texts of thirteen Calls and summaries of the contents of another nineteen, for a total of thirty-two of the first forty Calls.

22. Islamic Jihad issued a statement from Lebanon claiming responsibility for a July 6, 1989, bus crash that killed seventeen Israelis. The PLO later issued a statement deploring the incident. Even with the claims and disclaimers issued around the bus incident, responsibility for it remains murky.

23. Even when overt collaborators were still at work, their role changed. They were socially ostracized, so they could not work from within Palestinian society. They were reduced to being an armed adjunct to the occupation forces, eliminating their primary value to Israel. For a picture of the alienation of overt collaborators from their people, see Zvi Gilat, "And This Is Why They Are Called Collaborators and Hated," excerpts from "Collaborators in the Territories," *Hadashot,* July 28, 1989; in *Al-Fajr Weekly,* August 14, 1989, 10.

24. Based on interviews in the West Bank in 1989. Palestinians also claimed that the intelligence services created drug addicts and supplied drugs to control collaborators. On the other hand, Israeli claims that many of those killed as collaborators had no connection with the intelligence services were corroborated by Palestinian sources. Some members of popular committees admitted that retaliation got out of hand. A late UNLU Call stated that no killings should be carried out without specific prior approval of the leadership.

25. The other thirty actions could only be carried out by a government. Indeed, Israel uses some of them against Palestinians.

26. Only 24 are actions that were tried—and three of those would be counterproductive to the Palestinian cause. Of the remaining 57 actions, research reveals that many have been employed. These 87 categories range across Sharp's complete spectrum of actions.

27. This section is based on interviews and discussions with members of popular committees in various parts of the West Bank and Gaza conducted between 1992 and 1997, and on Salameh 1994.

28. For further information on the historical roots of the nonviolent resistance, see Crow, Grant, and Ibrahim 1990.

29. Many of the methods Sharp describes have been used in the Intifada: consumers' boycotts; a policy of austerity; a national consumers' boycott; traders' boycotts; refusal to let or sell property; merchants' general strikes; refusal to pay fees, dues, and assessments; revenue refusal; refusal of impressed labor; prisoners' strikes; professional strikes; general strikes; economic shutdown.

30. In dealing with Beit Sahur, Israel apparently realized that Palestinians could be determined, steadfast, and willing to sacrifice and work collectively for a goal, particularly when the punishment was indiscriminately meted out against a whole community. Dajani 1994, 65; Nojeim 1993.

31. For accounts of tax resistance in one village, see Finklestein 1990; Grace 1990.

32. We witnessed such a protest in different villages on Land Day from 1988 to 1991.

33. Many of Sharp's methods were used before and during the Intifada: withholding or withdrawal of political allegiance; refusal of public support for certain political figures imposed by Israel; literature and speeches advocating resistance; boycotts of legislative bodies, elections, government employment and positions, government departments and agencies, and government-supported organizations; refusal of assistance to enforcement agents; refusal to accept appointed officials; refusal to dissolve existing institutions; reluctant and slow compliance; nonobedience in the absence of direct supervision; popular nonobedience; refusal of an assemblage or meeting to disperse; sitdowns; noncooperation with deportation; hiding, escape, and false identities; civil disobedience of illegitimate laws; selective refusal of assistance by government aides.

34. For a partial picture of this process, see Kuttab 1988b.

35. For pre-Intifada incidents in which Palestinians disabled or returned weapons, see Kennedy 1984.

36. Many of the full range of Sharp's categories of nonviolent intervention have been employed in the Intifada: fasting; reverse trial; physical intervention; nonviolent invasion; nonviolent interjection; nonviolent obstruction; nonviolent occupation; establishing new social patterns; alternative social institutions; alternative communications systems; nonviolent land seizure; defiance of blockades; selective patronage; alternative markets; alternative economic systems; disclosing identities of secret agents; dual sovereignty and parallel government.

37. Many Palestinians despaired of the loss of at least two years' education for their children and feared the holding back of a generation. But others felt that the closing of the schools was a difficult but ultimately positive step, that the old educational system had to be destroyed and the Israelis only hastened the process.

As one educator stated, "My children (who are in their twenties) grew up with no idea of Palestinian culture, history, geography. Now every ten-year-old, every five-year-old, knows our heroes and our history, can name every village and town, can sing our songs. They have learned the practical skills of organizing and leading. And they have no fear: they know who they are and feel they can control their own destiny. This is education. Now it is our job to direct and build on that foundation."

38. Government hospitals are those built during Jordanian and Egyptian control of the West Bank and Gaza Strip. They are now administered by Palestinians but are funded and controlled by the Israeli Civil Administration. Israeli army and police feel free to enter these hospitals, search for people wounded in confrontations with soldiers, and arrest them, frequently taking them from the hospital immediately.

39. The politics of food was a topic of conversation at every home in the West Bank. Foreign visitors were given tours of the family gardens and vineyards, in which homeowners discussed the increased planting, production, and labor needed. They provided details on the source of every dish in a meal: what came from Palestinian sources, what was imported from Israel. While this reflected some of the deep, almost mystical love for the land that Fawaz Turki (1981) describes, the renewed emphasis on the land was born of necessity, not romanticism.

40. This information is based on personal interviews during a trip to the West Bank in 1988. It is difficult to assess how widespread or effective this system was, but several instances of dispute settlement were observed by researchers as well as outsiders. See Nojeim 1993; Dajani 1994. This had resulted in a changed attitude among some Palestinians at least. One claimed: "Before the Intifada, if a man beat his wife, we would say it's his business. If it gets bad enough, she will go to the authorities. Now we feel that such behavior undermines our solidarity. If I hear that my neighbor beats his wife, I will confront him and demand that he stop. If he continues, then I will speak to the local committee about it. We have much less domestic trouble than we used to." Julie Peteet (1987) describes similar developments in refugee camps in Lebanon.

41. The popular committees lost control over the shabab, the youth who fought the Israeli military in the streets. The shabab conducted the punishment of the collaborators, or security informants. They also established rules for moral conduct and killed women who "compromised their virtue."

42. A violent revolutionary movement may have the luck or luxury of assuming power before the creation of alternative structures. For example, the Cuban revolution was successful before much structural development had occurred. But in a protracted conflict, which is usually the case with both violent and nonviolent revolutions, the development of alternative social structures is the key to sustaining the struggle. When analysis focuses on direct confrontation and armed struggle, it misses the nonviolent aspects of most revolutions, whether they embrace violence or not.

43. Subsequent conversations with Israelis and American Jews have indicated that members of Israeli peace groups working with Palestinians would agree about the respect and lack of hate among Palestinians. See Kaminer 1996; Bar-On 1996.

44. Part of the reason for the respect is the recognition of the ideals of democracy and justice espoused by Israel and Judaism. The recognition also fuels frustration and resentment among Palestinians, who see the failure to apply these ideals to the present conflict.

45. The Palestinian attitude of mutuality and acceptance would be unlikely without Israeli peace groups actively attempting to alleviate and transcend the conflict by resisting the occupation and reaching out in reciprocal respect to Palestinians. See Kaminer 1996.

46. Interview with Mubarak Awad, American University, Washington, D.C., March 26, 2000.

47. Palestinians interviewed (both those sympathetic and those antagonistic to Islamic groups) consistently said that about 10 percent of the population followed Hamas and another 10 to 20 percent were influenced by that group. This seems to coincide well with Shadid's figures of 10 percent support for the Muslim Brotherhood's political program and significantly broader support for them on social and cultural issues.

48. The comments on the ideology of Hamas is based on interviews with Hamas supporters in the West Bank in March 1989. Also see Taraki 1989; Fashah 1982.

49. Islamic Jihad also insisted that all Calls open with the traditional salutation, "In the name of Allah the merciful," but the leftists would not hear of adding a religious note to what were essentially political manifestos. Schiff and Ya'ari 1989, 214.

50. Anyone visiting the Ibrahim mosque in Hebron is struck by the Israeli affront to religious sensibilities: a shrine holy to both Islam and Judaism is surrounded by gun towers; soldiers guard the doors and patrol the mosque, casually waving their automatic weapons and slapping riot clubs in their hands.

51. These attitudes are central components for nonviolence in both Quakerism and engaged Buddhism.

52. See esp. Call 12, "The Call of Al Qastel," *Democratic Palestine* 29 (1988): 10–11.

53. Based on limited interviews with supporters of Islamic organizations, West Bank, 1989.

54. Based on interviews with Palestinians who were sympathetic to progressive and secular organizations on the West Bank, 1989.

55. An individual was regarded as shahid (martyr) whether he/she was a stone thrower shot during demonstrations or a bystander caught in a crossfire, killed by stray bullets that hit him/her at home, or who died from the effects of tear gas. Visits to martyrs' homes made the complexity of causes and interpretations apparent.

56. These attitudes represent the traditional Muslims that were interviewed, not supporters of Hamas or Islamic Jihad. Obviously this does not indicate how extensive such openness is among Palestinian Muslims, nor would it suggest that there would be an easy reconciliation between Muslims and Jews if a settlement were reached.

57. The experience of a member of a group who visited the West Bank and Gaza in 1989 may best illustrate the process. In a northern Palestinian village, five young women who spoke limited English became frustrated trying to communicate their concerns to the American visitor. One of them decided to write a statement in Arabic that could later be translated. She wrote out the statement and read it to her friends, who requested some changes. After they had agreed on its content, they took it to two older women and asked them to look at it. The older women, after making a few minor modifications, agreed that it was a worthy statement, so it was given to the visitor to use.

58. See the documentary film *Struggle for Peace*, based on Fernea and Hocking 1992.

59. This specific cultural feature of the Islamic religion—keeping social and cultural norms and rules functioning instead of relying on the rules of the Israeli administration—was identified by Mubarak Awad as an important contribution of Islamic religion to the Intifada. Interview with Mubarak Awad, Nonviolence International, Washington, D.C., March 26, 2000.

60. An important exception is the work of the Palestinian Center for the Study of Nonviolence in Jerusalem. Its joint Muslim-Christian leadership has published several works on nonviolent resistance. While the practical steps of nonviolent resistance they have advocated have been widely adopted in the Intifada, their attempts to develop a broader philosophy of nonviolence among Palestinians has met with limited success.

61. Since the main concern in this chapter is Islam, the role of Christianity in the Intifada was not explored. Palestinian Christians generally share the same Islamicate social structure that Muslims do, so most of the observations hold true for them as well. Churches play much the same role as mosques; martyrs are revered in the same way; popular committees function similarly in Christian villages; and so on. Some writings propose a Christian foundation for dealing with the Israeli-Palestinian conflict (Chacour 1984; Ateek 1989).

62. Interview with Mubarak Awad, Nonviolence International, Washington D.C., March 26, 2000.

Chapter 6. Conclusions

1. Such conferences are new, considering that in the 1970s there was only one conference in New Delhi on the subject and that in the 1980s another conference was initiated by the University of Hawaii, led by Glenn Paige and Chaiwat Satha-Anand. Thus, it is important to highlight the need for a more focused discussion on this subject rather than one conference per decade.

Bibliography

The Arabic definite article (al-) is ignored in the alphabetization of authors' family names. For example, Jamal al-Suwaidi is alphabetized as Suwaidi.

Abdelkader, Deina Ali. 1993. "Jihad: Is It a Neglected Duty?" Paper presented at the National Conference on Peacemaking and Conflict Resolution.

Abed, Shukri. "Islam and Democracy." 1995. In *Democracy, War, and Peace in the Middle East,* ed. David Garnham and Mark Tessler, 16–132. Bloomington: Indiana University Press.

Abu-Amr, Ziad. 1989. "The Palestinian Uprising in the West Bank and Gaza Strip." *Arab Studies Quarterly* 10.4: 402–5.

Abu Dawud Sulayman ibn al-Ash'ath al-Sijistani. 1998. *Kitab al-Sunan: Sunan Abu Dawud.* Jiddah: Reprinted by Dar al-Qiblah lil-Thaqafah al-Islamiyah.

Abu-Hassan, Mohammed. 1995. "Islamic Criminal Law." *Al-nadwah* 6.3 (July).

Abu-Lughod, Janet L. 1989. *Before European Hegemony: The World System,* A.D. *1250–1350.* New York: Oxford University Press.

Abu-Nimer, Mohammed. 1996a. "Conflict Resolution Approaches: Western and Middle Eastern Lessons and Possibilities." *American Journal of Economics and Sociology* 55.1: 35–53.

———. 1996b. "Conflict Resolution in an Islamic Context." *Peace and Change* 21.1: 22–40.

———. 1998. "Conflict Resolution Training in the Middle East: Lessons to Be Learned." *Negotiation Journal,* no. 3: 99–116.

———. 1999. *Dialogue, Conflict Resolution, and Change: Arab-Jewish Encounters in Israel.* New York: SUNY Press.

Abu-Rabi', Ibrahim. 1996. *Intellectual Origins of Islamic Resurgence in the Modern Arab World.* New York: SUNY Press.

Ahmad, Razi. 1993. "Islam, Nonviolence, and Global Transformation." In *Islam and Nonviolence,* ed. Glenn Paige, Chaiwat Satha-Anand, and Sarah Gilliatt, 27–53. Honolulu: Center for Global Nonviolence Planning Project, Matsunaga Institute for Peace, University of Hawaii.

Ahmed, Akbar. 1988. *Discovering Islam: Making Sense of Muslim History and Society.* London: Routledge and Kegan Paul.

Ajami, Fouad. 1981. *The Arab Predicament: Arab Political Thought and Practice since 1967.* New York: Cambridge University Press.

al-Albani, Muhammad Nasir al-Din. 1988. *Da'if Sunan Ibn Majah*. Beirut: al-Maktab al-Islami.

Ali, Abdullah Yusuf. 1991. *The Meaning of the Holy Qur'an*. Brentwood, Md.: Amana Corporation.

Ali, F. 1993. "Conflict: Its Psychological Cause, Effect, and Resolution through the Qur'an." Paper presented at Conference on Conflict Resolution in the Arab World, Cyprus.

Ali, Muhammad. 1944. *A Manual of Hadith*. Lahore: Ahmadiyya Anjuman.

Anderson, Lisa. 1994. "Liberalism, Islam, and Arab State." *Dissent* 41.4: 439–44.

Antoun, Richard. 1979. *Low Key Politics: Local-Level Leadership and Change in the Middle East*. Albany: SUNY Press.

———. 1997. "Institutionalized Deconfrontation: A Case Study of Conflict Resolution among Tribal Peasants in Jordan." In *Conflict Resolution in the Arab World: Selected Essays*, ed. Paul Salem, 140–75. Beirut: American University of Beirut.

Arabi, Osama. 1993. "Constitutional Aspects of Conflict Resolution in Classical Islam: Koranic Text and Prophetic Sunna as Means of Facing Political Crisis, Legal Conflicts, and Power Abuse." Paper presented at the Conference on Conflict Resolution in the Arab World, Cyprus.

Armanazi, Ghayth. 1974. "The Rights of Palestinians: The International Dimension." *Journal of Palestine Studies* 3.3: 93–94.

Ateek, Naim Stifan. 1989. *Justice, and Only Justice: A Palestinian Theology of Liberation*. Maryknoll, N.Y.: Orbis Books.

Augsburger, David. 1992. *Conflict Mediation across Cultures: Pathways and Patterns*. Louisville: Westminister/John Knox Press.

Avruch, Kevin. 1998. *Culture and Conflict Resolution*. Washington, D.C.: United States Institute of Peace Press.

Avruch, Kevin, Peter Black, and Joseph Scimecca, eds. 1991. *Conflict Resolution: Cross-Cultural Perspectives*. New York: Greenwood Press.

Awad, Mubarak. 1984. "Nonviolent Resistance: A Strategy for the Occupied Territories." *Journal of Palestine Studies* 8.2: 49–64; 8.4: 22–36.

———. 1988a. "Nonviolence Is the Better Way." *Middle East International*, January 9: 21.

———. 1988b. "The Strategy of Disobedience." *Middle East*, February: 24–25.

'Awwa, Muhammad Salim. 1983. *Fi al-nizam al-siyasi lil-dawlah al-islamiyyah* (The political system of the Islamic state). Cairo: al-Maktab al-Misri al-Hadith.

Ayoub, Mahmoud. 1996. "The Islamic Concept of Justice." In *Islamic Identity and the Struggle for Justice*, ed. Nimat Barazangi, M. Raquibuz Zaman, and Omar Afzal. Gainesville: University Press of Florida.

———. 1997. "Nonviolence in Islam: A Dialogue between Muslims." Paper presented at conference on nonviolence and peace in Islam sponsored by the Nonviolence International Center and Mohammed Said Farsi Chair of Islamic Peace, American University, Washington, D.C., February.

al-Baladhuri, Ahmed ibn Yahya. 1866. *Futuh al-buldan* (Conquest of countries). Ed. M. J. de Goeje. Leiden: E. J. Brill.

Barakat, Halim. 1993. *The Arab World: Society, Culture, and State.* Berkeley: University of California Press.

Barazangi, Nimat, M. Raquibuz Zaman, and Omar Afzal, eds. 1996. *Islamic Identity and the Struggle for Justice.* Gainesville: University Press of Florida.

Bar-On, Mordechai. 1996. *In Pursuit of Peace: A History of the Israeli Peace Movement.* Washington, D.C.: United States Institute of Peace Press.

Beinin, Joel, and Joe Stork, eds. 1997. "The New Orientalism and Democracy." In *Political Islam: Essays from Middle East Report,* 35–45. Berkeley: University of California Press.

Bennet, Brad. 1990. "Arab-Muslim Cases of Nonviolence Struggle." In *Arab Nonviolent Political Struggle in the Middle East,* ed. Ralph Crow, Philip Grant, and Saad Ibrahim. Boulder: Lynne Rienner.

Bennis, Phyllis. 1990. *From Stones to Statehood: The Palestinian Uprising.* New York: Olive Branch Press.

Bjorkman, Len. 1988. "Control's Observation during the Curfew." *Fellowship,* October–November, 11–13.

Brumberg, Daniel. 1991. "Islamic Fundamentalism, Democracy, and the Gulf War." In *Islamic Fundamentalism and the Gulf Crisis,* ed. James Piscatori. Chicago: American Academy of Arts and Sciences.

al-Bukhari, Muhammad ibn Isma'il. 1959. *Al-adab al-mufrad.* Cairo: n.p.

———. 1983. *The Translation of the Meaning of* Sahih al-Bukhari: *Arabic-English.* By Muhammad Muhsin Khan. 6th rev. ed. Jami' al-sahih. English and Arabic. 9 vols. Lahore, Pakistan: Kazi Publications.

———. *Sahih al-Bukhari.* 1998. 8 vols. Beirut: Dar al-Kutub al-I'lmiya. (Arabic)

Burgess, Heidi, and Guy Burgess. 1994. "Justice without Violence: A Theoretical Framework." In *Justice without Violence,* ed. Paul Wehr, Heidi Burgess, and Guy Burgess. Boulder: Lynne Rienner

Burns, J. Patout, ed. 1996. *War and Its Discontents: Pacifism and Quietism in the Abrahamic Traditions.* Washington, D.C.: Georgetown University Press.

Burton, John. 1990. *Conflict: Resolution and Prevention.* New York: St. Martin's Press.

Bush, Robert, and Joseph Folger. 1994. *The Promise of Mediation.* San Francisco: Jossey-Bass.

Carmody, Lardner, and Tully Carmody. 1988. *Peace and Justice in the Scriptures of the World Religions: Reflections on Non-Christian Scriptures.* New York: Paulist Press.

Catholic Relief Services (CRS). 1999. *Report on Islam, Peace, and Justice.* Baltimore: n.p.

Chacour, Elias. 1984. *Blood Brothers.* Grand Rapids: Chosen Books.

Cheragh Ali, Moulavi. 1977. "The Popular *Jihad* or Crusade; According to the

Muhammadan Common Law." In *Critical Exposition of the Popular "Jihad,"* 114–61. Karachi: Karimsons.

Childress, James. 1982. *Moral Responsibility in Conflicts: Essays on Nonviolence, War, and Conscience.* Baton Rouge: Louisiana State University Press.

Clawson, Patrick. 1994. "Liberty's the Thing, Not Democracy." *Middle East Quarterly* 1.3: 1–2.

Cole, Donald Powell. 1975. *Nomads of the Nomads: The al-Murrah Bedouin of the Empty Quarter.* Chicago: Aldine.

Collins, Frank. 1988. "Destroying the Network of Palestinian Collaborators." *Washington Report on Middle East Affairs,* November, 20.

Commins, David. 1986. "Religious Reformers and Arabists in Damascus, 1885–1914." *International Journal of Middle Eastern Studies* 18.4: 405–25.

Crow, Douglas Karim. 1998. "Nurturing an Islamic Peace Discourse." Visiting fellow publication, Center for Global Peace, American University, Washington, D.C.

Crow, Ralph, Philip Grant, and Saad Eddin Ibrahim, eds. 1990. *Arab Nonviolent Struggle in the Middle East.* Boulder: Lynne Rienner.

Dajani, Souad. 1993. "Towards the Formulation of a Strategy of Nonviolent Civilian Resistance: The Occupied Palestinian Territories as a Case Study." *International Journal of Nonviolence* 1.1: 35–53.

———.1995. *Eyes without Country: Searching for a Palestinian Strategy of Liberation.* Philadelphia: Temple University Press.

Daraz, Mohammad Abdullah. 1972. *Nazarah fi al-Islam.* Cairo: n.p.

Dessouki, Ali. 1998. "Crisis in Muslim State and Society." Paper presented at the Islam and Cultural Diversity Conference, Center for Global Peace, American University, Washington, D.C.

Diamond, Louise, and John McDonald. 1991. *Multi-Track Diplomacy: A Systems Guide and Analysis.* Grinnell: Iowa Peace Institute.

Donner, Fred. 1991. "The Sources of Islamic Conceptions of War." In *Just War and Jihad: Historical and Theoretical Perspectives on War and Peace in Western and Islamic Traditions,* ed. John Kelsay and James Turner Johnson, 31–69. New York: Greenwood Press.

Dunn, Michael. 1992. "Revivalist Islam and Democracy: Thinking about the Algerian Quandary." *Middle East Policy* 1.2: 16–22.

Easwaran, Eknath. 1984. *A Man to Match His Mountains: Badshah Khan, Nonviolent Soldier of Islam.* Petaluma, Calif.: Nilgiri Press.

Emerson, Steve. 1993a. "Accidental Tourist." *Washington Post,* 13 June.

———. 1993b. "Islamic Fundamentalism Terrible Threat to the West." *San Diego Union-Tribune,* 27 June.

Engineer, Ashgar. 1994. "Sources of Nonviolence in Islam." *Nonviolence: Contemporary Issues and Challenges,* ed. Mahendra Kumar. New Delhi: Gandhi Peace Foundation.

Esack, Farid. 1997. *Qur'an, Liberation, and Pluralism: An Islamic Perspective of Interreligious Solidarity against Oppression.* Oxford: Oneworld.

———. 1998. "Religion and Cultural Diversity: For What and with Whom?" Paper presented at the Islam and Cultural Diversity Conference, Center for Global Peace, American University, Washington, D.C.

———. 1999. *On Being a Muslim: Finding a Religious Path in the World Today.* Oxford: Oneworld.

Esposito, John. 1988. *Islam: The Straight Path.* New York: Oxford University Press.

———. 1992. *The Islamic Threat.* New York: Oxford University Press.

Esposito, John, and James Piscatori. 1991. "Democratization and Islam." *Middle East Journal* 45.3: 427–40.

Esposito, John, and John Voll. 1996. *Islam and Democracy.* New York: Oxford University Press.

Fadl, Atiawa Khir Allah. 1982. *Rehlat Alf Sanal ma Qaba'l Awlad Ali* (One thousand years journey with Awlad Ali tribes). Alexandria, Egypt: n.p.

Fashah, Munir. 1982. "Political Islam in the West Bank." *Middle East Report* 12.2: 15–17.

Feffer, John. 1988. "All but Guns." *Nuclear Times,* November–December, 21–24.

Ferguson, John. 1978. *War and Peace in the World's Religions.* New York: Oxford University Press.

Fernea, Elizabeth Warnock, and Mary Evelyn Hocking, eds. *Struggle for Peace: Israelis and Palestinians.* Austin: University of Texas Press.

Finklestein, Norman. 1990. "Bayt Sahur in Year II of the Intifada: A Personal Account." *Journal of Palestine Studies* 19.2: 62–74.

Fisher, Roger, and William Ury. 1981. *Getting to Yes: Negotiating Agreement without Giving In.* Boston: Houghton Mifflin.

Fisher, Ronald. 1997. *Interactive Conflict Resolution.* Syracuse: Syracuse University Press.

Friedmann, Yohanan. 1989. *Prophecy Continuous: Aspects of Ahmadi Religious Thought and Its Medieval Background.* Berkeley: University of California Press.

Galtung, Johan. 1969. "Peace Violence and Peace Research." *Journal of Peace Research* 6: 167–91.

Garnham, David, and Mark Tessler, eds. 1995. *Democracy, War, and Peace in the Middle East.* Bloomington: Indiana University Press.

Gauhar, Altaf. 1978. "Islam and Secularism." In *The Challenges of Islam,* ed. Altaf Gauhar. London: Islamic Council of Europe.

al-Ghazali, Sa'id. 1987. "Islamic Movement versus National Liberation." *Journal of Palestine Studies* 17.1: 176–81.

Gilat, Zvi. "And This Is Why They Are Called Collaborators and Hated." *Hadashot,* July 28, 1989.

Ginat, Joseph. 1997. *Blood Revenge: Family Honor, Mediation, and Outcasting.* Portland, Ore.: Sussex Academic.

Grace, Anne. 1990. "The Tax Resistance at Bayt Sahur." *Journal of Palestine Studies* 19.2: 99–107.

Groves, Joseph W. 1991. "Islam and Nonviolence: A Case Study of the Palestinian Intifada." Paper presented to the Religion, Peace, and War Group of the American Academy of Religion, Philadelphia.

Hall, Edward. 1976. *Beyond Culture.* New York: Anchor Books.

Haddad, Yvonne. 1980. "The Arab-Israeli Wars, Nasserism, and the Affirmation of Islamic Identity." In *Islam and Development: Religion and Sociopolitical Change,* ed. John Esposito. Syracuse: Syracuse University Press.

Hammeed, Sayed Saiyidain. 1994. "Nonviolence in Islam." In *Nonviolence: Contemporary Issues and Challenges,* ed. Mahendra Kumar. New Delhi: Gandhi Peace Foundation.

Hamzeh, Nizar. 1997. "The Role of Hizbullah in Conflict Management within Lebanon's Shi'a Community." In *Conflict Resolution in the Arab World: Selected Essays,* ed. Paul Salem, 93–121. Beirut: American University of Beirut.

Hanafi, Hassan. 1987. "Life in Peace: An Islamic Perspective." *Bulletin of Peace Proposals* 18.3: 433–48.

———. 1988. "The Controversy of Violence and Nonviolence in Islam." In *al-Muqawama al-Madaniyah fi al-Nidal al-Siyasi* (Nonviolence in political struggle), ed. Saad Eddin Ibrahim. Amman: Muntada al-Fikr al-Arabi (Center for Arab Thought).

———. 1992. "Secularism and Islam." *al-Hewar baiyna al-Mashrig aul Maghrib* (Dialogue between eastern and western Arab world), ed. Hassan Hanafi and Mohammed Abid el-Jabri. Cairo: Madbouli Bookshop.

Harris, Rabia Terri. 1994. "Islam 101: A Primer." *Fellowship,* May–June.

Hashmi, Sohail. 1996. "Interpreting the Islamic Ethics of War and Peace." In *The Ethics of War and Peace: Religious and Secular Perspectives,* ed. Terry Nardin. Princeton: Princeton University Press.

Hassan, Riffat. 1987. "Peace Education." In *Education for Peace: Testimonies from World Religions,* ed. Hayim Gordon and Leonard Grob. Maryknoll, N.Y.: Orbis Books.

al-Hibri, Aziza. 1992. "Islamic Constitutionalism and the Concept of Democracy." *Journal of International Law* 24: 1–27.

———. 1999. "Islamic and American Constitutional Law: Borrowing Possibilities or History of Borrowing?" *Journal of Constitutional Law* 1.3: 491–527.

Hijab, Nadia. 1989. "The Strategy of the Powerless." *Middle East International,* 12 May: 17–18.

Hiltermann, Joost. 1991. *Behind the Intifada: Labor and Women Movements in the Occupied Territories.* Princeton: Princeton University Press.

Hippler, Jochen, ed. 1995. *The Next Threat: Western Perceptions of Islam.* London: Pluto Press.

Ibn Hisham, ʿAbd al-Malik. 1992. *Al-sirah al-nabawiyah.* Beirut: Dar al-Fikr.

Hodson, Marshal. 1974. *The Venture of Islam: Conscience and History in a World Civilization.* Vol. 1, *The Classic Age of Islam.* Chicago: University of Chicago Press.

Homer, Jack. 1968. *World Religion and World Peace.* Boston: Beacon Press.

Hourani, Albert. 1947. *Minorities in the Arab World.* London: Oxford University Press.

Hourani, George. 1985. *Reason and Tradition in Islamic Ethics.* London: Cambridge University Press.

Howeidy, Fahmi. 1993. *Al-Islam wa al-Demugratiah* (Islam and democracy). Cairo: Cairo Center for Translation and Publication.

Hudson, Michael C. 1977. *Arab Politics: The Search for Legitimacy.* New Haven: Yale University Press.

Hurwitz, Deena, and R. Scott Kennedy. 1988. "Al-ʿawdah, the Palestinian Ship of Return." *Resource Center for Nonviolence Center Update,* Spring, 1–4.

Ibrahim, Saad Eddin. 1990. "Why Nonviolent Political Struggle in the Middle East?" Introduction to *Arab Nonviolent Struggle in the Middle East,* ed. Ralph Crow, Philip Grant, and Saad Ibrahim. Boulder: Lynne Rienner.

———. 1994a. "Arab Elites and Societies after the Gulf Crisis." In *The Arab World Today,* ed. Dan Tschirgi, 77–91. Boulder: Lynne Rienner.

———. 1994b. *Racial, Ethnic, and Religious Minorities in the Arab World.* Cairo: Dar al-Amin and Ibn Khaldun.

———. 1995. *Egyptian Childhood: Past and Present, and Images and Practices.* Cairo: Ibn Khaldun.

Inglehart, Ronald. 1997. *Modernization and Postmodernization: Cultural, Economic, and Political Change in Forty-three Societies.* Princeton: Princeton University Press.

Iqbal, Muhammad. 1930. *Six Lectures on the Reconstruction of Religious Thought in Islam.* Lahome: Kapur Art.

Irani, George, and Nathan Funk. 2000. "Ritual of Reconciliation: Arab-Islamic Perspective." Occasional Paper #19. Kroc Institute. South Bend, Ind.: Notre Dame University Press.

Ibn Is'haq, Muhammad. 1978. *Kitab al-siyar wa-al-maghazi.* Beirut: Dar al-Fikr.

Ismaʿil, Mustafa Faruq. 1986. *Ethnic Groups: A Study in Cultural Adaptation and Representation.* Alexandria: General Egyptian Book Organization.

Jabbour, Elias. 1996. *Sulha: Palestinian Traditional Peacemaking Process.* Ed. and comp. Thomas C. Cook Jr. Montreat, N.C.: House of Hope Publications.

Jaggi, O. P. 1974. *Religion, Practice, and Science of Non-Violence.* New Delhi: Munshiran Manoharlal.

Janner, Janice. 1997. "Toward a Christian Understanding of Nonviolence in Islam." Eastern Mennonite University. Unpublished paper.

Jansen, G. H. 1992. "Islam and Democracy: Are They Compatible?" *Middle East International.*

Jansen, Johannes. 1986. *The Neglected Duty: The Creed of Sadat's Assassins and Islamic Resurgence in the Middle East.* New York: Macmillan.

Johansen, Robert. 1997. "Radical Islam and Nonviolence: A Case Study of Religious Empowerment and Constraint among Pashtuns." *Journal of Peace Research* 34.1: 53–71.

Johnson, James. 1987. *The Quest for Peace: Three Moral Traditions in Western Cultural History.* Princeton: Princeton University Press.

———. 1991. "Historical Roots and Sources of the Just War Tradition in Western Culture." In *Just War and Jihad: Historical and Theoretical Perspectives on War and Peace in Western and Islamic Traditions,* ed. John Kelsay and James Turner Johnson, 5–30. New York: Greenwood Press.

Juergensmeyer, Mark. 1986. *Fighting Fair: A Nonviolent Strategy for Resolving Everyday Conflicts.* San Francisco: Harper and Row.

Kadi, Wadad. 1998. "Reflections on Islamic Perspectives on Cultural Diversity." Address to the Cultural Diversity and Islam Conference, Center for Global Peace, American University, Washington, D.C.

Kaminer, Reuven. 1996. *The Politics of Protest: The Israeli Peace Movement and the Palestinian Intifada.* Brighton, England: Sussex Academic Press.

Ibn Kathir, Abi al-Fida ' Ismail. 1983. *Mukhtasar Tafsir Ibn Kathir.* Beirut: Dar al-Ma'rifah (Muhammad Kurayyim Rajih).

Kelman, Herbert. 1990. "Interactive Problem-Solving: A Social-Psychological Approach to Conflict Resolution." In *Conflict: Readings in Management and Resolution,* ed. John Burton and Frank Dukes. New York: St. Martin's Press.

Kelsay, John. 1993. *Islam and War: A Study in Comparative Ethics.* Louisville: Westminster/John Knox Press.

Kennedy, R. Scott. 1984. "The Druze of the Golan: A Case of Nonviolent Resistance." *Journal of Palestine Studies* 13.4: 22–36.

Kepel, Gilles. 1994. *The Revenge of God: The Resurgence of Islam, Christianity, and Judaism in the Modern World.* University Park: Pennsylvania State University Press.

Khadduri, Majid. 1955. *War and Peace in the Law of Islam.* London: Oxford University Press.

———. 1984. *The Islamic Conception of Justice.* New York: Johns Hopkins University Press.

Khalidi, Rashid. 1988. "The Uprising and the Palestinian Question." *World Policy Journal* 5.3: 497–518.

Khan, Abdul Ghaffar. 1969. *My Life and Struggle.* Delhi: Hind Pocket Books.

Khan, Mohammed Muqtedar. 1997. "Peace and Change in the Islamic World." Address to the Forum on Islam and Peace in the Twenty-First Century, Washington, D.C., February.

Khoury, Philip, and Joseph Kostiner, eds. 1990. *Tribes and State Formation in the Middle East.* Berkeley: University of California Press.

Khuri, Fuad. 1997. "The Ascent to Top Office in Arab-Islamic Culture." In *Con-*

flict Resolution in the Arab World: Selected Essays, ed. Paul Salem, 121–40. Beirut: American University of Beirut.

King, Martin Luther, Jr. 1957. "Nonviolence and Racial Justice." *Christian Century,* 6 February, 165–67.

Kishtainy, Khalid. 1990. "Violent and Nonviolent Struggle in Arab History." In *Arab Nonviolent Political Struggle in the Middle East,* ed. Ralph Crow, Philip Grant, and Saad Ibrahim. Boulder: Lynne Rienner.

———. 1998. *Dalil al-Muwatin Lil Jihad al-Madaui* (Citizen manual for civil jihad). London: Al-Radid.

Korany, Bahgat, Rex Brynen, and Paul Noble, eds. 1998. *Political Liberalization and Democratization in the Arab World.* Vol. 2, *Comparative Experiences.* Boulder: Lynne Rienner.

Korejo, Muhammad Soaleh. 1993. *The Frontier Gandhi: His Place in History.* Karachi: Oxford University Press.

Kramer, Martin. 1993. "Islam vs. Democracy." *Contemporary* 95.1: 2–35.

Kriesberg, Louis. 1991. "Conflict Resolution Applications to Peace Studies." *Peace and Change* 16.4: 400–417.

———.1998. *Constructive Conflicts: From Escalation to Resolution.* Lanham, Md.: Rowman and Littlefield.

Kuttab, Daoud. 1988. "The Struggle to Build a Nation." *The Nation,* 17 October, 336–40.

Kuttab, Jonathan. 1988a. "Nonviolence in the Palestinian Struggle." *Fellowship,* October–November, 7–8.

———. 1988b. "The Children's Revolt." *Journal of Palestine Studies* 17.4: 35.

Laue, James. 1991. "Contributions of the Emerging Field of Conflict Resolution." In *Approaches to Peace: An Intellectual Map,* ed. W. Scott Thompson and Kenneth Jensen, 299–332. Washington, D.C.: United States Institute of Peace Press.

Laue, James, and Gerald Cormick. 1978. "The Ethics of Intervention in Community Disputes." In *The Ethics of Social Intervention,* ed. Gordon Bermant, Herbert Kelman, and Donald Warwick. New York: Halsted Press.

Law in the Service of Man. 1988. *Punishing a Nation: Human Rights Violations during the Palestinian Uprising, December 1987–December 1988.* Jerusalem: al-Haq/Law in the Service of Man.

Lawrence, Bruce. 1986. *Defenders of God: The Fundamentalist Revolt against the Modern Age.* New York: Harper and Row.

Lederach, J. Paul. 1995. *Preparing for Peace: Conflict Transformation Across Cultures.* Syracuse: Syracuse University Press.

———. 1997. *Peace Building in Divided Societies.* Syracuse: Syracuse University Press.

Lewis, Bernard. 1988. *The Political Language of Islam.* Chicago: University of Chicago Press.

———. 1993. "Islam and Liberal Democracy." *Atlantic Monthly* 271.2: 89–98.

Lockman, Zachary, and Joel Beinin, eds. 1989. *Intifada: The Palestinian Uprising against Israeli Occupation*. Boston: South End Press.

Luego, Andrea. 1995. "The Perceptions of Islam in Western Debate." In *The Next Threat: Western Perceptions of Islam*, ed. Jochen Hippler. London: Pluto Press.

ibn-Majah, Muhammad ibn Yazid. n.d. Vol.2. Beirut: Dar al-kutub al-I'LMiyah.

Martin, Richard. 1991. "The Religious Foundation of War, Peace, and Statecraft in Islam." In *Just War and Jihad: Historical and Theoretical Perspectives on War and Peace in Western and Islamic Traditions*, ed. John Kelsay and James Turner Johnson, 93–117. New York: Greenwood Press.

Marty, Martin E., and R. Scott Appleby, eds. 1993. *Fundamentalisms and the State: Remaking Polities, Economies, and Militance*. Chicago: University of Chicago Press.

Mayer, Elizabeth Ann. 1991. *Islam and Human Rights*. Boulder: Westview Press.

McDonald, John W., and Diane B. Bendahmane, eds. 1987. *Conflict Resolution: Track Two Diplomacy*. Washington, D.C.: Institute for Multi-Track Diplomacy.

McDonough, Sheila. 1994. *Gandhi's Responses to Islam*. New Delhi: D.K. Printworld.

McDowall, David. 1989. *Palestine and Israel: The Uprising and Beyond*. Berkeley: University of California Press.

———. 1994. *The Palestinians: The Road to Nationhood*. London: Minority Rights Publications.

McLaurin, R. D., ed. 1979. *The Political Role of Minorities in the Middle East*. New York: Praeger.

McReynolds, David. 1988. "Report on the Ship of Return." *Nonviolent Activist*, June, 11–12.

Mehdi, Syed Sikandar. 1994. "Islam and Nonviolence." In *Nonviolence: Contemporary Issues and Challenges*, ed. Mahendra Kumar. New Delhi: Gandhi Peace Foundation.

Melman, Yossi, and Dan Raviv. 1989. *Behind the Uprising: Israelis, Jordanians, and Palestinians*. New York: Greenwood Press.

Mernissi, Fatima. 1975. *Beyond the Veil: Male-Female Dynamics in Modern Muslim Society*. Cambridge, Mass: Schenkman.

———. 1992. *Islam and Democracy: Fear of the Modern World*. Reading, Mass.: Addison-Wesley.

Merton, Thomas, ed. 1965. *Gandhi on Nonviolence*. New York: New Directions.

Migdal, Joel, and Baruch Kimmerling. 1993. *Palestinians: The Making of a People*. New York: Free Press.

Miller, Judith. 1993. "The Challenge of Radical Islam." *Foreign Affairs* 72.2: 43–56.

Moaddel, Mansoor, and Kamran Talattof, eds. 2000. *Contemporary Debates in*

Islam: An Anthology of Modernist and Fundamentalist Thought. New York: St. Martin's Press.

Moghadam, Valentine. 1993. *Modernizing Women: Gender and Social Change in the Middle East.* Boulder: Lynne Rienner.

Mursi, Fuad. 1989. *Nazarah thaniyah ila al-quwmiyah al-Arabiyah* (A second look at Arab nationalism). Cairo: al-Ahli Publications.

Musa, Muhammad. 1967. *Nizam al-hukum fi al-Islam* (The governing system in Islam). Cairo: n.p.

Musá, Sulayman. 1984. *Rihlat fi al-Urdun wa Filastin* (Journeys in Palestine and Jordan). Amman: Dar Ibn Rushd.

Nagler, Michael. 1996. "Is There a Tradition of Nonviolence in Islam?" In *War and Its Discontents: Pacifism and Quietism in the Abrahamic Traditions,* ed. J. Patout Burns. Washington, D.C.: Georgetown University Press.

Naqvi, Syed Nawab Haider. 1994. *Islam, Economics, and Society.* New York: Kegan Paul International.

Nardin, Terry, ed. 1996. *The Ethics of War and Peace: Religious and Secular Perspectives.* Princeton: Princeton University Press.

Nasr, Sayyed Hussein. 1998. Keynote speech to the Islam and Cultural Diversity Conference, Center for Global Peace, American University, Washington, D.C.
———. 2000. *Ideals and Realities of Islam.* 4th ed. Chicago: ABC International Group.

Niebuhr, Reinhold. 1960. *Moral Man and Immoral Society.* New York: Scribner's.

Nisan, Mordechai. 1991. *Minorities in the Middle East: A History of Struggle and Self-Expression.* Jefferson, N.C.: McFarland.

Nojeim, Michael. 1993. "Planting Olive Trees: Palestinian Nonviolent Resistance." Ph.D. dissertation, American University, Washington, D.C.

Nonini, Don. 1988. "Everyday Forms of Popular Resistance." *Monthly Review, 7,* no. 6: 25–36.

Norman, Daniel. 1993. *Islam and the West: The Making of an Image.* Oxford: Oneworld.

Norton, Augustus Richard. 1993. "Inclusion Can Deflate Islamic Populism." *New Perspectives Quarterly* 10.3: 50–51.

Nurbakhsh, Javad. 1983. *Tradition of the Prophet.* 2 vols. New York: Khaniqahi-Ni'matullahi Publications.

Nusseibeh, Sari. 1989. "The Uprising: A Critical Appraisal." *Arab Affairs* 6:31.

Owadi, Ahmad. 1982. *Al-Qanun al-Qabali Fi al-Urdan* (Law among Jordanian tribes). Amman: Bashir Publications. (Arabic)

Paige, Glenn, Chaiwat Satha-Anand, and Sarah Gilliatt, eds. 1993. *Islam and Nonviolence.* Honolulu: Center for Global Nonviolence Planning Project, Matsunaga Institute for Peace, University of Hawaii.

Pasha, Sabri. 1983. *Mira'at al-Jazira Al-Arabiyah* (Arabian peninsula mirror). Trans. Mitwali Ahmad and Safafi al-Mursi. Riyadh: al-Riyadh Publication House.

Peretz, Don. 1994. *The Middle East Today.* Westport, Conn.: Praeger.

Peteet, Julie. 1987. "Socio-Political Integration and Conflict Resolution in the Palestinian Camps in Lebanon." *Journal of Palestine Studies* 16.2: 29–44.

Pipes, Daniel. 1992. "Fundamental Questions about Islam." *Wall Street Journal,* 30 October.

Pruitt, Dean, and Jeffery Rubin. 1986. *Social Conflict: Escalation, Stalemate, and Settlement.* New York: McGraw-Hill.

Pryce-Jones, David. 1992. *At War with Modernity: Islam's Challenge to the West.* London: Alliance Publishers for the Institute for European Defense and Strategic Studies.

Pyarelal, Nayar. 1966. *Thrown to the Wolves: Abdul Ghaffar Kahn.* Calcutta: Eastlight Book House.

Qleibo, Ali. 1990. "Tribal Methods of Conflict Resolution: The Palestinian Model: Atwa or Sulh Asha'iry." Unpublished paper. Bethlehem, Palestine.

Rahman, Fazlur. 1996. "Islam's Origin and Ideals." In *Islamic Identity and the Struggle for Justice,* ed. Nimat Barazangi, M. Raquibuz Zaman, and Omar Afzal. Gainesville: University Press of Florida.

Robinson, Glenn. 1997. "The Logic of Palestinian State-Building after Oslo." In *Building a Palestinian State: The Incomplete Revolution.* Bloomington: Indiana University Press.

Rosen, Lawrence. 1984. *Bargaining for Reality: The Construction of Social Relations in a Muslim Community.* Chicago: University of Chicago Press.

Rothenberger, John. 1978. "The Social Dynamics of Dispute Settlement in a Sunni Muslim Village in Lebanon." In *The Disputing Process: Law in Ten Societies,* ed. Laura Nader and Harry Todd, 152–81. New York: Columbia University Press.

Rubenstein, Richard. 1992. "Dispute Resolution on the Eastern Frontier: Some Questions for Modern Missionaries." *Negotiation Journal* 8.3: 205–13.

Sachedina, Abdulaziz. 1996. " The Justification for Violence in Islam." In *War and Its Discontents: Pacifism and Quietism in the Abrahamic Traditions,* ed. J. Patout Burns. Washington, D.C.: Georgetown University Press.

———. 2000. *The Islamic Roots of Democratic Pluralism.* New York: Oxford University Press.

Ibn Sa'd, Muhammad. 1957. *Al-Tabaqat al-kubra.* 9 vols. Beirut: n.p.

el-Sa'dawi, Nawal. 1982. *The Hidden Face of Eve: Women in the Arab World.* Boston: Beacon Press.

Said, Abdul Aziz. 1994. "Cultural Context of Conflict Resolution: With Reference to an Arab-Islamic Perspective." Unpublished paper, American University.

Said, Edward. 1981. *Covering Islam.* New York: Pantheon Books.

Sai'd, Jawdat. 1997. "Peace—Or Nonviolence—in History and with the Prophets." Paper presented at the Forum on Islam and Peace in the Twenty-First Century, American University.

Saiyidain, Khwaga Ghulam. 1976. *Islam, the Religion of Peace.* New Delhi: Islam and Modern Age Society.

————. 1994. *Islam, the Religion of Peace.* 2d ed. New Delhi: Har-Anand.

Salameh, Noh. 1994. "Nonviolence in the Intifada." George Mason University, unpublished paper.

Salem, Paul. 1994. *Bitter Legacy: Ideology and Politics in the Arab World.* Syracuse: Syracuse University Press.

————, ed. 1997. *Conflict Resolution in the Arab World: Selected Essays.* Beirut: American University of Beirut.

Sandole, Dennis, and Hugo van der Merwe. 1993. *Conflict Resolution Theory and Practice: Integration and Application.* Manchester, England: Manchester University Press.

Satha-Anand, Chaiwat. 1987. *Islam and Violence: A Case Study of Violent Events in the Four Southern Provinces, Thailand, 1976–1981.* Tampa: University of South Florida.

————. 1993a. "Core Values for Peacemaking in Islam: The Prophet's Practice as Paradigm." In *Building Peace in the Middle East: Challenges for States and Civil Society,* ed. Elise Boulding. Boulder: Lynne Rienner.

————. 1993b. "The Nonviolent Crescent: Eight Theses on Muslim Nonviolent Actions." In *Islam and Nonviolence,* ed. Glenn Paige, Chaiwat Satha-Anand, and Sarah Gilliatt, 7–26. Honolulu: Center for Global Nonviolence Planning Project, Matsunaga Institute for Peace, University of Hawaii.

————. 1994. "The Islamic Tunes of Gandhi's Ahimsa." In *Nonviolence: Contemporary Issues and Challenges,* ed. Mahendra Kumar. New Delhi: Gandhi Peace Foundation.

————. 1998. "Muslim Communal Nonviolence Actions: Examples of Minorities' Coexistence in a Non-Muslim Society." Paper presented at the Islam and Cultural Diversity Conference, Center for Global Peace, American University, Washington, D.C.

Sayigh, Yezid. 1989. "The Intifada Continues: Legacy, Dynamics, and Challenges." *Third World Quarterly* 11.3: 35.

Schiff, Ze'ev, and Ehud Ya'ari. 1989. *Intifada: The Palestinian Uprising—Israel's Third Front.* New York: Simon and Schuster.

Schulze, Kirsten E., Martin Stokes, and Colm Campbell, eds. 1996. *Nationalism, Minorities, and Diasporas: Identities and Rights in the Middle East.* London: Tauris Academic Studies.

Scimecca, Joseph. 1991. "Conflict Resolution in the United States: The Emergence of a Profession?" In *Conflict Resolution: Cross-Cultural Perspectives,* ed. Kevin Avruch, Peter Black, and Joseph Scimecca. New York: Greenwood Press.

Scott, James. 1985. *Weapons of the Weak: Everyday Forms of Peasant Resistance.* New Haven: Yale University.

Segal, Jerome. 1989. *Creating the Palestinian State: A Strategy for Peace.* Chicago: Lawrence Hill Books.

Shadid, Mohammed K. 1988. "The Muslim Brotherhood Movement in the West Bank and Gaza." *Third World Quarterly* 10.2: 658–88.

Shaheen, Jack. 1985. "Coverage of the Middle East: Perception and Foreign Policy." *Annals of the American Academy of Political and Social Science* 482:160–75.

Shahih, Muslin Ibi-Sharh al-Nawawi. 1972. *Jami al-Shahih.* Beirut: Dar Ihya' al-Turath al-Arabi.

Shalaby, Ibrahim M. 1978. "Islam and Peace." *Journal of Religious Thought* 44:42–49.

Sharabi, Hisham. 1988. *Neopatriachy: A Theory of Distorted Change in Arab Society.* Oxford: Oxford University Press.

al-Sharif al-Radi, Muhammad ibn al-Husayn. 1978. *Nahj al-balaghah.* Beirut: Mu'assasat al-A'alami lil-Matbu'at. (Reviewed and classified by Muhammad Baqir al-Mahmudi.)

Sharp, Gene. 1973. *The Politics of Nonviolent Action.* 3 vols. Boston: P. Sargent.

———. 1987. "Nonviolent Struggle." *Journal of Palestine Studies* 17.1: 37–55.

———. 1989. "The Intifada and Nonviolent Struggle." *Journal of Palestine Studies* 19.1: 3–13.

al-Shawi, Tawfiq. 1992. *Fiqh alshura wa-al-istishara.* Al-mansura: Dar al-wafaa.

Shaybani, Muhammad ibn al-Hasan, and Majid Khadduri. 1966. *The Islamic Law of Nations: Shaybani's Siyar.* New York: Johns Hopkins University Press.

Shayegan, Daryush. 1992. *Cultural Schizophrenia: Islamic Societies Confronting the West.* Trans. John Howe. Syracuse: Syracuse University Press.

Shehadeh, Raja. 1982. "The Land Law of Palestine." *Journal of Palestine Studies* 11.2: 82–99.

———. 1985. "Some Legal Aspects of Israeli Land Policy in the Occupied Territories." *Arab Studies Quarterly* 7.2–3: 42–61.

———. 1988a. *Occupier's Law: Israel and the West Bank.* Rev. ed. Washington, D.C.: Institute for Palestine Studies.

———. 1988b. "Occupier's Law and the Uprising." *Journal of Palestine Studies* 17.3: 24–37.

Sibley, Mulford. 1944. *The Political Theories of Modern Pacifism: An Analysis and Criticism.* Philadelphia: American Friends Service Committee.

Siniora, Hanna. 1988. "An Analysis of the Current Revolt." *Journal of Palestine Studies* 17.3: 3–13.

Sisk, Timothy. 1992. *Islam and Democracy: Religion, Politics, and Power in the Middle East.* Washington, D.C.: United States Institute of Peace Press.

Sivan, Emmanuel. 1990. *Radical Islam: Medieval Theology and Modern Politics.* New Haven: Yale University Press.

Smith, Daniel. 1989. "The Rewards of Allah." *Journal of Peace Research* 26.4: 385–98.

Sonn, Tamara. 1996. *Islam and the Question of Minorities.* Atlanta: Scholars Press.

Strum, Philippa. 1992. *The Women Are Marching: The Second Sex and the Palestinian Resolution.* Chicago: Lawrence Hill Books.

al-Suwaidi, Jamal. 1995. "Arab and Western Conceptions of Democracy." In *Democracy, War, and Peace in the Middle East,* ed. David Garnham and Mark Tessler, 82–115. Bloomington: Indiana University Press.

al-Tabari, Mohammad B. Jarir. 1969. *Kitab al-umam wa-al-muluk.* Cairo: Dar-ul-Ma'arif.

Tabarsi, al-Fadl ibn al-Hasan. 1958. *Majma' al-bayan li-'ulum al-Qur'an.* Cairo: Dar al-Taqrib bayna al-Madhahib al-Islamiyah.

Taraki, Lisa. 1989a. "The Islamic Resistance Movement in the Palestinian Uprising." *Middle East Report* 156:30–32.

———. 1989b. "Mass Organizations in the West Bank." In *Occupation: Israel over Palestine,* ed. Naseer Aruri, 431–63. Belmont, Mass.: Association of Arab-American University Graduates.

Ibn Taymiyya. 1949. "Qa'da fi qital al-kuffar" (The Basis for fighting the nonbelievers). In *Mujmu'at rasail* (Collections of letters), ed. Hamid al-Faqqi, 115–46. Cairo: n.p.

Tendulkar, Dinanath. 1967. *Abdul Ghaffar Khan: Faith Is a Battle.* Bombay: Times of India Press.

Tessler, Mark, and Marilyn Grobschmidt. 1995. "Democracy in the Arab World and the Arab-Israeli Conflict." In *Democracy, War, and Peace in the Middle East,* ed. David Garnham and Mark Tessler, 135–70. Bloomington: Indiana University Press.

Thompson, Henry. 1988. *World Religion in War and Peace.* Jefferson, N.C.: McFarland.

Tibi, Bassam. 1988. *The Crisis of Modern Islam: A Preindustrial Culture in the Scientific-Technological Age.* Salt Lake City: University of Utah Press.

———. 1990. "Old Tribes and Imposed Nation-States." In *Tribes and State Formation in the Middle East,* ed. Philip Khoury and Joseph Kostiner, 127–53. Berkeley: University of California Press.

———. 1994. "Redefining the Arab and Arabism in the Aftermath of the Gulf Crisis." In *The Arab World Today,* ed. Dan Tschirgi. Boulder: Lynne Rienner.

———. 1996. "War and Peace in Islam." In *The Ethics of War and Peace,* ed. Terry Nardin. Princeton: Princeton University Press.

Al-Tirmidhi, Muhammad ibn Isa. 1965. *Jam'i al-Tiridhi.* Beirut: n.p.

Tschirgi, Dan. 1994. *The Arab World Today.* Boulder: Lynne Rienner.

Turki, Fawaz. 1981. "Meaning in Palestinian History: Text and Context." *Arab Studies Quarterly* 3.4: 371–83.

Turpin, Jennifer, and Lester Kurtz, eds. 1997. *Web of Violence: From Interpersonal to Global.* Urbana: University of Illinois Press.

Voll, John. 1994. "Islam as a Special World System." *Journal of World History* 5.2: 213–26.

Voll, John, and John Esposito. 1994. "Islam's Democratic Essence." *Middle East Quarterly* 1.3: 3–19.

Wahid, Abdurahman. 1993. "Islam and Nonviolence: National Transformation." In *Islam and Nonviolence,* ed. Glenn Paige, Chaiwat Satha-Anand and Sarah Gilliatt, 53–59. Honolulu: Center for Global Nonviolence Planning Project, Matsunaga Institute for Peace, University of Hawaii.

Wahiduddin Khan, Maulana. 1998. "Nonviolence and Islam." Address to the Forum on Islam and Peace in the Twenty-First Century, American University, Washington, D.C.

Wehr, Paul, Heidi Burgess, and Guy Burgess, eds. 1994. *Justice without Violence.* Boulder: Lynne Rienner.

Weigel, George. 1992. "Religion and Peace: An Argument Complexified." In *Resolving Third World Conflict: Challenges for a New Era,* ed. Sheryl Brown and Kimber Schraub, 172–92. Washington, D.C.: United States Institute of Peace Press.

Wilsnack, Dorie. 1986. "Mubarak Awad: Nonviolence in the Middle East." *Nonviolent Activist,* October–November, 91–101.

Witty, Cathy. 1980. *Mediation and Society: Conflict Management in Lebanon.* New York: Academic Press.

Wolfe, Alvin, and Honggang Yang, eds. 1996. *Anthropological Contributions to Conflict Resolution.* Athens: University of Georgia Press.

Wright, Robin. 1985. *Sacred Rage: The Wrath of Militant Islam.* New York: Simon and Schuster.

———. 1988. "The New Dimension of Palestinian Politics." *Middle East Insight* 5.6: 20–29.

———. 1991. "Islam's New Political Face." *Current History* 90.552: 6–25.

———. 1992. "Islam, Democracy, and the West." *Foreign Affairs* 71: 131–45.

Yoder, J. Howard. 1992. *Nevertheless: The Varieties and Shortcomings of Religious Pacifism.* Rev. ed. Scottdale, Pa.: Herald Press.

Zaman, Raquibuz M. 1996. "Economic Justice in Islam, Ideals and Reality: The Cases of Malaysia, Pakistan, and Saudi Arabia." In *Islamic Identity and the Struggle for Justice,* ed. Nimat Barazangi, M. Raquibuz Zaman, and Omar Afzal, 47–58. Gainesville: University Press of Florida.

Zartman, William. 1992. "Democracy and Islam: The Cultural Dialectic." *Annals of the Academy of Political and Social Science* 524:223–42.

Zinati, Mahmud. 1992. *Nuzum al-Arab al-qabaliyah al-muʿsirah* (Current Arab tribal laws). Cairo: Madbouli Publications.

Zubaida, Sami. 1992a. *Islam, the People, and the State: Essays on Political Ideas and Movements in the Middle East.* New York: I. B. Tauris.

———. 1992b. "Islam, the State, and Democracy: Contrasting Conceptions of Society in Egypt." *Middle East Report* 22.6: 2–10.

Index

Mohammed Abu-Nimer is associate professor at the International Peace and Conflict Resolution Program, American University, Washington, D.C. He is author of *Dialogue, Conflict Resolution, and Change: Arab-Jewish Encounters in Israel* (1999) and editor of *Reconciliation, Justice, and Coexistence: Theory and Practice* (2001). As a practitioner of peace building, Abu-Nimer has been conducting workshops in conflict resolution and diversity training since 1982 in the United States, Israel, Palestine, Jordan, Egypt, Turkey, Ireland, Sri Lanka, and the Philippines.